LET GO FORE 'N' AFT

Captain A.J. Roberts,
'The Old Man'

MINERVA PRESS
MONTREUX LONDON WASHINGTON

LET GO FORE 'N' AFT
Copyright © Captain A.J. Roberts 1996

ISBN 1 86106021 1

First Published 1996 by
MINERVA PRESS
195 Knightsbridge,
London SW7 1RE

Printed in Great Britain by
B.W.D. Ltd, Northolt, Middlesex.

LET GO FORE 'N' AFT

Acknowledgements

This is a non-fiction story with some fictitious names. The author wishes to record his thanks to his wife, daughter and helpful friends, for their encouragement and support.

Contents

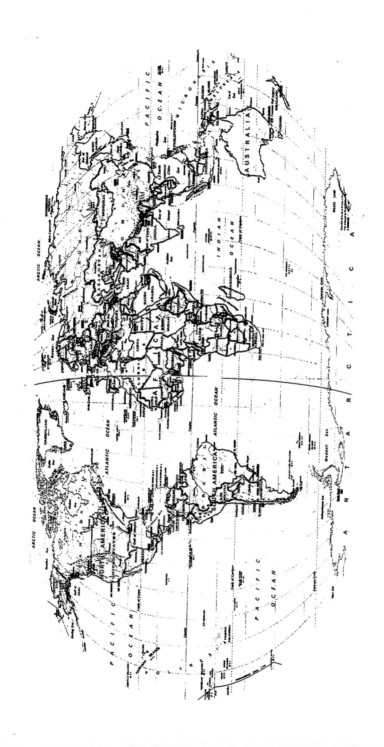

The Call Of The Deep

When the Robson family: father, mother, son Dan, and daughter Connie, moved to the Sussex seaside resort of Brighton, Dan saw the sea for the first time and promptly fell in love with it. Thereafter, Dan spent most of his free time revelling in it one way or another, sometimes helping the pleasure boatmen, and at other times swinging over the surging waves from the girder supports of the West Pier. Since the Robsons owned a commercial hotel in Cannon Place within a hundred yards of the esplanade, Dan was ideally situated for spending time on the beach.

Sadly for him, they moved a few years later to the West Sussex cathedral city of Chichester, and he left school at the age of fifteen. His parents, having noted his growing fascination with the sea, tried to get him interested in some useful trade around the city. Being a dutiful boy, he did his best to find a job and applied for any vacancy advertised in the Chichester Daily News. His rosy cheeks and robust countenance did not find favour with a firm of Funeral Directors seeking a junior hearse attendant, or with the Cathedral Prebendary School, requiring an assistant janitor, but he was successful in landing a trainee's job with the local branch of a large company supplying bakers' needs throughout West Sussex.

For the next three months, Dan did his best to satisfy his employers and got along very well with the manager and his wife; he particularly enjoyed travelling with the manager on his rounds of country bakeries in an old Model T Ford van. Kind-hearted baker's wives often favoured him with cakes, buns and pastries to share with his boss at their tea-breaks. This all came to a halt when Dan arrived to start work one morning and found the shop closed, with police in attendance. The shocking news was that his manager had committed suicide overnight, his poor wife was too distraught and unable to carry on, so the branch was closed pending investigations and Dan joined the ranks of the unemployed.

He now urged his parents to allow him to go to sea, they felt sorry that he had tried to please them and through no fault of his own had failed, so they sympathised with his pleas. Anyone coming into the restaurant they owned wearing a nautical uniform was a target for his eager questioning.

On one of these occasions, the man said he would take Dan to see his Marine Superintendent in Southampton, but Dan's father insisted on accompanying him and it was just as well that he did, as the man turned out to be a rogue. On the train, the man had asked for five pounds to arrange the interview, which while it seemed a lot of money, Dan's father agreed to pay after the introduction but not before. At Cunard House, the man had told the Robsons to wait outside until he had organised things, he then went into the building and they never saw him again. Half an hour later, when father and son went into the offices to make enquiries, the mean trick was exposed.

For Dan, it was like a shower of cold water to his dreams, another dampener to get started in a career, but he would have to learn to cope with disappointment. Father and son retraced their steps to the Docks' Station and returned home, glad at least that they hadn't yielded to the man's demands for money.

From his own enquiries, Dan had learned that many ships in the British Merchant Service carried from one to six youths, variously named Apprentices, Cadets or Midshipmen, according to the style of the company employing them. They were the trainee officers of the future. With the fierce competition between ship owners for charters, they sought to make economies wherever they lawfully could to gain an advantage over their rivals; this included using cheap labour. This state of affairs was understood by the seafarers of the day: better to be housed and fed under poor conditions than to be out of work with no dole. Many men had families to support and could see the pitiful sight of fellow citizens of the great British Empire, survivors of the war to end wars, maimed, crippled or blinded, begging in the city streets. This was the situation in 1926, when the stringent measures of the Tory Government spawned the eruption of a national strike by the long-suffering workers.

One afternoon, when he had finished helping his parents and was at a loose end, he got the idea to cycle to Dell Quay, a jetty on the foreshore of Chichester Harbour about four miles away. There might be some sort of coaster there, and lo and behold, when he got there, a small steamer was preparing to sail. She was just one of many such vessels trading around the coasts of the British Isles carrying cargoes to out of the way places.

Sitting on a wharf bollard, Dan studied every detail: the battered bow, the dented plating, the seaman lowering a derrick from the solitary mast, and the bearded man leaning over the forepart of the tiny bridge. The tall Woodbine funnel was belching forth thick black smoke in a very businesslike manner, hinting of the mighty power lurking down below in the engine-room.

Dan's eyes drank it all in, to him she was as a crown jewel, and he sat gazing at her as a lover to his beloved. Recognising the signs, the bearded Skipper called out to him, "Would you like to come down to Itchenor with us lad: we could put you and your bike ashore with the pilot."

"Oh yes please sir I would," answered Dan, hardly able to believe his ears.

"Lift your bike aboard then and come up to the bridge," and heaving his bicycle over the bulwarks, he wasted no time in accepting the invitation. "Let go for'ard, let go aft" called out the pilot, and off they went. Dan watched the wharf move away, the churning wake and belching funnel and felt he was on his way across the world instead of a few miles down the estuary. His future career was settled at that point: nothing else would do. He thanked the Skipper profusely, while he and the pilot exchanged meaningful grins. Cycling home, he decided to ask his parents to write to some shipping lines for information about apprenticeship for their son.

Hearing of his afternoon adventure, his parents finally yielded to his eagerness, explaining their natural reluctance to part with their only son. His mother was particularly sad and confided to Dan that her father and older brothers had served at sea as Mates and Master of some of the famous clipper ships, and from experience she knew the heartbreak of long separations.

Shortly after this, the Robsons met an elderly man who recommended a nautical training school that would prepare Dan for a seafaring career in the best possible way. For Dan, that was almost too good to be true: what a providential coincidence! The next step was to take medical and eyesight tests, and then the enrolment for a six months' course. The curriculum was like drink to a thirsty man, and Dan revelled in it all. An ex-German North Sea pilot schooner owned and operated by the school provided valuable experience in the practical aspects of seamanship, trips around the North Sea as far as Cromarty Firth in the north, and Boulogne, Calais, Antwerp and Flushing on the Continent were undertaken. At the various ports of call, local dignitaries came on board to inspect both the ship and her complement of young boys. There was also a number of parades ashore to war memorials, churches and civic buildings.

At the end of the course, Dan managed to pass the qualifying exams without undue difficulty, and then awaited the next step. During the six months, the school's officers had carefully assessed each boy's character and temperament to try and determine whether he was better suited for the Royal Navy or the Merchant Service. They decided the latter service for Dan, and that proved to be the correct assessment in the course of time.

By decree of King George the Fifth, 'The Sailor King' the name Merchant Service, had been changed to Merchant Navy and it has remained so named ever since.

The University Of Experience
Stage I

Following the completion of his course, Dan was indentured to a well-known trampship company with a fleet of vessels ranging from very old to brand new, and then sent home to spend time with his family before embarking on his first deep sea voyage. The end to cosy home life came one day with a letter from Head Office instructing Mr Dan Robson to report to Captain D. Davies on *Canadian City* at the Wm. Gray Shipbuilders yard in West Hartlepool on the following Tuesday.

What a hotchpotch of emotions that letter aroused: excitement and eager expectancy on Dan's part, sadness and foreboding for his mother and when departure time came, she was heartbroken. She might have had a premonition she would not see her son again in this life.

It was a typically dull, dismal winter's afternoon when Dan and his father walked down the street from the station to the shipbuilding yards, enshrouded in mist. On the way, they met a man wearing a brass-buttoned patrol jacket uniform, with a peaked cap and a Merchant Navy badge. He was gazing into a Naval outfitter's shop window, so they asked him the way to *Canadian City*.

As Dan was also in uniform, complete with brass-buttoned bridge overcoat, the man took in the situation at a glance, saying "If you can hang on for a minute I'll take you there, I'm going that way myself." He introduced himself as Mr Thomas, Second Mate of *Canadian City*, and right from that first meeting Dan had the utmost respect for Tudor Thomas, which lasted through the many years he knew him. When asked if Dan would need a sextant, they were on display in the shop-window, the hint of a smile flickered on the face of the Second Mate, then, "No... not just yet anyway, but he will need dungarees, and if he hasn't already got one, order a donkey's breakfast while you are about it." With those significant remarks in their ears, the trio continued towards the Yards now not very far away.

The ship was 'flying light' (completely empty) and looked enormous to Dan when the three of them came on to the wharf alongside her. Father and son said their goodbyes on the quayside, Mr Robson watched while Dan climbed the long ladder to step on board, then Dan watched while his Dad walked slowly away, turning to wave before disappearing around the corner of a wharf building. With a sad heart, Dan turned as Mr Thomas approached with a young man of about twenty, whom he introduced as Dusty Miller, the senior apprentice. As such, Mr Thomas said, he was to be obeyed at all times. 'That sounds grim,' thought Dan.

With a jerk of his head, Dusty indicated that Dan was to follow him across the deck to a small cabin facing aft in the midship part of the bridge superstructure. Stepping over the high sill of the space he would later learn to call the 'half-deck', Dan was surprised at the small size of the place that was to accommodate six apprentices. Dusty nodded towards a lower bunk near the door. "That's yours," he said, adding that the small locker at deck level next to it was also Dan's. Then he told Dan to unpack as much of his gear as he could before the other four cabin mates arrived.

Among these there was one other junior, Jim, who was to become Dan's friend and fellow drudge. It was made plain to the pair that they had no rights or privileges, but that if they did as they were told with no backchat they would get on all right. Dusty Miller told Jim and Dan that it was part of their job to wait on their seniors, which meant that at meal times they had to collect the food for all of them from the galley and bring it to the half-deck.

Somehow, this did not seem to match their concept of brass-buttoned cadets, and was very dispiriting for the newcomers. After a miserable meal in the feeble light of a single kerosene lamp, clearing away and washing up afterwards, both boys crawled into their bunks for the night, wondering if this was really what they had had in mind.

It seemed no time before the night watchman, an old 'shellback', called them with, "Wakey, wakey, rise and shine." He brought a billy of steaming hot coffee to help restore the circulation in their chilled bodies and to prepare them for the day's work ahead.

That first day was full of activity, with thick swirling coal dust being stirred up by coal being poured into the bunkers, supplies being stowed in lockers and storerooms and men hurrying everywhere. Later in the morning, all six apprentices were summoned to the lower bridge to be inspected by Captain Dan Davies, a fine, middle-aged, fatherly man, who talked about what was expected of them and warned them about some of the dangers of life on board and ashore.

The Captain, the First Mate, Chief Engineer, the Chief Steward and the Second Mate were all from Wales. Two of the engineers were from Belfast, one was from the Clyde and two were Geordies. The Cook was a Greek from Barry called Mr Papadopoulus. The Bos'n and the Ship's Carpenter were Norwegians, the seamen were all Scandinavians, the donkeyman and the stokers were Geordies, and to complete the list there was a galley boy, a messroom boy and a cabin boy.

There was one other officer, the Wireless Officer engaged on contract from Marconi Communications Ltd., he was from Hull.

Sailing day came, and from early morning until late in the afternoon *Canadian City* underwent a series of checks to engines and steering gear, followed by speed trials, as required by the Board of Trade. Finally, the navigational aids, especially the compasses, were corrected by a qualified compass adjuster. Then he and all the other shore-based personnel were taken ashore by launch and *Canadian City* set off on her maiden voyage.

She headed out into the choppy North Sea on a darkening winter's afternoon, bound for Vancouver, to load timber for New York. By evening, the twisting, corkscrew motion of the ship, light in the water, had ruined Dan's appetite and while carrying food from the galley the smell of the stew wafting into his nostrils almost made him add to it.

Being first trippers, Dan and Jim were put on day work, so they could sleep all night. The seniors, however, working four hours on and four hours off, made sure the boys were woken at midnight, at four in the morning, and often enough in between to rob them of the bliss of undisturbed slumber. Soon though, Dan and Jim were put on watch like everyone else and learned to sleep in three and a half hour shifts.

The ship bowled along down the North Sea and the English Channel, soon to meet the lift of the Atlantic as she emerged from the chops of the Channel. The North Atlantic is not renowned for good weather in winter, and it was not until the ship had passed the Azores that sunshine warmed and cheered the first trippers' hearts.

Improved weather conditions gave the sadistic Third Mate and his willing cohorts, the senior apprentices, the opportunity to indulge themselves in one of their favourite pastimes, by announcing an initiation ceremony designed to degrade, embarrass and humiliate the victims.

Despite spirited resistance, Dan, Jim, the cabin boy and the messroom boy were stripped and plastered all over with black grease into which galley refuse had been mixed.

Needless to say, special attention was paid to their private parts, and when the sordid assault was over, the boys had to clean themselves up, first by scraping off the muck, then wiping themselves down with cotton waste soaked in kerosene, and finally finishing off with a chemical soft soap used for cleaning paintwork. By this time they had become used to having an adequate bath with the rationed half bucket of water usually collected scalding hot from the scavenger pump in the engine room, and left in bucket-holding brackets in the bathroom, to cool off.

Soon afterwards, the ship was passing through the Sargasso Sea where the surface of the water was so thickly covered by weed that it looked like a field. In the old days, the progress of sailing ships was severely hampered until a strong wind blew them clear. Even steamships have had trouble with the weed binding around the tailshaft and propeller, but *Canadian City* crossed the area safely and entered the Caribbean. They sighted the West Indies as they passed through the Windward Passage and arrived at the Panama Canal a few days later.

Dan was captivated when the American pilot, smoking a cigar, came on board with a special team of West Indian seamen to handle the ship's mooring lines in cooperation with the electric 'mules' to take the ship through the Gatun Locks. Seeing the ship being lifted sixty feet and then looking back and down to Colon, restored Dan's spirit of adventure, which had been dented in the passage from England. He watched as the ship made her slow but steady way through the chain of natural lakes that formed part of the fine engineering marvel that was the Panama Canal. To save time and money, *Canadian City* pumped this canal water into her fresh water tanks as she steamed through, but the practice was later stopped as being a danger to health.

The West Indian seamen had brought bananas and limes on board for sale; a welcome change of diet for Jim and Dan as they gazed at the jungle-clad banks slipping by. Eventually, they reached Mira Flores, the first of the descending locks, and then San Pedro Miguel, the second, after which they were back at sea level.

This time it was the Pacific: how romantic it all seemed. Apart from slowing down to let the pilot and his men depart by launch, the ship did not stop at Balboa, but entered the Gulf of Panama and on into the wide Pacific Ocean.

They had beautiful weather for the whole eighteen days run up the long western seaboard of North America, then through the Straits of Juan de Fuca to Victoria, where, with the Vancouver pilot on board, the ship headed through the sweet-smelling pine-clad islands of Strait of Georgia.

At Burrard Mills, up harbour from Vancouver, the ship was to load a part cargo of Oregon pine and to get there she had to pass through a low-level harbour bridge with a mid-section that could be swung open.

Canadian City passed through without incident, but one of the company's other ships had not been so lucky. She had steamed downstream fully-laden, helped along by a particularly strong current to arrive at the bridge before the mid-section had been swung aside. She swept beneath the bridge but the masts, the top of her bridge and the funnel were sliced off. The swing-bridge was also extensively damaged.

From Burrard Mills, the ship sailed for the picturesque coves of Nanaimo and Chemainus on Vancouver Island, where the men who worked the timber were Native American Indians. Dan half-expected them to whoop into a war dance, but instead of wielding tomahawks, those fellows handled their timber hooks dextrously to stow the cargo, and instead of puffing on clay pipes, they smoked Camel cigarettes and spoke with broad American accents. They were expert lumberjacks and longshoremen, stowing the cargo so tightly that none of it moved. When the holds were full, the ship was still not down to her load line, so she took on a deck cargo as well, lashed with heavy gauge chains and bottle-screws to prevent movement.

After loading her timber, *Canadian City* sailed for New York and Newark. Fine weather followed them all the way down the west coast, through the Panama Canal and out into the Gulf of Mexico, heading for the straits between Cuba and the Florida coast. All went well until the ship neared Cape Hatteras, when the sky filled with heavy black clouds.

Later that night a frightening electrical storm surrounded the ship, which seemed to be the focal point of almost continuous sheet lightning, and forked lightning which ran along the ironwork of the ship, up and down the masts, along the crosstrees, skipping along the chain lashings, hissing as it went.

In fact, *Canadian City* was crossing a corner of the notorious Bermuda Triangle, where so many ships and aircraft have disappeared without trace. Dan was doing his lookout stint on the fo'c'sle head, the forepart of the ship, when the Captain sent the standby man with a message that he was to spend the rest of his watch on the bridge. Actually, he was in serious danger, since he was standing barefoot on a wet steel deck.

Dan was happy to be out on the wing of the bridge, in the dark: at least he was not alone, and the reason he was wet through and his feet were freezing, was the fact that the seniors had grabbed his new wet-weather gear for their own use. Suddenly he felt warmth, he could wriggle his toes, the circulation was returning, what bliss, how delightful, but how come? Then, slowly the warmth stopped, what a shame! What a pity it couldn't continue!

It took a minute for Dan's chilled brain to work out what had happened. The Old Man, not wanting to leave the bridge in the awful conditions, had moved alongside in the inky blackness between the lightning flashes and had relieved himself, not realising that Dan's bare feet would give the game away.

Nearing New York, Dan and Jim got excited at the prospect of going ashore and sampling the free suppers at the Mission to Seamen or the Apprentices Club, the tables loaded with cakes and buns, chocolate-coated dates, figs, ginger and ice cream – all the delicious food they had heard about. But the Third Mate and his cohorts decided to give the juniors haircuts to smarten them up for the big city. They sat the innocents down and sheared the hair off their heads until they looked like a pair of scrubbing brushes. Then they vigorously applied what they called a hair tonic, which turned out to be kerosene: they might have planned a singe, but, at that precise moment, the Second Mate, hearing the hullabaloo, poked his head around the door to see what all the noise was about. The bullies looked rather sheepish when Mr Thomas asked them if they had nothing better to do instead of acting like kindergarten children.

Nothing was going to deter Dan and Jim from going ashore, so the first evening, they visited both the Mission and the Apprentices Club. Taking off their caps as they entered, they not only displayed their convict-style haircuts but released a pungent odour of kerosene as well. They certainly cleared a space around themselves which was very useful when supper was served... it's an ill wind!

It was June, and the weather was hot and oppressive, but no one swam in the dock water which was thick with muck from the sewers and drains. After a week in Brooklyn, when even the attraction of the delicious free suppers was waning, the ship sailed for Newark, not far away in New Jersey, to discharge the remaining timber. There the dock water was relatively clean and inviting, but even here the tomfoolery of the Third Mate nearly cost Dan his life: he had swum up behind Dan, pushed him under, and stood on his shoulders.

Tudor Thomas, the Second Mate, was watching, saw the danger and shouted at the stupid man to release Dan, who shot to the surface with his lungs bursting for air.

It seemed as though the two juniors had a guardian angel in the shape of the Second Mate, and it was just as well, as the seniors never tired in harassing their younger cabin mates.

When the last of the fragrant timber had been off loaded at Newark, the ship sailed in ballast down the eastern seaboard of the United States, around the Florida coast close in to Miami, across the Gulf of Mexico to Galveston in Texas. This port was at the seaward end of a ship canal connecting it to Houston, fifty miles inland. At the Houston end, a turning basin enabled ocean-going ships to turn around and head out again after being loaded or discharged.

Canadian City was to load a full cargo of scrap iron and cotton for Shanghai, Yokohama and Kobe. The iron came alongside the ship in huge railway trucks and then, with powerful electromagnets on the end of crane wires, the scrap was lifted in clumps from the trucks, swung over the ship's gaping hatchways and the current cut to let the load fall into the hold.

It was rather a tedious process, but almost three thousand tons were loaded in two weeks. On the 4th July, Independence Day, the waterfront workers had a holiday and Dan spent the day helping the Ship's Carpenter forage for useful bits of cargo. By accident, Chips, who would have made the proverbial Scotsman look like a reckless spendthrift, dropped a fifty cent coin in among the scrap iron. Most people would have written it off, but not Chips, and with Dan's help he carefully shifted the iron, piece by piece, until at last he saw the coin and retrieved it. He was so excited, he impulsively gave Dan twenty five cents.

For Dan, the windfall meant a banana split for fifteen cents plus two five cent candy bars. He and Jim had already spent their pocket money, but Dan remembered the milk bar uptown, advertising the biggest and best banana splits in town so he invited Jim along. They were no sooner in the main street when they were faced by a pretty girl shaking a collection box, right under their noses. Her sparkling eyes and dazzling smile were too much for Dan, and before he realised what he was doing he dropped his precious twenty-five cent piece into her box!

As she moved on, the full horror of what he had done hit him. "What a fool, a complete idiot!" he said to himself and with heavy hearts he and Jim turned to go back to the ship. They had only gone a few paces, when Dan saw the glint of something falling right in front of his face. It tinkled as it fell and with the zest and zeal of a rugby forward diving for a try, he pounced upon it before it had a chance to bounce a second time. To their amazement it was a fifty cent piece! Talk about 'pennies from heaven' and with a bonus as well. They resolved to head for the milk bar without further distraction and there, they were able to indulge in their heart's desire better than they would have been able to do originally.

During the sojourn in Houston, Dan's mate Jim required medical treatment, which the Captain was not qualified to perform. Both went uptown to a doctor's surgery where, following an examination, it was decided circumcision was the best remedy. Poor Jim, without further ado, was laid out on the surgery table, given a local anaesthetic, and operated on right away. The only trouble was, as Jim confided to Dan later, the anaesthetic did not take effect until much later with the result that Jim screamed with agony and needed the bulky weight of the Captain to keep him on the table. Jim was bandaged and sent back to the ship with the restriction that he was to be put on 'light duties only' for a couple of days.

On a happier note, while still in Houston, a group of people came on board to invite anyone interested to attend an evangelical meeting at their hall.

Neither Dan nor Jim had any idea what an evangelical meeting was, but hearing that there would be a free supper, both boys decided to take up the invitation. Being accustomed to the brusque, unfriendly treatment on board, it was an agreeable surprise for the pair to be greeted with real warmth. They didn't understand what was said during the meeting, and were puzzled at the frequent shouts of "Hallelujah!", "Praise the Lord!" and "Amen!", but they were impressed by the joy that animated these people. They lapped up the motherly attention of the women and the splendid spread of cakes and coffee that was served after the meeting.

The boys were delighted they had come and even enquired if there would be more meetings. When a family offered to collect them from the ship the following Sunday, and take them to church, they readily agreed. These kind and loving people were hoping the preaching of the Gospel would make an impact on the boys, but at this stage in their lives fodder for the inner man was a priority. The spiritual would come later.

One thing did remain in Dan's mind for years. Those were the Depression days, unemployment was making life difficult for thousands of people, and it seemed that the preacher's livelihood depended to a large extent on the weekly collection. The poor man was lamenting the fact, as he told the congregation, that he knew times were hard, but there were, "too many nickels and dimes on the plate and not enough quarters and halves!"

With the loading of scrap iron completed, the ship sailed down the canal to Galveston, to top off with bales of cotton for Shanghai. In Galveston Dan was impressed with the superb physique of the black cargo workers. He was keen on physical fitness and body-building himself and envied them their powerful frames. He reckoned that if he was built on similar lines himself, he would have the greatest pleasure in cleaning up the Third Mate and the four senior apprentices single-handed.

There were also some equally big and buxom black women who sold juicy water melons which were cheap enough for the boys to buy. It was rumoured that these women were themselves also available at a very reasonable price, but it seemed that even the most amorous of the crew were not keen to be embraced by those massive arms and outsize bosoms.

The loading was finished, with the bales of cotton making a neat and compact stow for the long voyage ahead, so it was down to the Panama Canal for Dan's third transit. The long, thirty-six day Great Circle track across the North Pacific was uneventful, with good weather all the way, but after seeing no ships at all throughout the passage, the Sea of Japan seemed congested. From the Hakodate Strait in northern Japan, all the way to Shanghai, there was a wide variety of ships, and after entering the Yangtze Kiang river, countless dhows and sampans joined the crowd. The pilot who boarded at this point revealed his nationality by his broad Scottish accent, "Harrrd a' starrrboarrrd, full ahead," giving Dan's Scot's blood a thrill.

The sleek P&O liners, and white-painted, yellow-funnelled CPR ships connecting the Orient with Vancouver and the Canadian Pacific Railway, fascinated Dan: ships can be every bit as beautiful as women; maybe that is why they are called 'she', he pondered.

As *Canadian City* approached Shanghai's port at Woosung, the oriental atmosphere thrilled Dan's romantic nature to the core. He was in China! They steamed up the busy Woosung river, past a string of warships representing the various concessions into which the city was divided at that time. There were British – the smartest and best, naturally – then American, French, Japanese, Italian and Portuguese. There was even a four-funnel Russian cruiser, of pre-World War One vintage.

China had been exploited by those nations for many years and there were many levels of existence there, from the sophisticated prosperity of the commercial districts, to the extreme poverty of the sampan people, and derelicts lying in the gutters of side streets and alleyways.

Discharging the cotton began as soon as the ship berthed alongside a pontoon in the river, and instead of heavy, muscular blacks heaving the bales around, the skinny Chinese coolies seemed just as capable, a point Dan thoughtfully noted, keen as he was on physical culture.

Mail was distributed and hungrily read and reread by the crew. There was a letter from Dan's mother and he became aware of her great love for him, as when she said goodbye to him, she sensed, she would not see him again in this life.

That in fact, was quite true, her heart and spirit had been broken by Dan's departure and she never fully recovered. Luckily Dan was unaware of this, or he would have been shattered had he known: he had his mother's soft disposition.

When they were able to go ashore, Dan and Jim were naturally excited, and on their way to the Seamen's Mission they passed many exotic-looking places of entertainment. One such place was a dance-hall-cum-cabaret, the 'Palace of the Moon', and peering through the open entrance into the colourful interior, they saw gorgeous slant-eyed Chinese girls dressed in ravishing ankle-length gowns with thigh-high splits. Neither Dan nor Jim could dance, even if they had had the money to spend in such a place, so they walked on to the Mission where there was a concert and, of course, supper – always the high point of the boys' shore excursions.

While ashore, they often witnessed brawls. One night, on their way back to the waterfront and the sampans waiting to take them back to the ship, they saw a drunken Navy man arguing over the cost of a rickshaw ride. A big Sikh policeman, his turban making him look like a giant, strode over and walloped the Chinese rickshaw wallah with his cane, then he picked up the rear end of the frail vehicle to bang it down with such force that both wheels buckled with the tyres hanging loose. The distressed and weeping coolie, still protesting, was kicked up the backside and chased away.

Dan nearly wept too at the injustice of it all, but he couldn't help the poor man. He was sickened at this show of racism and weight of authority, but felt that some day it would all be corrected. How right he would prove to be.

The cotton discharged, the ship sailed for Kobe and Osaka, Japanese ports on the Inland Sea where the scrap iron was to be offloaded. Although it was only 1928, the joke was that one day the Japanese would fire it all back at the Americans, and of course, the time came when they did just that.

Kobe and Osaka were busy seaports, with most commodities cheap enough for Dan and Jim to buy, so they bought some tinned fish and fruit, and small presents for their families. Even their limited funds had considerable buying power in the Japan of those days: that was what made the visits to this thriving country so popular.

It might be thought that the boys seemed unduly concerned about their stomachs, it should be pointed out that *Canadian City*, like all British ships, was obliged to comply with the minimum Board of Trade Scale of Provisions, so crews were not likely to starve, but economic concerns did not allow for any extras. Young men, especially growing young men at sea, have ravenous appetites. The weekly ration for every man on board was: tea one ounce, coffee one ounce, sugar ten ounces, tinned butter two ounces. There was one tin of condensed milk per man for three weeks, one pound of bread or the equivalent in dry biscuit, and one pint of drinking water per man per day. This was known as 'the pound and pint' a legitimate claim for all.

There were also three cooked meals each day at 8 a.m., noon and 5 p.m., but it needed a good cook doing his best to provide palatable meals with the limited resources available to him. In Dan and Jim's case, by the time the four seniors had taken their share out of the kitties, the remains were somewhat meagre. Breakfast was burgoo, the cheapest oatmeal available, and was full of weevils, but everyone turned a blind eye to that, and stirring in a spoonful of molasses, would demolish the lot. There were no refrigerators on board those ships then, only an icebox, so fresh meat, apart from the weevils, lasted barely a week. After that it was either tinned meat of unknown origin, or 'salt junk' (beef or pork). Fresh vegetables also disappeared from the menu after a few days, but potatoes sometimes lasted for two weeks.

The fish for Friday afternoon tea was dried salted hake, which looked more like thick cardboard, and was so hard, that it had to be hacked into pieces and soaked for a day before it was needed. It was then boiled for hours, and though the smell was repulsive, the fish was eaten, though sometimes with lack of enthusiasm. The white sauce that accompanied the fish to try and make it more palatable was similar to wallpaper paste in appearance and probably in taste too.

To eke out the condensed milk, Dan learned to make two small holes diametrically across the top of the tin, and to blow out a dollop into his tea or coffee mug. Then he plugged the holes till the next time, to keep out the cockroaches who would otherwise gorge themselves to death on the contents.

After Kobe, the ship sailed to Yokohama to finish off the discharge of scrap iron. While in port, she was caught in a severe typhoon. She was anchored in the bay and had to drop a second anchor and use the main engines to ease the strain on both anchor cables. This manoeuvre saved *Canadian City* from the fate of two other vessels, which were blown on to the breakwater and badly damaged. When the weather abated, unloading was resumed and completed, and then she sailed for Vancouver to load grain for Lisbon.

By this time, Dan and Jim had grown in physical strength and confidence, they could not be so easily intimidated or manhandled, and the days of horseplay by the seniors were coming to an end. Dan was of medium height, weighed ten stone and was well-proportioned, he had regular features, dark-brown hair, blue eyes and had a cheerful, optimistic nature. He was also developing an interest in women and had been fascinated by the demure daintiness of the oriental girls.

It was now autumn and there was considerable fog in the North Pacific since the Great Circle course had taken them up into the vicinity of the Aleutian Islands, to take advantage of the favourable current, and it was very cold.

One perishing morning, when the empty ship was bowling along with hatches open, while the holds were being prepared for the grain, the Cook's kitten, frisking around as kittens do, lost its balance and fell fifty feet down on to the steel floor of number two hold. The poor little animal was badly injured, so the Bos'n put it into a bucket to be hauled up and thrown overboard. Someone must have told the Cook what had happened, for he arrived at the scene just in time to save his pet from a watery grave. He was not a man to take liberties with and he had a violent temper, but he was as concerned about the kitten as if it had been his child. He made splints for the forelegs which were both broken, bathed and tended its small mouth and nose which were also damaged, and made the animal as comfortable as possible. He crooned over his pet as a mother would over her baby. Yes, Dan had seen the same cook in a furious argument over food, eyeball to eyeball with the ferocious Norwegian Bos'n, the Cook with a raised cleaver, and the Bos'n with a steel marline spike aimed an inch away from the Cook's ample belly, but fortunately such squalls blow over and peace returns. Seafarers, on the whole, are real softies where animals and birds are concerned, so everyone was delighted when a couple of weeks later the kitten was able to leave its cosy nest and soon resumed its playful habits, hopefully having learned to look before it leapt.

The whole eighteen days passage across the Pacific was spent erecting shifting boards to partition the holds, and feeders in the 'tween decks, to stop the bulk grain shifting with the rolling of the ship.

Approaching the coast of Vancouver Island, seagulls in their hundreds accompanied the ship, wheeling and shrieking over any food thrown overboard. One day, when Dan was doing some washing on deck, he put the soap on the hatch while he rubbed the clothes. Instantly, a bird swooped down, swallowing it as it rose into the air. This led to scraps of old food from the galley being tied by a fishing line and thrown to the birds, who when they had swallowed it and flown away, lost it again when the line reached its limit, but this practice was quickly stopped.

In Vancouver, Dan and Jim soon located the Mission to Seamen, known also as the Flying Angel, because of the one shown on their flag. They were warmly welcomed by the kind missioner and his helpers, and graciously attended Sunday morning service with an eye to the lunch that followed.

In the afternoon, they explored the town, and while gazing through the window of a milk bar, they were approached by a pleasant man who asked if they would like a milk shake. Vancouver had a reputation for friendliness in those days, so Dan and Jim accepted the man's invitation. Over their milk shakes, the man said that his family liked to meet English boys and would they come home with him? They were pleased and flattered so followed their new friend into the street and headed for the nearest streetcar stop. In spite of the year at sea, they were still too trusting and could not see anything wrong in going to see this man's family on a Sunday afternoon.

While the three of them waited for the tram Dan was surprised to see their friend the missioner coming down the street, and even more surprised when he came up to their would-be host and said in a brusque manner: "Okay mister, I'll take over now."

To the boys' amazement the man turned away without a word. The missioner explained that the man was a notorious seducer of young boys and had only recently been released from prison.

In spite of their naïveté, Dan and Jim were not entirely ignorant of such depravity. On board they had often heard that someone or other was 'after their ring' and they knew that they had to be on guard against lecherous shipmates, especially when stripped off in the bathroom.

When loading was finally completed after a pleasant six days in Vancouver, they sailed for Lisbon in company with another tramp steamer, *Ramon de Larrinaga*. They remained in sight of one another for the twenty day run to the Canal, and the eighteen day crossing of the Atlantic to the ancient and very busy port of Lisbon. There, when Dan saw the way their golden grain was discharged, he was disgusted. The workers often spat and sometimes urinated into the wheat and the thought of the wheat being milled into flour for human consumption put him off eating shoreside bread.

One evening, towards the end of their three week stay, Dan and Jim went ashore by launch for a look-see. During the course of their wanderings, they came across Chips sitting at a pavement table. He invited them to join him and share his vino, which Dan thought tasted more like vinegar than wine.

They had no sooner settled down at the table than a voluptuous, dark-eyed youngish woman sidled into the remaining seat. She ignored the two boys and concentrated on Chips, propositioning him in broken English as Dan and Jim watched, fascinated. When however, she displayed the same repulsive habits of the cargo workers, clearing her nose and throat and spitting, they decided a kiss from her would not be so pleasant after all. Apparently, Chips did not suffer from such scruples, because a little later he and the girl left the table and disappeared. The next day, Dan asked him how he had got on.

Apparently, the girl had thought Chips was tipsy and had taken him to her apartment for the sort of reception all too common for unsuspecting clients, especially drunken seamen. As they entered, two men waiting behind the door pounced on Chips, intending to rob him and then beat him up before dumping him in some alley to recover or whatever.

Unfortunately for them, Chips was neither drunk nor just another seaman, he was as strong as an ox and exceptionally fit. He could put his long arms around a four hundred pound barrel of salt beef and walk away with it. So when his would-be assailants made their move he just reached out, grabbed their throats and banged their heads together with such force it knocked all the fight out of them. Then he threw them like rag dolls down a flight of stone steps into a basement. The girl ran screaming after them, but not before Chips was able to land a well-aimed kick to her backside as she went. He felt he had taught the trio a lesson they wouldn't forget in a hurry.

There had been heavy fog during their three weeks at anchor. For the apprentices, that meant keeping two hour watches throughout the night on the fo'c'sle head to ring the ship's bell for five seconds every two minutes – the required signal for a ship at anchor in fog. In Lisbon, the tedious task was made very unpleasant because the cargo workers used the ship's hawse-pipes as toilets, and despite the fact that the area was scrubbed down every morning, the stench was such that the apprentices rang the bell with one hand while holding their noses with the other.

No one was sorry when the ship sailed, this time for the Red Sea to load phosphate for Korea. This was disappointing for those who had hoped she would head for some UK port to pay off, but such is life for men on trampships: all right maybe for single men, though not so good for the married. Dan always felt sorry for both husbands and wives when sailing from a home port on a voyage lasting perhaps two years. On this occasion, it so happened that before *Canadian City* reached Gibraltar, orders were received by wireless of a change of plans. They were to proceed to the River Plate for another cargo of grain. This was good news for all hands, because first, it saved them from having to dismantle the shifting boards and feeders, and second, there was the distinct possibility of a cargo for, perhaps the Continent or a United Kingdom port. So the ship changed course for Tenerife to fill her bunkers with coal and incidentally gave the crew a chance to see that very old, picturesque port, steeped in maritime history, although that aspect hadn't registered in the chartering plans of Head Office. Five hours of bunkering and they were on their way again, to cross the equator a few days later.

The new crew members were so used to all sorts of practical jokes by then, such as being sent down to the engine room in off duty time on a Sunday morning for a 'long stand', that when they were told to listen for the bump as the ship crossed the line, they were smart enough to ignore the instruction. However, as several of them had not yet been south of the equator, they had to submit themselves to the time-honoured ceremony of Crossing the Line. Naturally, the weather through the tropics was hot, but the speed of the ship created a cooling breeze unless they had a fair, or following, wind which would bring out the sweat when working hard. Flying fish skimmed the surface of the sea or leapt high out of the water onto the deck.

Then it was Christmas, Dan's second at sea, although as far as meals went it was hardly different from any Sunday. The officers, deck and engine-room personnel had ham and some titbits, bought in Tenerife. For a change, the rest of the crew were treated to fresh pork, although they reckoned that it was actually the flesh of an old wild boar, grown too old and muscle-bound to escape the hunters: it would have made good boot leather.

The ham was delicious according to the officers. That was too much for the apprentices who had noticed the gammon hanging in the pantry six feet in from the open porthole. If the porthole was left open overnight, they planned to take advantage of the fact, and for just one night it was. Ingeniously, they lashed a razor-sharp sheath knife to the end of one broomstick and a fork to the end of another and managed to saw off chunks of ham which was, they agreed, delicious. Christmas pudding was just Sunday plum duff with a few extra currants thrown in, covered with the usual sauce that tasted like sweetened wallpaper paste.

The River Plate, when they arrived, was crowded with shipping. At Buenos Aires, the pilot guided them to a berth at a wheat-loading silo, then the customs and immigration formalities were completed, including a medical examination known colloquially as a 'short arm' inspection. In the evening Dan and Jim headed for the Flying Angel as was their custom, and as usual their lack of funds kept them on the straight and narrow, away from the temptations of vivacious, dark-eyed señoritas, who seemed to abound in every window.

The missioner in Buenos Aires was Canon Brady, well known in shipping circles. One of his activities was the training of young Argentineans in the art of boxing. In his prime, he would challenge any visiting seaman or stoker to a few rounds in the ring and he had the reputation of being a tough and capable fighter. It was said that he started Luis Firpo, the Wild Bull of the Pampas, world heavyweight boxing contender, on his way to the record books and his two hectic clashes with world champion Jack Dempsey. They spent most of their bouts knocking each other over the ropes and out of the ring, but Dempsey prevailed in the end.

The three weeks it took to load the wheat passed quickly enough, then they sailed 'Falmouth for orders', meaning the final destination of the cargo would be determined en route by the charterers in London. Everyone was happy at the prospect of seeing their loved ones and as they approached the English Channel, this rosy glow developed into the well-known euphoria: the 'Channels'.

While in Buenos Aires, the hull of the ship had been given a fresh coat of gleaming black paint, so that she would end her maiden voyage looking reasonably respectable to the critical eye of the company's marine superintendent. Now, with the good weather expected during the run through the tropics the whole ship was freshly painted. The First Mate took extreme care about this and in consultation with the Bos'n they chose the right men for the various jobs. Only the most competent A.B.'s were entrusted with giving the upper and lower bridge structure a gleaming coat of white enamel: lesser lights could do the remaining parts of the superstructure. The senior apprentices would be given the masts, derricks and shrouds, while the two juniors were assigned to the messy task of making a start on painting the ten steam winches. An attractive rich tan colour was used for the masts and applied by brush, but the shrouds and stays were coated with a white lead compound applied by a wad of cotton-waste dipped into the mixture, a messy job swinging from a bos'n's chair. Of course, the winches were the messiest job of all and with no hints or tips as to the best way to go about it, Dan and Jim, each with a bucketful of black paint and crude oil mix, and wads of cotton-waste, were left to their own devices. Each had been secretly told to race against his mate, but they were close enough friends to ignore such suggestions, and by the time they started their third winch, it dawned on them the best way to go about the job was to paint the innermost parts first and work out from there, not the reverse, which they had been doing. On the most suitable day for the job, the four A.B.'s were allotted the task of painting the funnel, the upper quarter black, and the lower three quarters a special red. Since the funnel casing was very hot, the painters suspended in bos'n's chairs needed thick burlap kneepads and boots sitting right up to the hot surface as they were, and the paint had to be applied quickly. Finally, the steel decks, one side at a time, were given a coat of black paint and oil mixed, to complete the picture of a well-run, well-cared-for ship and so enhance the chances of promotion for the First Mate. Flying fish landed on the decks and many were caught, passed to the Cook and ended up boiled, steamed or inside a fish pie – there was no fat for frying, so sadly, there was no fish 'n' chips.

Approaching the Azores, the Captain received orders to proceed to Antwerp to discharge their cargo. This was good news, though the last week of the voyage was typically wintry and cold. They arrived off the mouth of the great River Scheldt, picked up a pilot and proceeded upstream to the docks of Antwerp, one of the largest and busiest on the European continent.

The discharge of the bulk wheat there was much more efficient than it had been in Lisbon. It was sucked up long, flexible tubes into huge containers on the wharves and, since the work went on for sixteen hours a day, the ship rose almost visibly out of the dock water.

With the trampships being away from their homelands for such long periods, the wives of the senior officers were allowed by the company to visit their husbands while the ship was in home waters. On this occasion, the wives of the Captain, Chief Engineer and Chief Steward travelled to Antwerp from Wales. When Dan remarked that two large people in one bunk would not leave room to turn, he was told that the officers' bunks could be extended and an extra section of mattress fitted. 'Nice for some,' thought Dan.

It was while the ship was in Antwerp that Dan got one of the most shattering blows of his life. He was awakened from a deep sleep early one morning, to be told by Captain Davies that his mother had died. He had been looking forward so much to seeing her, and surprising her with a small Japanese trinket box, but now he felt that the bottom of his world had fallen through. At breakfast time, it seemed unbelievable that, apart from briefly expressing sorrow at hearing the news, his cabin-mates could laugh and joke and carry on as usual. It dawned on Dan that he, and he alone, must carry the burden of grief.

During the morning, he was summoned to the Captain's cabin to be told he would be going home on compassionate leave as soon as the ship reached Hull, so he had better get his gear packed and ready to go. While he was not sorry to leave those who had made his life a misery early on, he was sorry at parting from Jim: he had been such a stalwart friend through the experiences they had shared together. He would have three new mates on his next voyage, and would no longer be a junior.

Canadian City was to proceed from Hull to Archangel, in Arctic Russia to load timber for Noumea, New Caledonia, almost diametrically on the opposite side of the world, but for Dan it was farewell to his first ship.

The University Of Experience
Stage II

Dan travelled from Hull to Chichester with mixed emotions; he was happy at the prospect of seeing his father, sister and friends again, yet melancholy at the thought of home without his mother. His father and sister were pleased to see him and Dan appreciated the good food, comfort and peace of home after being cooped up with five other youths in the half-deck. But, home wasn't the same without his mother, and after the initial warm welcome from his friends, he realised that he no longer spoke the same language. Everything seemed the same, but he had changed. His month's leave passed all too quickly, then one morning a letter arrived telling Dan to join *Atlantic City* at Newport, the following Friday.

When he saw his new ship for the first time, he could see she was a very old one, and she looked terribly drab and woebegone. She had been under the tips loading coal and was smothered in its dust everywhere.

He soon learned from his new shipmates she had been chartered for ten trips to take Welsh steam coal, the best of its kind in the world to the bunkering port of St Vincent off the coast of West Africa. These trips were so uninteresting and monotonous as to be unworthy of mentioning, but one thing was worth it all: his new cabin-mates were a happy-go-lucky group of lads who compensated for the tedium. At the end of the charter, *Atlantic City* was given a change, a load of coal for Port Said in Egypt, and there was a replacement of the Welsh fireman by six Liverpool men.

So, instead of pressing southwards when abreast of Gibraltar they passed through the Straits and on into the sparkling blue waters of the Mediterranean Sea, heading eastwards towards their goal.

It was Dan's first visit to Port Said and he was intrigued by the antics of the bum-boat men hawking their wares, and by their Arab or Egyptian appearance, complete with fez, contrasting with their names, painted proudly on the stern-sheets of their dinghies: Sandy McNab or Jock McGregor and Hamish Macpherson. They were equally proud of the 'references' given them by earlier customers along the lines of "This fellow is a rogue and vagabond, do not deal with him," or "This lying blackguard would steal the milk out of your tea, watch him!"

Dan felt that these fellows could tell by the way their testimonials were received that they were phoney, but they were such a shrewd lot they just rode along with them to humour the customers.

They didn't get things all their own way. Dan heard of a fireman who swapped a tin of fifty cigarettes for a canary which turned out to be a sparrow dyed yellow, but the fireman wasn't worried. He had carefully removed the cigarettes and filled the space with ash from the galley fire, then just as carefully re-sealed the tin.

Dan also got used to these traders whispering "You come sleep with my daughter, eh? Vaaary clean, vaaary sweet, vaaary pleasant."

Before arriving at the port, everything of value that was portable was either removed to safekeeping or nailed, screwed or bolted down and sealed. But there were also industrious Arabs, boatmen who patiently waited as the coal was being discharged into barges, ready to dive to the seabed to recover any coal spilled into the harbour. When they had gathered a sackful, they would row ashore to sell it. These fellows would often get a bit of help from the winchmen on board who would accidentally bump the ship's side with the loaded baskets and cause a spillage. This 'Robin Hood' code of robbing the rich to help the poor is well-established in ports around the world. When the holds were empty of coal, they were swept thoroughly and made ready to load bulk phosphate at Safaga.

The Suez Canal was full of ships passing through: smart passenger liners, cargo ships, deeply laden tankers homeward bound, most of them piloted by the British or French personnel of the Suez Canal Authority. They were said to be the most highly-paid pilots in the world, but in 1956 President Nasser of Egypt changed all that by nationalising that vital waterway.

When Dan first went through, it was 1930, when camel trains were still a common sight, shambling along the road alongside the canal. They seemed oblivious to what was going on around them, and were part of a different world altogether.

Safaga in those days was just a rock-phosphate crushing works, with a few sheds, a primitive rail-track down to the jetty and nothing but dry brown hills all around. The Arab workers, with a minimum of mechanisation, set about their task, in the terrible heat and dust, to load over eight thousand tons of phosphate in three weeks.

There was nothing to do ashore, but one evening the Scottish manager of the works produced a soccer ball, and challenged the ship to a match. With over thirty Britishers to choose from, they expected to be more than a match for the locals, but the Arabs, barefooted and fleet-footed, ran rings round them. They were like sunburnt Glasgow Rangers, filled with the same dedication and verve, and *Atlantic City* United team, humbled and disunited in defeat, returned to their ship.

The ship sailed for Japan, but a few days later the engineer's messroom boy began to behave in a peculiar fashion, howling like a wolf at night. At first it was thought that the Red Sea heat had unbalanced him, but his condition deteriorated even in the cooler temperatures of the Indian Ocean, and he was taken out of the small cabin he shared with two others and locked up in the lazaret aft.

Before he was restrained, it was found that he had suddenly developed tremendous strength. He could tear up heavy canvas, and wrench solidly-built racks and shelving off the bulkhead. It took the Bos'n and two hefty seamen to handcuff the boy to an iron ladder, but then he started bashing his head against it. The Bos'n's men made a large mattress out of an old tarpaulin and straw, and on this the boy was spreadeagled, to prevent him scratching, gouging himself and masturbating. He was wild-eyed and drooling, and much of the time howling or screaming with bouts of maniacal, spine-chilling laughter.

Fortunately, he had periods of calmness and then the Steward managed to feed him and dress his wounds. As he seemed to have no control over his bowels or bladder he was kept naked, and the messes he made were hosed away by the watch on deck. It was the duty of the watchkeepers to keep an eye on him at night, and Dan found that no matter how quietly he crept up to peep over the hatch coaming, he found the boy looking at him with an evil leer as though to say, "You can't catch me off guard!" He was finally taken off the ship at Singapore to be properly cared for, and hopefully released from the demonic power that had possessed him.

The galley boy had taken over the messroom boy's work and four of the apprentices took turns to work in the ship's galley or kitchen. Dan enjoyed the change: watching the Cook kneading dough for bread, his sweat and cigarette ash sometimes dropping into the mixture, was just one of many diversions. Another ruse, to rid the galley of unwanted callers at dishing-up times, was to drop a dollop of burnt sugar on the red-hot stove; the acrid fumes soon had the desired effect. One morning during Dan's stint helping the Cook, the Captain, having his daily stroll around the ship, watched him peeling potatoes. Then, asking Dan to hand the peeler to him, he took a penknife from his pocket and proceeded to flatten the depth of cut and handed it back stressing the need for economy. When Dan mentioned this to the Cook, he also took a knife and returned the cut to what it had been, explaining that he depended on those potato peelings for making his yeast and would let the Captain know that. The call at Singapore was solely to land the demented messroom boy, then it was on with the voyage, up through the China Sea to Japan.

Arriving at Moji, Dan was impressed by the demure femininity of the girls in their kimonos and geta – quaint wooden sandals with cleats underneath which raised them a couple of inches off the ground. Japan then was largely untouched by western influences and both the men and women wore traditional Japanese clothing. The women were regarded as little more than chattels and still walked deferentially three or four paces behind their husbands, or masters.

In Wakamatsu, women came on board with kimonos, sashes, silk pyjamas and other pretty things for sale, 'For girlfriends at home', they said with shy smiles. They had brown, almond-shaped eyes, milk-white complexions, a gentle charm and their clothes seemed impregnated with a sweet smelling powder. Dan thought they were absolutely gorgeous, and to his great surprise and pleasure they showed no reluctance in being friendly to him; they were not aloof as he had expected them to be.

At eighteen he had had very little contact with girls, apart from with his sister and her friends, they were just part of the background scenery to him, but he was to discover that he would enjoy a rapport with the opposite sex throughout his life and really enjoy their company. So far though, he had never had a girlfriend.

There was, he remembered, Marlene. She was the nineteen year old daughter of the headmaster of the Sea Training School and one quiet Sunday afternoon he had found himself alone with her. She was sprawled on a settee reading the newspaper and she called Dan over. His mind was on the Morse Code which he was trying to memorise, so when Marlene asked him what he thought of some drawings of ladies' underwear advertised in the newspaper, he truthfully said that he wasn't interested. He was just fifteen years old.

"Don't you feel something," Marlene had asked

"No" said Dan. Whereupon she told him to sit down beside her and then she slid his hand under her skirt on to her bare thigh.

"What now?" she asked, drawing close to him.

Suddenly Dan's whole being was stirred, electrified: he found his hand moving up her leg, 'I would never dream of doing this,' he thought. His heart was thumping, his blood racing, and his whole body was tingling with excitement. Then, GREAT SCOTT!

"What's this... no knickers!... how rude!" So that was why she had been so interested in those advertisements! His mind and emotions were in a complete whirl, yet he was aware of Marlene fumbling to unbutton the flap of his bell-bottom trousers, and he had been at a loss with no idea what to do next: oh dear!

At that critical moment, the door in the hall had slammed loudly. Marlene leapt from the settee and in a flash was over at the bay window gazing out to sea.

Curley, Dan's best friend, bounded into the room to say in an aggrieved tone, "I've been looking for you all over the place!" Dan had had just enough time to drop on his knees beside the settee and pretend he was reading the newspaper. He was still aroused and shaking like a jelly, but wrapping his erring hand in his handkerchief, he got to his feet, picked up his signals book to follow his mate through the door. Looking across to Marlene to say 'bye, bye', before he left, she gave him a quick glance which clearly said, 'Not a word, eh?'

Later, Dan heard that Marlene had been home on holiday from her finishing school in France, and he often wondered just how proficient she became in later years at the end of her course. It was several minutes after leaving the house before Dan could settle to take in what Curley was rattling on about; it all seemed so unimportant: he had just discovered that it is not only a girl's pretty face that captivates a man but something much more gripping.

However, back in the Japanese ports, Dan and his mates who were completely different to his former ones enjoyed themselves within the limited range of their funds and felt the Japanese race akin to their own, the British.

Experiencing the daily spartan life of their calling, they truly relished the cosy, welcoming friendship of the 'table-masters', as the Japanese waitresses were called in those days. To be attended to with such dedication was something completely new and nice to Dan and his mates. Apart from concentrating on their service, the girls remained demurely quiet, but at one stage, after the young men had been swapping yarns about the fog and its prevalence in certain parts of the world – there was thick fog outside the door – they were surprised when their attendants told them they were very bad boys. Thinking they were in high favour, the lads enquired, "Oh! what makes you say that, what have we done wrong?"

One of the girls then shocked them by saying, "You are bad boys because you all-the-time talk, fog, and foggy-foggy." It took a few seconds for this to register on their minds, but when it did, they roared with laughter, and then they were faced with the ticklish task of explaining the difference between a meteorological phenomena and a common swearword, not normally used in mixed company. Thus ended their pleasurable, all too brief sojourn in Wakamatsu, then back to the sea.

Leaving Japan, *Atlantic City* set forth on her Great Circle course across the North Pacific. It was a cold and foggy trip at that time of the year and long before radar, so the risk of collision was always present. The fog signals – a prolonged blast on the steam whistle every two minutes – made the engineers grumpy at what they regarded was a waste of their precious steam pressure.

However, the need for such precautions was dramatically revealed one morning when, after a night of dense fog, a shaft of sunshine broke through and was reflected from the wheelhouse windows of a loaded Shell oil tanker fine on the port bow on a reciprocal course. The crew of both ships got quite a shock at being so close in mid-ocean, and so much further north than the normal shipping lanes.

It was at this time that the apprentices and seamen were given a job that modern seamen would refuse to do because it was too dangerous and unhealthy: cleaning out the sediment of the oil that was carried in the double bottom tanks of the ship. After years of carrying crude oil, this sediment, the consistency of butter, seriously reduced the capacity of the tanks and had to be cleared out.

The tanks were constructed in cells to provide maximum strength for the ship and before the men entered, the space had to be aired to allow as much of the gas as possible to escape. Then the first group of six men, wearing only a sack with holes cut in the lower corners for leg-holes and the top laced over the shoulders with rope-yarn, entered the dark, smelly, sticky compartment. They squeezed through the oval manhole into a space with three feet of headroom and sediment eight inches deep. It was as black as the inside of a cow, as someone quipped, and Dan began to understand about claustrophobia, and the panic it can produce: it was awful. They were supposed to empty each bay into the one next to it through gaps in the steel partitions, so that the sludge could eventually be suctioned out into the sea from the end bay. Sitting on the cold steel plating with the muck up to his waist, and the freezing North Pacific swishing past less than an inch below, Dan thought of nicer places he could be. At first it was thought too risky, because of the gas, to have even an electric light down there, but later one was installed. That restored a measure of confidence and made the wretched operation much easier and quicker, and as a result, it was completed in three days in a series of two three-hour shifts per day. Still, they had breathed in noxious fumes and suffered some after-effects, and in spite of vigorous washing it took a while to get rid of the smell of the oil and the corrosive effects of the acids on their skin.

Everyone was thankful to reach Vancouver and to commence loading a full cargo of grain for Europe. One of their first calls on getting ashore was to head for the Empire Café in Hastings Street, their favourite eating spot, where the speciality was ham, eggs and chipped potatoes in generous helpings for seventy-five cents.

The voyage down the west coast was interesting, in that they had another trampship doing the same, *Ullapool,* belonging to the Ropner Line, which was where Dan's friend Curley had been indentured.

Though sometimes only a mile apart and at others hull down on the horizon, they remained in sight of each other all the way to the English Channel where they parted company, *Ullapool* for Rotterdam and *Atlantic City* to Victoria Docks, London. For Dan, his first round the world voyage was successfully completed, but on arrival he was transferred to *Prince Rupert City* which was also discharging cargo in another part of London's vast docks.

Atlantic City went on to serve her owners well, whoever they were – the Chinese just before World War Two, and then the Japanese Yusen Kaisha line, before finally being torpedoed and sunk by an American submarine in the Caroline Islands in 1942.

The University Of Experience
Stage III

While *Prince Rupert City* was discharging her cargo in London, Dan was allowed to visit his old home in Chichester to see his sister, following the unexpected death of their father during Dan's last voyage. He was beginning to see how self-centred he had been with scarce a thought about his sister, his sole next of kin. Father had died suddenly on the operating table, having a cataract removed from his left eye.

It was good to see how well she was fitting in with her temporary adopted family, and comforting to find that the family finances were sufficient to enable him to complete his apprenticeship. The coming voyage should do that very nicely.

During Dan's absence, the ship changed articles – the old crew were paid off, some were invited to sign on for another voyage and those not wanted were replaced. This did not apply to the apprentices who had signed their indentures for four years and now, he was about to begin the last trip of his apprenticeship, another round-the-world voyage lasting over eight months. Sailing from London, *Prince Rupert City* proceeded to Cardiff to complete the discharge of her cargo and to prepare for the next one. After restocking with supplies, the ship sailed for Tampa and other Gulf ports to load cased oil and cotton for the Far East.

The transatlantic run was uneventful and after rounding Key West, *Prince Rupert City* proceeded up the Florida coast to Tampa and from there to Mobile in Alabama. There Dan and Mac, one of his new cabin-mates, decided to explore uptown, although as usual they had very little money.

The road was a long and dusty one and as they trudged along, an old Ford jalopy pulled up and two female occupants offered them a lift. The lads jumped into the back seat as the driver, in a broad Southern drawl, asked, "Where u'r youse guys goin'?"

"Nowhere in particular," answered Dan.

"Wud youse like to come to our place?"

"If it's anywhere near town it's okay with us," said Mac.

It was rather dark by the time they reached a ramshackle house, Dan and Mac could see that the girls were much older than they had thought and were heavily made up.

When they got inside the house, the driver put her hand out saying, "It'll be faive darllors each for a 'short-time,' okay?" Any illusions the lads might have had were now shattered.

Dan said, "FIVE dollars! We haven't got that much between us," whereupon the woman swore, then said,

"Well how much yuh got anyway?"

Mac piped up, "About forty cents," which wasn't exactly true and this prompted both women to mouth a few choice American oaths.

In disgust, one said to the other, "Come on, Hett, let's change 'n' see what's cookin' uptown" and then and there they stripped down to their underwear.

At that point, a couple of rough-looking men appeared at the door, and said, "I see ya gotta coupla suckers here!"

Hettie replied, "Hell no, they're a coupla Limeys and they ain't got it, what the heck."

"Yuh silly bitches, peaked caps don't mean they got money: you'll be picking up cops next, stupid gits." With that gentle tirade, the men disappeared, the women got dressed and drove Dan and Mac back to the main street of town. There they found a milk bar which served their favourite gastronomic delight, banana splits. Chuckling over their escapade, they were thankful for their release from what could have been a ticklish predicament.

Their other loading ports were New Orleans: too expensive, and Beaumont, where Dan met a group of friendly people leaving a hall who asked, "Are you saved?" They were Pentecostalists, and Dan remembered the people who had been so kind to him and Jim in Houston three years before. So, when these people in Beaumont invited Dan to attend their meeting, he persuaded Mac and the four younger apprentices to go along too. Again, it was a pleasurable experience, and they were entertained at various homes by these hospitable people. They certainly seemed to be following the lifestyle of what they preached: brotherly love.

With a full cargo of cased oil and cotton, *Prince Rupert City* set off once more down to the Panama Canal, and the long haul across the broad Pacific to Japan. This passage introduced a habit that was to benefit Dan for the remainder of his life. The new carpenter was a Geordie from South Shields, and he was a physical fitness fanatic. He took it upon himself to organise keep fit classes daily among those members of the crew who were interested. His physique was lean and muscular – whipcord would be an apt description – and his programme was varied and thorough. Dan lapped up every minute of the system, rapidly developing a good muscular figure of his own, which was to prove of great value later on.

At Shanghai, Dan was again distressed by the plight of the Chinese people. There always seemed to be a disaster of one sort or another: civil war, flood, revolution or plague. This time it was famine, and there were peasants dying of starvation in the streets, corpses floating down the river, and *sampan* families competing with the seagulls for the scraps thrown overboard from the ships moored in midstream.

Dan pondered on the unfair distribution of the world's ample food supply, and the greed that caused the dire poverty of these poor innocent people.

Prince Rupert City was to help alleviate in a small measure, the shortage of food, by sailing for Sydney, Australia, to load a full cargo of wheat. As a senior apprentice, Dan now enjoyed some minor privileges, and one of these was to watch the plotting of the route from Shanghai to Sydney. The Captain chose a route out of the East China Sea, then well into the Pacific, clear of land before proceeding on a southward curve to enter the Coral Sea south of the Solomon Islands, then to pick up the Australian coast at Cape Byron and on to Sydney.

During the trip, they conducted a crossing-the-line ceremony for the uninitiated. Mac volunteered for the role of King Neptune's wife, a flaxen-haired siren with a wig of rope-yarn, flour for face powder, red lead for rouge and lipstick, and burnt cork for his eyebrows and eyelashes. His singlet had to be upholstered with an ample bosom on which poor shipwrecked sailors could rest their weary heads when they reached their watery graves. It was all good clean fun!

The ship arrived off Sydney Heads, picked up the pilot and entered Port Jackson. The route took them past picturesque coves, bays and inlets with Aboriginal or early settlers' names. Then there was Circular Quay with its trans-harbour ferries, then of course, The Rocks and under the brand new Harbour Bridge which was at that time under construction, and the subject of many protests as being an eyesore. Later it became affectionately known as The Coathanger, and many Australians considered it to be the eighth wonder of the world: the writer adds Amen to the latter. It was and still is a fine example of British engineering.

Dan and his friends loved the free and easy style of Sydney and spent much of their time at a dance academy, where the entrance fee was only 2s/6d (25 cents). Dan was particularly intrigued by the boldness of the lovely Australian girls. As soon as the music started, a girl would come over, stand in front of him and say, "Dense?" He soon picked up the Sydney accent and learned that girls in Australia were called 'sheilas'. What a range of beauties that name covered!

When one of his dance partners said she lived at Bondi, he asked if he could see her home, so they later set off on a Bondi tram and when they arrived at the famous beach, he asked if they could have a stroll along it so that he could tell his friends back home that he had been on Bondi beach with a fair young maiden. It was a balmy moonlit evening, and Dan felt romantic, but he was brought back to earth when Debbie said, "No, you can't tell them THAT, because I'm neither fair, nor a maiden." He was taken aback by her interpretation and chuckled, but didn't try to exploit it. He was unsure how to react so, after a kiss and a cuddle at her front gate he returned to the city and the wharf at Glebe.

The agents had told the Captain that all sorts of things could disappear from the ship overnight, so the apprentices had to take turns being night watchman. On the last night, one of the sailors offered to take the place of the duty apprentice and with the First Mate's permission, the kind offer was accepted. However, this was found to be not the unselfish gesture it appeared to be, and although this night watchman was very much in evidence at the top of the gangway when Dan returned at midnight, the following morning the ruse was revealed, creating a heated discussion between the Captain,

Steward and Cook. It transpired that the previous afternoon, the ship's icebox had been filled with enough meat, fish and eggs to last for about ten days of the passage back to Shanghai. However, when the Cook went to get some provisions for breakfast, he found the padlock wrenched off the icebox, which was now completely empty. The night watchman and his gear had also disappeared. The police were called, but it was clear the seaman had collaborated with shoreside thieves who had helped him desert in return for his part in the theft.

The Old Man decided that the company, having paid for one lot of fresh food, could not be expected to provide another. It was just unfortunate, and they would all have to suffer the consequences. Nowadays, a shipmaster would have no hope of getting away with such a decision, the crew would refuse to sail, but it was a different era then, and *Prince Rupert City* sailed on schedule with a A.B. who was 'on the beach' and who signed on with no questions asked.

The eighteen day passage through the tropics with glorious weather all the way soon passed, and arriving safely in Shanghai, the ship discharged her precious cargo of wheat. When at last the holds were cleaned out again, it looked as if every grain had been swept up or eaten where it lay, it was the cleanest 'clean-out' that had ever been seen.

The galley-wireless or 'ship's grapevine' spread the news that her next destination was to be Vladivostock, to load timber and soya beans for Hamburg and London. The Russian Customs and Port Authority were very strict, it seemed. A complete inventory of everything each crew member possessed had to be made, and every one had to be medically examined. This was a new experience for even the most senior officers and men, who had visited the world's ports for years.

In addition, the ship's wireless office had to be sealed and any messages to or from the ship had to go through the Port Authority. There would be no issue of Russian money, because of tight international currency regulations. They later found there was nothing to buy ashore anyway, so money was superfluous, a welcome change for Dan and his mates. Apart from that, Vladivostock looked grim indeed.

However, soon after their arrival, an elderly Russian official came on board to invite all hands to attend the International

Seamen's Club on the waterfront. They offered indoor sports, dancing and a theatre, and there would be hostesses to help them enjoy themselves. After he had gone, the lads decided to put his advertising to the test that evening.

A large group of healthy young women waited at the club to welcome them, and all spoke English. The men were shepherded into a hall and the women explained that first they must listen to a talk on the benefits of Communism. During the course of these evening lectures, the distinguished diplomat type speaker with his perfect Oxbridge accent announced the astonishing news that the British Navy had mutinied at Invergordon. All the British present absolutely rejected that as wild propaganda, but many years later, Dan learned there had been serious trouble spinning off from the 1926 General Strike throughout the whole Navy, and mutiny had taken place.

The girls were keen on physical culture: some were excellent gymnasts and acrobats and all took part in a combination of dancing and exercises, or aerobics, to keep in shape. They put on a display of their various routines and rhythmic dancing, and Dan was very impressed, now being an enthusiastic physical culturist himself. He was also impressed by the equally striking physiques of the virile young men, whose sleek muscular bodies reminded him of magazine pictures of Mr Universe, though not so muscle-bound.

Dancing, both Russian style and ballroom, was very popular and Dan and his friends were taught the polka and other lively Russian dances. They thoroughly enjoyed themselves, although Dan found that if one of the girls gave his hand a playful squeeze, his fingers would feel as if caught in a vice. He reckoned a slap on the face would probably loosen a few teeth, and he kept this in mind when he accompanied one of them to her apartment block, at closing down time. En route, Trishka told him they were being followed and to prove it they sat on a roadside seat until the 'shadow' passed, and waited till they resumed their homeward trek.

Nevertheless, a warm kiss is nice in anyone's language, in fact, so nice, that on turning back, Dan lost his way. Seeing a large building with lights and a hum of machinery he thought it might be a factory working a night shift, so he headed for it to ask the way to the docks area. As he got nearer he could see a sentry on duty at the entrance.

Wracking his brain for the Russian equivalent of 'English ship' Dan approached the man saying, "Angleesti paraquod, Angleesti paraquod," hoping it made sense, but the man's reaction horrified him. He barked something in Russian, grabbed his rifle, which carried a bayonet, and lunged it towards him. Dan leapt backwards as if struck by lightning, deciding not to parley any further. He eventually located the docks and told his mates next day that he felt sure he would have been skewered if he hadn't managed to jump out of range in time, and that the pleasure of escorting hostesses home wasn't worth the risk involved.

When one evening some of the fine specimens of Russian manhood invited anyone on the ship to take part in a series of boxing contests, everyone scoffed at the very idea of being matched against these superb athletes.

"No, no, no!" they chorused in alarm; they knew their limitations.

Their hosts were not so easily put off, saying, "We always think of the British as a fearless race which had won the mighty British Empire. Surely they would not balk at a friendly spar with the nation they defeated in the Crimea?" Everyone laughed at the obvious bait, wondering if the Russians were seeking revenge for that defeat, and they were not blind to the fact that their hosts were in tiptop shape whereas they were not. Nevertheless, they were finally cajoled into accepting the challenge, with the assurance that the bouts would be friendly exhibition ones. Dan felt obliged to take part even though slightly fearful of getting a battering.

When Dan saw his opponent on the evening of the tournament his fears were confirmed, and while these fellows boxed almost nightly, Dan had only had bouts at the Sea Training School and a few bare fist fights since. He managed to keep on his feet and the only damage he did to his opponent was to remove a scab from his cheekbone, a rather rash thing to do for, in so doing, he was caught with several left jabs and, ducking one of these, he collected a beautifully timed right uppercut full on his nose, which put a bit of colour into the bout.

The Russians were correct in claiming the contests were exhibitions only. They were exhibitions of their superb fitness and boxing ability. The club organisers graciously declared all bouts a draw and complimented everyone for their willingness to take part, so British honour was preserved.

The ship finally completed loading timber in the lower holds and bagged soya beans on top and in the 'tween decks. The six weeks sojourn in Vladivostock had been much more pleasant than expected, and what Dan and his friends liked best was the fact that it cost absolutely nothing, so for once their impoverishment went unnoticed, and unfelt.

Now they were homeward bound. Before sailing, the inventories were checked and a rigorous search was made for stowaways. Then once again they were at sea, down past Japan, Formosa (now Taiwan) and on to the South China Sea, where the only stowaway to beat the search put in an appearance: a mottled ginger cat who was promptly named Red.

There were already three other cats on board: Boxer from Houston, Whiskey from Sydney, and the veteran Smokey from Cardiff. Strangely, these cats chose different parts of the ship for their territory. 'Smart-alec' Smokey had established himself in a corner of the galley, Whiskey chose the firemen's quarters, with Boxer a close neighbour in the sailors' fo'c'sle, while the new boy adopted the chief engineer. They appeared to be isolationists, but once they did meet, as though by arrangement for a conference, sitting at each corner of number three hatch dreamily viewing one another through half-closed eyes. Throughout the whole passage to Europe they were never seen to shape-up for a fight or even to sniff one another. They were all, apparently, disciplined seafaring veterans.

It was fine weather all the way, until the Atlantic changed it with nasty cold winds and rain from Gibraltar all the way to Hamburg. On opening the hatches it was a shock to see the bags of soya beans alive with big fat maggots, but the dockers ignored them and got on with the job. Then it was on to London to discharge the remaining cargo of timber.

It was also the end of Dan's apprenticeship in the 'University of Experience': four years' hard labour to qualify him to sit for his Second Mate's Foreign-Going Certificate. A very welcome benefit for Dan was the fact that for the four months he had exceeded his apprenticeship term, he was paid a full A.B.'s rate, and this windfall provided a helpful bank balance until he could find another job.

The Royal Yacht Squadron

After *Prince Rupert City* paid off, Dan was free to choose his own future. The Depression was biting hard and ships everywhere were laid up. The crews were left to hang around shipping offices on the off-chance of a job. Deck officers and engineers, fully qualified men, were on the disposable heap too, and many, being married men, were desperate for any job and prepared to take lower ranking positions to support their families. There was no inducement for Dan to attend navigation school with such a prospect.

One day, while Dan was visiting Connie and staying at The Golden Fleece, he was drawn into conversation with a rugged-faced man built like a bulldog who said he had known him as a schoolboy, and that it was he who had suggested the Sea Training School to his parents. He introduced himself as Captain Rogers and asked Dan how his career was progressing.

Dan warmed to this bluff, hearty character and told him how he had just finished his apprenticeship and was trying to make up his mind what to do next. It was February 1932, in the middle of the Depression, so when Captain Rogers asked if he would like to work on the large yacht belonging to Lord Stanton, of which he was the Skipper, Dan could hardly believe his ears and promptly said he would. The Skipper explained that the yacht was laid-up on the slipway at Northam, Southampton, but Dan could live on board as ship-keeper and help to look after her. 'What a God-send,' thought Dan, unaware of how truly he spoke.

Dan was to meet Captain Rogers at Chichester railway station two days hence, so they could travel to Southampton together. Dan was neatly dressed in a navy blue Fifty Shilling Tailor's suit, with trilby hat and carrying his suitcase.

While waiting for their train, the Skipper spotted one of his old shipmates on the opposite platform and much to Dan's discomfiture, he called out in a booming voice, "Look at the seaman of today,

George, all geared up like a Bombay tart, suitcase and all. And look at this – a wristwatch!" he continued, pushing up Dan's sleeve. "What's the world coming to, eh George?" Dan's face was as red as a railway porter's tie, but the Skipper gave him a hefty thump on the back to show he meant no ill-will.

Even in her bare winter garb, *Centaurus* looked sleek and graceful with her fine lines and clipper bow. She was a three masted Bermuda-rigged schooner, quite a smart up-to-the-minute rig in those days, needing a minimum of work when beating to windward and speedier in going about. She had plenty of brasswork – twenty skylight gratings and all cleats, leads, bollards and belaying pins were brass – and with white pine decks, richly varnished teak deckhouses, bulwarks and scuppers, *Centaurus* was an eye-catching vessel.

Dan's main duties at first were to be on call during the day and caretaker at night during the week. His pay was two pounds a week – five times his fourth year senior apprentice rate – and he felt like a millionaire. He had to live on board and provide his own food, which suited him very well, but from midday Saturday when the Camper Nicholson yard was closed and a watchman came on duty, he was free to do as he pleased.

He knew he could always regard The Golden Fleece as home, so he sometimes went to Chichester for the weekend, an added attraction being former schoolfriends, to impress with his world travels. Other weekends he elected to stay in Southampton, to attend ballroom dancing lessons in a nearby Northam hall, and in the course of these, he developed a warm friendship with a Welsh girl named Brenda. Her parents were from Cardiff, so they welcomed Dan to their home to share an evening meal and reminisce about the beauty of South Wales. Dan appreciated this taste of family home life. An incident during one of these weekend visits nearly caused a rumpus with the girl's parents.

Dan and Brenda had been left alone one Saturday evening while her parents went to the cinema. They were in the front room, a sort of parlour reserved for visitors in those days, and everything was highly polished, especially the lino covered floor. After kissing and cuddling for a while, they got an impulse to play a little more dangerously, so they got down on the floor to try and do what they felt would be nice to do... after all, everyone else seemed to be doing it.

They soon found IT wasn't usually done on cold, highly polished floors, and what was claimed to be a pleasantly serious activity, became hilarious. They slithered and slid all over the floor, bumping their heads on table legs, armchairs and the settee, all the time laughing at their inability to get going.

In the midst of all this, they heard the sound of a key being fitted into the lock of the front door not six feet from the parlour. Dan pulled up his trousers, straightened the floor rug and dropped into an armchair while Brenda, with only one leg in her pants, pulled them up and flopped into his lap, hiding with her skirt the evidence that he had not had time to button the front of his trousers. There being no zippers in those days. A split second later Brenda's mother opened the door and switched on the light.

When she saw her daughter on Dan's lap she almost screamed "Brenda! What are you doing sitting there, like that? Get up immediately and sit in your own chair!"

Dan's reaction was to put his arm tightly around Brenda and say, "Oh she's all right, Mrs Turner, it's a bit chilly this evening, and we're only trying to keep warm."

Mrs Turner was not wholly convinced, but muttering her disapproval, joined her husband who had gone into the kitchen. This gave the young ones just enough time to adjust their clothing before Mr Turner, heralding his approach with a discreet cough, opened the door to ask if they would like a cup of tea.

"My word, yes please!" they said, thankful for their narrow escape, and soon they were all in the kitchen sharing a nice supper. Even so, Dan had a distinct feeling Mrs Turner would encourage her daughter to look elsewhere for a boyfriend.

The weeks at Northam flew by, Dan enjoyed the best of two worlds, being aboard ship and yet not at sea. In April, the Mate, a middle-aged man from Poole in Dorset, joined; he was employed on a seasonal basis, and when not yachting, he was a crab-fisherman. His broad Dorset brogue was enriched by expressions Dan had never heard before: a 'fore and aft jacket' was a single-breasted one, a frocktailed coat was a 'claw-hammer' coat, a butterfly collar was a 'Come-to Jesus' collar, and so on. If someone was listening to their conversation, 'he had his ventilators on the wind', to describe his having intimacy with a female, he would say, 'so I just gets foul of her' meaning entangled.

Early in May, five other members of the crew arrived to speed up the fitting-out programme. These fellows were older: Cornishmen from Loo, Mousehole and Penzance and immediately it became obvious they were not pleased to find an outsider in their midst. They didn't like the fact that Dan, a single man, was earning the same wage as themselves, married men.

They were a clannish lot, proud of being regarded as tough fishermen and good yachtsmen, but Dan was not overawed by them: why should he be. He was an able-bodied seaman with worldwide experience behind him, he was sturdy and strong, so could look after himself, and could afford to ignore the sly jibes directed at him.

Centaurus was put through her sea trials on Southampton Water, and private stores from Fortnum and Masons of Piccadilly, were loaded and stowed in his lordship's quarters. Lord Stanton's butler was in charge of these provisions and his head chauffeur was on board to look after the yacht's auxiliary motor, the speedboat and a launch. These two shared a small two-berth cabin adjoining his lordship's quarters, they were 'specials', regarded as petty-officers by the crew.

Lord Stanton provided a uniform for every member of the crew: navy blue uniform jacket and trousers, two peaked caps, two navy blue jerseys, one pair of black go-ashore shoes, two sets of khaki overalls for working round the decks, and two pairs of sandshoes. In addition, each man got a complete set of wet-weather gear – yellow oilskin, sea-boots and sou'wester. Dan regarded this as outstanding generosity after the extremely lean conditions on his last ships.

At last, Lord Stanton boarded *Centaurus* as she lay at anchor off the Royal Pier and with just enough sail set for steerage way, and with Captain Rogers at the wheel, she glided gracefully through Southampton Water to the Solent, where she anchored again in Cowes Bay.

Dan, being the youngest, sprightliest and most presentable of the crew, was chosen by his lordship to be his special launchman on his latest model speedboat. Captain Rogers was pleased that his choice of an outsider was thus approved by his lordship, so he gave Dan special tuition in boat-handling and the etiquette of helping ladies to embark and disembark. This further needled Dan's Cornish shipmates, especially as it relieved Dan of the never-ending task of polishing brass.

Although Lord Stanton used *Centaurus* for entertaining his society friends and as a grandstand at the various regattas they attended, she also took part in the King's Cup race around the Isle of Wight, but unless a gale was blowing, in which case the race was usually cancelled, she didn't stand a chance against the racing yachts *Britannia*, *Shamrock*, *White Heather*, *Velsheda*, *Candida* and other speedsters of that time.

Because of his aristocratic background, Lord Stanton was a member of the Royal Yacht Squadron, said to be the most exclusive club in the world, and he was entitled to fly the white ensign on *Centaurus*. The navy blue jerseys worn by the crew had 'R.Y.S. CENTAURUS' in gold lettering across the chest and the same colours, gold and navy blue, were his lordship's racing colours – he owned a first class stud-farm near Newbury and racing stables at Newmarket. One windy day, Dan couldn't help noticing that one of the young lady guests sported the same colour combination for her underwear!

The international yachting fraternity of those days included some of the richest people in the world and, apart from their racing vessels, they owned the finest collection of luxury yachts. There were superb steam yachts such as *Nahlin*, *Sapphire*, *Hieropulus* and *Erin*, and the King's own flagship *Victoria and Albert* manned by selected Royal Navy personnel. Another eye-catcher was the three-masted square-rigger *Westward* owned by the Guinness family of Dublin, and an equally imposing vessel was the smart *Saratoga* whose owner, the financier J. Pierpont Morgan, was said to be the richest of them all at that time.

Sir Thomas Lipton, the millionaire tea planter and grocery chain owner, built a series of yachts in a vain effort to regain the America's Cup for Britain. It was said that the Americans had inserted a clause in the rules governing the race that gave them an unfair advantage over any British or European challenger, in that any such yacht had to sail across the Atlantic to the race venue. This meant the challenger had to be strong enough to cope with the usually adverse winds and rough ocean crossing, and then had to compete with a yacht designed solely for racing in calm waters.

Those restrictions were later abandoned, but not before Sir Thomas Lipton had spent a fortune on his *Shamrocks*. He did, however, get his reward in the form of publicity for his chain-store empire and a knighthood for his efforts.

After the festivities of Cowes Week had petered out, Captain Rogers informed his crew that they were to depart for the west of Scotland and the Hebrides. They called at Holyhead in Anglesey and then at Kingston, now Dunlaoghaire. Here Dan and his lordship's chauffeur visited the world famous Guinness Brewery and sampled the stout that gave he-men the strength to lift huge girders with one hand, so the advertisements claimed. Since being encouraged by Chips on *Prince Rupert City*, Dan had kept up his daily physical exercises: not easy in the confines of the yacht as he found out. One evening, Dan, resting his backside against the scuttle covering the ladder down into the crew's quarters, was swinging his upper torso vigorously from side to side with his arms outstretched. Unseen by him, an elderly man, one of the least friendly of his shipmates, had just got his pipe drawing to his satisfaction and, with peaked cap over his eyes, had decided to go up on deck for a breath of fresh air.

He had no sooner poked his head above the scuttle when the edge of Dan's hand caught him full in the face, knocking his pipe down his throat, propelling him backwards down the ladder. He thought he had been hit by the staysail boom, and although Dan apologised and helped him recover, he never forgave Dan for the burnt lip and bruised face he suffered, not to mention his damaged ego.

While at Loch Laxford, the Duke of Sutherland visited *Centaurus* with a group of friends and Dan had to ferry them to and from the yacht at anchor. It had been easy enough boarding the party in good weather, but when the time came to return them to the shore, there was a boisterous rise and fall alongside the gangway and what was more, the guests were somewhat unsteady on their feet.

With Captain Rogers and the Mate doing their best to help the visitors down the shaky steps into the heaving launch, with much good humoured advice from his lordship, they were safely, though in some cases rather inelegantly, deposited on board at last and landed at a more sheltered jetty further up the loch.

On clearing the rugged Sutherland coastline, *Centaurus* encountered light winds and a flat-calm sea, with an accompanying long, low swell that heralded a distant storm. Gale force winds and tempestuous seas were far more prevalent in that area than flat calms and the Skipper assured Lord Stanton that he would soon get all the wind he wanted and more.

En route to St Kilda, *Centaurus* glided into a shoal of basking sharks. The engines were stopped so as not to disturb the huge creatures, which looked as though they were sleeping just below the surface of the sea, mouths wide open to allow plankton to flow in. It was a picture of peace and contentment, but his lordship had a sudden desire to play the role of Captain Ahab in *Moby Dick* and produced a harpoon with heavy fishing line attached.

He tried to spear the creatures as the ship moved silently over them, but either his aim was bad or he hadn't allowed for the refraction in the water and he missed. He ordered the hack boat to be launched, transferred his harpooning gear into it and, with Dan at the helm, tried to get close to his quarry, he had invited the fishermen to take part but they had declined.

Lord Stanton hadn't the strength, the skill or the experience of the real Captain Ahab, his harpoon wasn't nearly sharp enough, and he probably underestimated the toughness of the shark's skin. He succeeded only in arousing the beast from its sleep to thrash the waters into a turmoil. This almost swamped the launch and nearly threw its occupants into the sea, but it took two more futile attempts to convince his lordship to call it a day and order the launch back to the yacht. The professionals, thus vindicated, were smugly satisfied at the lack of success.

A breeze sprang up and, with rising sea and falling barometer, Captain Rogers was able to persuade his lordship to head for their next port of call. So, with all sails set, they headed for the north-western corner of Ireland and the following morning, under full sail, they roared past a small steamer going in the same direction.

Lord Stanton was delighted. 'Sail overtaking steam' was the caption on a series of photographs that he took of the occasion. They raced on into Donegal Bay and then, with reduced sail, proceeded first into McSwynes Bay and finally to a sheltered anchorage off a delightful little fishing village called Killybegs.

Lord Stanton was related to the then occupant of Donegal Castle and wasted no time in going ashore. During his absence, the sails and running-gear were overhauled and in their free time, some of the crew did some fishing. Dan went ashore to explore. As he gazed through the old-fashioned shop window of the general store trying to decide whether to buy some Fry's Whipped Cream Walnuts or a bar of Cadbury's Dairy Milk Flake, he became aware of the reflection of two village girls standing wistfully behind him. Soft-hearted Dan understood very well that they too would love to be able to buy something but hadn't the money: how often he had been so placed.

He went into the shop and bought several bars of chocolate and when he came out he shared them with the girls with a smile, as though to say, "I read your thoughts." They seemed embarrassed but they accepted the chocolate with a few words of Gaelic which he didn't understand, but that didn't matter: the appreciation was unmistakable.

Lord Stanton told the Skipper to set course down the west coast to Shannon, then on again to Bantry Bay and another sheltered spot, Glengariff. His lordship, who gloried in bad weather, got a full measure of gale force winds and heavy seas rounding the south western extremity of Eire. Even in Glengariff Bay, which they eventually reached in blinding rain and a howling westerly, it was not altogether calm, and Dan felt that it was Providence more than good navigation, and seamanship that brought the yacht safely to anchor in the hair-raising conditions.

In fact, the preceding night, a steel block had sheared off its shackle at the masthead and crashed into the deck at Dan's feet, missing his face by a cat's whisker. Apparently, it was not yet time for him to meet his Maker.

While in Glengariff, Dan visited Blarney Castle to kiss the famous stone and to be endowed with the legendary gift of eloquence. Whether it was this, or an inherited trait, he developed a valuable fluency of speech to help him through life. From Glengariff, where his lordship went ashore to see other friends on their estates, *Centaurus* was ordered to Cork, where he planned to rejoin her for the return to the Solent and the next stage of her cruising itinerary. With a new group of friends joining the yacht, his lordship told the Skipper to proceed to Cowes, but to call at Torquay en route. Then he wanted to continue to Kiel Canal in Germany.

This was foreign-going to the Cornishmen and they muttered and groaned even more when it was rumoured that the trip would be extended to Stockholm.

Captain Rogers was glad that he had chosen Dan to join his crew because now he had Dan's four years' deep-sea experience to help him as Second Mate as they navigated the busy shipping lanes of the North Sea and Baltic. After Stockholm they visited Visby, capital of the Island of Roses, Gotland, then Malmö and Ystad in southern Sweden, and to complete the tour, Copenhagen. What Dan most enjoyed about this voyage was the abundance of the richest layered gateaux he had ever seen in the cake shops ashore, a treat in which he could now afford to indulge himself.

Centaurus, flying the white ensign, was the centre of great interest at all those ports of call, but especially so at Kiel Bay where a large regatta was being held and yachts large and small of many different nationalities were assembled. After a week of festivities ashore and on board, his lordship and his guests seemed to have had enough and Captain Rogers was ordered to return to Southampton.

With the yacht back at anchor off the Royal Pier, Lord Stanton and his party left for their country homes, Mediterranean villas or London clubs and the laying-up programme to protect the yacht and her valuable equipment over the winter months was commenced. Later, all hands except the Skipper were paid off, the Cornishmen went home, the Mate retired to Poole, Captain Rogers was left to his solitary role, and Dan went to visit his sister Connie at Chichester.

The Cruising Liner

While it was good to spend time with his sister, now an attractive young woman of eighteen, his thrifty nature inherited from his mother would not allow him to remain idle and use up the money he had saved from his yacht earnings. Captain Rogers had been a great help in providing employment for eight months, and with no improvement at all in the shipping world, he had suggested to Dan that a popular cruise liner was about to restart her cruising programme following refit, why not try his luck there? Knowing that former shipmasters were prepared to take lower ratings, Dan wasn't very hopeful, but nevertheless joined the milling throng outside the Shipping Office in Canute Road. The well-drilled regulars naturally filled their former jobs, possibly with the help of a backhander in the right quarter, and then the remaining less desirable posts were made known. Dan was prepared to accept an Ordinary Seaman's role, a step backward, but even those were already earmarked, so when he was finally offered the role of a Stillroom Scullion, he took it on without really knowing what was involved. He later discovered it was a glorified name for a dishwasher. Oh well, it would be a new experience, and he would be housed, fed and paid the modest sum of six pounds ten shillings per month, less tax, of course. After a strict medical where he found he only got the job because another fellow had failed, he joined his new shipmates and boarded the liner.

He was one of twelve inhabitants of a space deep in the bowels of the ship known as a 'peak' which Dan thought was incongruous, it should be called a 'pit', and a man known as a pantryman told him his duties commenced at 6 a.m. and finished at 10 p.m. with a two hour break from 2.30 to 4.30 p.m. There was no mention of meals or mealtimes, and it soon became apparent to Dan that it was largely a matter of surreptitiously grabbing whatever leftovers were still edible when brought into the stillroom by the saloon waiters. Before

Dan was attuned to this state of affairs, he marvelled at his co-worker Jack who 'wolfed' everything that remained on the silver platters that were brought in to be washed. He must have been starving while out of work, reckoned Dan. However, the same fellow was a few hours later rushed to the ship's hospital with acute appendicitis, making more work for Dan but also no competition for the leftovers.

Dan was surprised, at first, to note that greater deference was shown by his colleagues to the Second and Chief Stewards than his mates had showed on the trampships towards the Captain and Mates. Their livelihoods apparently depended on this good relationship. He also noticed a well-established 'pecking-order' and was careful not to cross its boundaries. The Second Steward was quite an imperious person, and would take up a commanding position to survey every activity of the saloon stewards, pantrymen and cooks attending to the passengers orders. Frequently, he would test the washing-up water in Dan's trough by running his fingers through the suds, then call over the Chief Pantryman to tell him it was either too soapy or not soapy enough, completely ignoring the washer as though absent. Even in the heat, steam and general clatter of the stillroom, Dan always knew when his 'lordship' was around. He moved in an atmosphere of his own: a pungent but pleasant deodorant, a badge of experience in dealing with his 'paying-guests', the passengers.

There was so much activity down below in the catering section of the ship that apart from the throb of her engines, Dan would not have known whether the ship was still alongside the wharf or at sea. For the first few nights, Dan's restless dreams were of stacks of besmeared silverware pouring into his trough to be scoured and placed in racks for drying; at other times, it was visions of the delicious-looking veal and ham pies, or pork pies conjured up by the Larder Cook. In the course of chats with his fellow workers, mostly married Southampton men, Dan got a glimpse of some aspects of liner life, hitherto unknown territory to him. He was very surprised to learn that the saloon Stewards who worked long hours, and depended to a large extent on the gratuities received from their batch of passengers at the end of each trip, were obliged to pay the Chief Pantryman for their own daily meals. 'What a strange set-up,' thought Dan, 'Was it approved company policy or some sort of fiddle he didn't understand?' He smiled listening to one waiter's story of the 'dear old lady' passenger who told him at 'tipping time' she had noticed a hole in his socks so she had knitted him a pair which she felt sure he would prefer to money. Another incident occurred which taught him a lesson for the future, to be kind and considerate to those who have control over your food.

An irascible old man, prone to complaining about everything, arrived at his table for lunch at 2.15 p.m. when all other diners had long since departed, and demanded the menu. The waiter's gentle reminder that it was past lunchtime hours was ignored and he ordered Brown Windsor soup, to be followed with Ham and Tongue salad. The waiter came into the stillroom wondering how he was going to deal with this order when all such items had been returned to cold-store until the next meal. Ever conscious of incurring complaint by a passenger to some 'bigwig' in the company, when their jobs would be on the line, the Second Pantryman, without batting an eyelid, found a gravy jug not yet washed, mixed into it some boiling water, added a drop of H.P. sauce, and handed it to the waiter to serve to his client. Meanwhile out of the 'Rosie' where leftovers are deposited prior to being dumped overboard via the correct procedure, the Pantryman fished out pieces of lettuce, tomato, sliced cucumber and radish, washed them thoroughly, diced it all neatly to decorate a plate on to which pieces of likewise salvaged ham and tongue had been arrayed, all perfectly clean and edible. The waiter later reported his customer was delighted with the Brown Windsor and found the whole meal very satisfactory considering the lateness of his arrival, and coming from this gentleman, that was tantamount to an apology.

One day, during a lull in the work, Dan and others present were discussing the fact that some people resemble animals, dogs in particular, there are the Bulldog types, the Whippet types and so on. Dan ventured to suggest that the Second Pantryman reminded him of an Old English Sheep Dog intending it a rather kind view, complimentary at least. Fred was nonplussed for a moment or two, and then told Dan what he reminded him of, the trouble was none of it was the least bit flattering, with no mention of dogs at all.

On another occasion, when Dan was heading for his workplace along the working alleyway in the lower regions of the ship, he saw some sort of commotion blocking the passage ahead so turned into a side alley to bypass the trouble-spot. However, at the next corner, he came face to face, literally eyeball to eyeball, with one of the butchers holding aloft a cleaver in his right hand, with his left reaching out towards Dan for a stunned fraction of a second there was silence, then Dan heard himself saying, "Shall we dance?" It was such a ridiculous thing to say in the circumstances, that the ghost of a smile flickered across the man's face, he looked down at his boots, as he did so he was grabbed from behind by a Master at Arms, one of the ship's policeman. Dan then heard that the man had become mentally deranged following a quarrel with his mates and took to one of them severely wounding him.

On another trip through the same area, Dan noticed a weighing clock hanging from a nail outside a freezer door, and ever keen to exercise his strength, he pulled down steadily on the hook, eyes intent on getting the needle to the end of the dial. He was thus absorbed right under the clock when the nail broke off and he got the lot full in his face. He had to go to the Sick Bay for treatment and felt rather sheepish when he had to explain how the accident happened. His facial features were somewhat marred for a few weeks but not permanently. Anyway, it didn't matter much because in the whole three months of cruising to such places as Gibraltar, Cadiz, Barcelona, Naples, Palermo, Messina, Venice, Dubrovnik, (the pearl of the Adriatic), Corfu, Constantinople and through the Bosphorus to enter the Black Sea, and the north African ports of Algiers, Tangier and Casablanca, Dan was able to go ashore on only three occasions: Venice, Algiers and Barcelona. It was hard work, work, work all the way, with very little time even to go up on deck for a breath of fresh air. It was anything but a pleasure cruise for those in the catering department. For the passengers, it was just the opposite and they got their money's worth. The ship was fully-booked throughout Dan's three months sojourn. This despite the Depression, because the rates were ridiculously low, from eighteen guineas for a twelve day cruise to sixty guineas up, for a twenty-four day cruise to the Black Sea and back via ports. However, a suspicious fire in the engine room put her out of action at the end of that time and Dan decided that style of life was not for him. He paid off and after a visit to Chichester decided to try his luck in London.

London Interlude

While serving on *Prince Rupert City* Dan had befriended the young cabin boy, barely fifteen years old, who was being subjected to the same treatment Dan had endured on his first voyage. Young Sid was from Bermondsey, with a Cockney accent you could cut with a knife. Dan had come across him one day on the verge of tears, "I ain't got no ring, I don't know what they're on abaht," he confided to Dan, clearly worried.

Dan's tender heart went out to the boy as he assured him the fellows weren't referring to jewellery, but to his rear end. They were really only joking, continued Dan, as they much preferred what girls by nature are endowed with, but in its absence amused themselves in this way. Nevertheless, it was best to be on guard at all times, especially in the bathroom. When the ship returned to the UK, to show his appreciation, young Sid had introduced Dan to his married sister, in case he should need lodgings while ashore in London.

Rose and her husband Bert lived in Walworth, just off the Old Kent Road. So now, returning to London after his service on *Centaurus*, and the cruise liner, Dan decided to pay them a visit. They said, "Why not try your luck ashore? You could stay with us here," and Rose suggested that Dan could have the back bedroom, breakfast every morning, Sunday dinner, and his washing done, all for thirteen shillings and sixpence a week! Naturally, Dan accepted the kind offer, Cockney hospitality indeed, and soon settled in.

Bert, who worked in the printing industry on Fleet Street, was able to give Dan a lot of useful advice which he put to good use. So, like thousands of others, Dan visited the front foyers of every newspaper office in Fleet Street to read the situations vacant columns, a service they provided free to the impoverished unemployed. It was more than a week before he saw an advertisement which read, "young men wanted for an exciting career with Airway."

Thinking it was something to do with aviation, Dan, with a crowd of others, hurried off to the Marble Arch address. By eleven o'clock there must have been at least fifty men assembled outside the front door of the Airway Company. A smartly dressed man appeared and announced that if anyone thought that Airway was in any way connected with the aviation industry they were mistaken. It was the trade name of a new type of vacuum cleaner. There were shouts of disapproval and, grumbling, the knowledgeable ones melted away, but Dan didn't know any better and he joined others trooping into the office to hear what was being offered. They were given a demonstration of the benefit of owning an Airway, the world's best home cleaner, and taught the patter necessary to convince a housewife that she could not possibly live another day without owning one. No doubt it was a top rate machine, but the drawback of the job was that a salesman's pay depended on sales – no wages or expenses were paid. If a machine was sold for cash at twenty-five pounds, the salesman's commission was five pounds. If one was sold on time payment, the commission was paid likewise.

Armed with a cleaner in a long black coffin-like case, Dan started off one morning for his area – Wallington, Cheam and Ewell, the stockbroker belt in the Surrey countryside. Most of his knocks went unanswered. When a lady did come to the door, she usually took one glance at the black case and hurriedly shut the door again, muttering "No thanks," as she did so.

Occasionally, he was invited in to give a free demonstration with no obligation to buy, as the patter went. Dan found that these well-to-do people were quick to have their lounges, halls and stairs vacuumed at no cost or trouble to themselves and then to say, "Yes, it seems a marvellous machine as you say, but I shall have to discuss it with my husband. If we decide to buy one we shall do so through his company and get a discount."

Other women, after Dan had vacuumed their houses, would say, "You look so hot and tired, do sit down and have a cup of tea," and later, "I don't think we could possibly afford to buy an Airway just now, but we'll think about it and let your company know. Incidentally, where did you get your lovely tan?"

After two weeks, all Dan got out of the job was a lot of train travel at his own expense, long walks with the heavy case, a few cups of tea and scones, but no sales or the likelihood of getting any. So he returned the Airway to the Marble Arch office and resigned.

Rose suggested that Dan should try the Alfred Marks Employment Agency in Frith Street, Soho, and there, after paying a small enrolment fee, he was given a note for the manager of the Leicester Square Theatre. It was two o'clock in the afternoon when he arrived breathless outside the Staff Manager's office in the theatre, having run non-stop all the way lest someone else should beat him to it. He was told Mr Cohen was away at lunch would Dan come back in an hour? "Oh no," Dan said, "I can easily wait here."

He wasn't going to take any chances on losing the interview. So, he waited and waited, and as the hours passed, staff going off and on, after meal breaks, would tell him that Mr Cohen would not as a rule keep people waiting like that, but actually it did not worry Dan at all. He had no other place to go, he was warm and dry and the passing parade of pretty girls was not hard to take, so he assured the concerned sympathisers he was all right. Eventually, at 6 p.m., someone located Mr Cohen and he actually apologised for being held up at a meeting and gave Dan a job as a checktaker, 11.30 a.m. till 11.30 p.m., six days a week, for thirty shillings a week, less unemployment and insurance tax. Dan felt the long wait had won him the job, he had no idea what a checktaker was, but no matter: it was something that paid a wage and that was all that mattered. He celebrated by having a pot of tea with crumpets and a fruit bun at a nearby Lyon's Café, for eightpence.

The Leicester Square Theatre provided non-stop variety performance from midday to midnight, Monday to Saturday. Dan's job was to stand at the entrance to the auditorium in a smart bottle-green uniform and tear patrons' tickets in half as they entered. Apart from tea breaks, this continued throughout the show, but was so full of interest for Dan, that the time flew. He could lie-in until nine in the morning and have breakfast with Rose in the kitchen, before taking the bus to the West End in plenty of time to start work. What a delightful change from his previous work experiences.

Dan was about to savour a completely different environment to any he had hitherto known, though he was in his twenty-second year with over four years of world travel behind him, he had much to learn from working in a mixed group of young men and women, and his eyes would be opened to many new aspects of life.

Dan enjoyed being in the stalls foyer among the milling theatregoers and sometimes he could talk to Dianne, the beautiful young woman who ran the chocolate kiosk nearby. Dianne had been Miss Earl's Court the previous year and certainly knew how to exploit her good looks and figure. She was, as the song had it, 'round and firm and fully-packed, that's my girl'. She was a mine of information about the theatre and life in the West End, and she loved to share titbits of scandal with Dan, a complete ignoramus in her eyes, to see the effect. Dan learned a lot about life ashore from her and realised how relatively innocent his so-called womanising seafaring colleagues really were, they were paragons of virtue compared to some of these people.

He didn't approve of the way Dianne treated the scores of besotted young men who made fools of themselves over her, bringing presents of flowers, perfume, fruit and liqueur chocolates. She accepted the young men's presents, but never accepted any of their invitations. She was madly in love with an out of work film extra named Leslie and she shared everything she got with him, she confided to Dan. Dan thought this was dishonest, but Dianne said airily that she didn't ask for the presents, and if men wanted to give her these things that was their problem. "Yes, I suppose so," conceded Dan: he was learning fast.

He soon became aware that some of the staff were cheating the management. Pretty usherettes thought nothing of beguiling a patron with a smile while short-changing him in the half light of the auditorium, they sometimes smoothed-out discarded programmes to sell again, or took a bribe to find a better seat. It was to supplement their meagre wages, they said, and Dan found how easy it was to fall in line.

One evening he was unwittingly drawn into one of these rackets when Paddy from the main foyer asked him to get a couple of five shilling tickets for him. When Dan asked how on earth he could do that, he only tore them in half, Paddy explained that by palming two five shilling halves and giving those to the next two five shilling patrons that came in, he would be left with two whole tickets. Dan didn't like the idea but, thinking it was only going to be a one-off affair for Paddy's friends, he agreed.

Little did he realise that such a simple act would develop into a sizeable swindle, involving not only the stalls but the dress circle as well. Paddy and his mate who actually sold the tickets, shared the ill-gotten proceeds with everyone else involved, and if it had been kept at a low level the deception might have continued unnoticed longer than it did. However, the management began to wonder why the receipts were lower than they should have been, and it became obvious to Dan that they had become suspicious. When they began standing nearby to watch what went on, and to ask if he put all the torn halves in the locked receptacle for the purpose. Dan really got the wind up, making sure he followed the correct procedure from then on, he told Paddy he was backing out. This wasn't as easy as he thought, he was cajoled to continue at first, then threatened, but that made Dan all the more determined to withdraw. He could see the axe falling up ahead, and warned the others, but to no avail.

At this point, the management decided to move some of the staff around, and Dan was made an usher in the Dress Circle, possibly to see if there was any difference, there was, relief for Dan! But the swindle continued with his replacement.

After about a month in his new role as an usher in the Dress Circle, Dan watched fearfully as Scotland Yard's Fraud Squad moved in and exposed the whole fiddle. All staff involved were instantly dismissed, although they were not prosecuted. Dan expected to be in trouble too, but nothing happened. In fact, because of another rearrangement of the remaining staff, he was put in charge of the Upper Circle – he was literally on the way up.

In his new role, Dan had to settle disputes between patrons and the six usherettes in his sphere of authority. Sometimes the girls complained that patrons were making improper suggestions, or making indecent gestures or acts in front of them. They also told him that certain members of management were not above trying their luck with them, either. Dan, at first, was amazed at the depravity of life ashore. Seafarers were far more moral than these landlubbers he reckoned.

Sometimes, the usherettes were dressed to match the style of the show, whether it was Caribbean, South American, Chinese or Italian, and the girls enjoyed the changes from their normal uniforms. Once they had to wear knee-length crinolines for a 'Ye Olde English' extravaganza. These short crinolines were fine in the

Stalls and Dress Circle, but not for the girls going up and down the steep stairs of the Upper Circle. It was found that the male patrons were paying more attention to their presentation, than to the stage. The girls complained to Dan they were not paid to expose their private parts to all and sundry, they had plenty to contend with as it was without inciting further harassment. Dan passed the message on to the Staff Manager who sympathised, and allowed the girls to return to their normal uniforms.

When Dan worked alongside the beautiful Dianne, she often remarked that she couldn't understand how he, surrounded by so many attractive girls, could remain oblivious to their charm and sex appeal. Dan explained he was a physical fitness fanatic committed to a body-building course with its slogan, 'Be a Vital, Virile He-Man;' how could he do that and play around with comely wenches at the same time? The truth was he was too scared to try, they all seemed so sophisticated.

He told her, not that she was the slightest bit interested, that he had bought a juice extractor and his diet consisted largely of fruit and vegetable liquids, Busy-Bee honey bread, nuts, raisins and anything else needed to achieve a Superman appearance. Of course, he had to have a daily measure of Yeast-Vite tablets, and a Guinness a day so that he too could one day hold a steel girder overhead with one arm. Dianne would then point to his pimply complexion and snort with disgust, "What on earth for...? What you need is a good woman!" He knew what she was getting at: it was sexual nourishment he needed, an efficient antidote for all the rich food he was indulging in, and that made him think. She might be right, she had a perfect complexion and figure, maybe the two went together?

The following Sunday happened to be the annual staff picnic day, and two charabancs conveyed a big group to Margate for a day at the seaside. Dan sat next to a smart young woman with nut-brown hair, brown eyes, a generous mouth and beautiful teeth. She was a friendly outgoing girl, one of the dress circle usherettes Dan had often seen, but never spoken to. Her name was Louise, she told Dan, who was nervous at being so close to her, but she put him at ease. Since she seemed to be unattended like Dan, they joined in with the day's festivities together, enjoying each other's company. On the way back to London they cuddled in their seats like everyone else seemed to be doing. 'How pleasant,' thought Dan, 'Going to sea was never like this.'

About the same time as this outing, Dan happened to overhear a violent quarrel between Rose and her husband, and what saddened him specially was to learn that he was the cause. Bert's workmates had undermined his faith in his wife's integrity by making such remarks as "I certainly wouldn't have a young sailor as a boarder in 'my' house. You know what sailors are!"

Poor Bert couldn't bring himself to believe that his Rosie would be like that, but the insinuations wore him down and he told Dan to go. Dan determined to put the matter right for Rose before he left and this he did, face to face with Bert. He was so fierce that Bert realised he was wrong and asked forgiveness from both Rose and Dan for allowing himself to be influenced by such mindless, wicked gossip. Dan was so concerned for them he made sure their rift was truly healed before he left, and to help it along he treated them to an evening out at their famous local pub, the Elephant & Castle. The party developed with others joining in, into a real old Cockney knees-up Muvver Brahn, (Mother Brown). A great time was thoroughly enjoyed by all!

Then he set about finding new lodgings nearer to the West End and eventually found a comfortable bedsitter in Smith Street, off the King's Road in Chelsea. It also happened to be on the bus route to Putney Common where Louise lived: this was not premeditated, it just happened.

The romance with Louise blossomed quite rapidly, but not beyond kissing goodnight at the bus stop, so he was pleasantly surprised late one Saturday night on the number seventeen bus when Louise said she would like to see where he lived.

"If I waited for you to invite me home, I don't suppose we would ever get there," she whispered. Getting off the bus at Smith Street heading for his first floor bedsitter, Dan's thoughts were too busy concentrating on getting past his landlady's room without being heard, to grasp the significance of her remark.

That night was the beginning of a new and turbulent experience for Dan. He discovered, among other things, that Louise was twenty-six, four years older than himself and by no means the novice that he was. Before meeting Louise, his weekends had been dull, staying in his lodgings until Sunday evening when he would go to

Kilburn to watch the boxing programme, where many up-and-coming champions made their debut. Now he found he needed his nuts, raisins and Guinness more than ever: life was exciting indeed getting 'foul of one another' as the old Dorset Mate used to say. Dianne would have approved, had she known, and later would notice a definite improvement in his complexion.

He was now earning two pounds ten shillings a week, enough to support a wife and family, but Dan was not sure he was ready for that.

Since Dan had six lively girls working with him, his days passed quickly and pleasantly, but Louise, in the Dress Circle, was just one of eight, and asked Dan if he would try and arrange a transfer for her to the Upper Circle. When he hesitated, thinking it might spoil their romance, Louise was quick to suspect the opposite – that Dan was succumbing to the charms of Sally, one of the prettiest girls in his team.

The result was a lovers' tiff which brought about a surprisingly abrupt ending to their fervent affair. Among other catty remarks, Louise told Dan he wasn't doing a real man's job anyway: real men didn't work alongside girls and so on, and Dan was immature enough to be hurt by her words. He thought of all the hard and sometimes perilous work at sea for a fraction of the money he was now enjoying in safe, warm and comfortable surroundings. Nevertheless, something told him that it was time to make a break and get out of an affair that was getting too serious. He had worked at the theatre for ten months and had managed to save a little money, so he gave a week's notice and put the Leicester Square Theatre behind him. Louise was flabbergasted when he told her that he was leaving to get a real man's job, especially when he added that he wouldn't be able to afford a girlfriend.

Resorting to the Alfred Marks agency again, he was able to land a job as a meat porter in Smithfield meat market right in the heart of London. Again, he had only a vague idea of what was involved, but soon found it was quite different from the cosy, well-paid work he had been doing, and he almost regretted his haste in quitting the theatre, and Louise. Instead of lying in bed till eight, then getting cleaned up for breakfast in unhurried peace, he had to get up at four o'clock in the morning, snatch a quick cup of tea, and then cycle across London to reach Smithfield by five-thirty. Instead of a smart uniform, he now had to wear a long meat porter's smock to handle frozen carcasses of beef, mutton, lamb and pork, to load heavy iron barrows and drag them like a donkey to the shops in the market. It was a drop from luxury to drudgery in one brief week. 'Oh well, it might change again,' thought Dan, to console himself.

He had grown soft at the theatre and at first could only lift carcasses of lamb and mutton, whereas his colleagues could handle hindquarters of beef weighing one hundred and seventy-five pounds with ease. He marvelled at their skill and strength as they ran with a hindquarter on their shoulders and then expertly threw it at a row of hooks to impale the hock so that the carcasses hung in a row like guardsmen on parade. Towards the end of two weeks he was regaining his former fitness and strength, but it took longer to cope without being exhausted at the end of the day, when he had to pedal his way back to Chelsea through the late afternoon traffic.

Instead of fifty shillings a week, his new wage was thirty shillings, less one and seven pence tax, which left just twenty-eight and five pence on which to live. His weekly rent was seventeen and sixpence, so with only ten and eleven pence for all other expenses he quickly learned to copy his workmates, and help himself to scraps of meat when he could. Every barrow load of meat was meticulously weighed and it wasn't easy to slice off a piece without the loss being detected, nevertheless, ways and means were found, without feeling the slightest bit of guilt. They were the poorest paid workers in the market, and their boss the wealthiest individual trader. With the scraps thus pilfered, Dan made a simple stew, supplemented with cheap vegetables, which, his mates assured him, had fallen off a lorry, and this was his daily evening meal throughout his term at Smithfield. Such a diet must have suited him, for he was never sick throughout the whole period of heavy physical work.

Usually, when Dan cycled to work, the city was deserted, apart from the odd milkman, policeman and a prostitute or two, but one morning he saw Piccadilly thronged with sheep. A couple of policemen were helping the drover to transfer the animals from Hyde Park to Green Park across the road and they were playfully pretending to ride the sheep. That spurred a couple of watching street girls to make some choice ribald remarks, and Dan wondered whether they were late or early on the job, it being just after five am!

At 5 p.m., the traffic in Ludgate Circus, Bridge Street, Victoria Embankment, Parliament Square, Victoria Street, and Buckingham Palace Road was just the opposite: it was dense, and sometimes Dan was so tired he rode through the traffic in a dream. He would suddenly come to, to find himself negotiating the maelstrom outside Victoria Station and marvel at his 'unconscious' progress.

Dan's workmates were a motley lot. One was a rebellious, Oxford-educated scion of an aristocratic family, sampling the harsher side of life. His accent made him stand out and not having done any manual work before, he could only handle the smaller and lighter items; flanks, clods, silversides or pigs' heads. The others included a professional boxer, an East End spiv who, it was said, spent regular terms inside Wandsworth or Pentonville prisons, and Dodger, an ex-Navy man with whom Dan had a fraternal relationship. There were also two New Zealanders, one was a shady customer, a womaniser, small and sharp-witted, the other was a burly dairy farmer on a working holiday, particularly well-suited for the work. Dan formed a close friendship with him that was to last for many years, and ultimately included the families that neither of them dreamed of at that time.

During their meal breaks, Dan's workmates patronised a nearby café where a cup of tea cost a penny, and coffee, made with essence, was a penny ha'penny. Some of them would then select a table, open up their own packets of sandwiches, help themselves to salt, pepper, mustard, pickle or tomato sauce and, if the proprietor's attention could be diverted for a couple of seconds, a cake or bun from the showcase as well. It was obvious to Dan that this café owner could not make any profit from their visits and hoped he had more honest customers.

Towards the end of six months at the market, with his reserve funds almost exhausted, a small accident, (he had caught the heel of his right shoe under the axle of the barrow he was pulling, ripping off the sole) ruined his one and only pair of shoes and forced him to consider returning to sea. Risking twopence he could ill-afford, he bought a shipping paper, the Journal of Commerce, which listed the whereabouts of ships, and was a mine of useful shipping information. Dan had reached the bottom as far as his resources were concerned, he could see no likely improvement in his situation, hence the need to read of his old environment.

Back To Sea And Shipwreck

As a consequence of his eighteen months ashore, Dan had truly had his eyes opened and his horizons widened, he had seen the inequality of life. The upper crust of society with their chauffeur-driven limousines, the wealthy, and the famous, engaged in the pursuit of entertainment, with the servile attention given them by his fellow workers in the hope of tips. One well-known identity secured the utmost grovelling obsequiousness on account of his habit of tipping with five pound notes, a distinctive white note in those days. These people always had a ready following, anxious to light their cigars, help them on with their coats, open doors and almost lick their shoes. There was even a hierarchy among these servers; near the top would be cloakroom attendants. It was rumoured that they bought these jobs from the management of the top clubs, hotels, and restaurants. Others near the top would be Linkmen, those outside these places who wielded a little bit of authority and were tipped for the favours they bestowed in calling taxis, opening cab doors, providing umbrella protection in rain and so on. They had 'arrangements' with favoured cab-drivers and to Dan it seemed as though everyone was in some wangle or another, and that the system was the cause through which the corruption flourished.

At the other end of the scale could be seen the destitute, at night lying on the kitchen-gratings of some high class hotel, club, or restaurant, seemingly only being kept alive by the warmth and nourishing odours from the cooking below. He had also watched on one occasion, the operation of capitalism at a lower level when an old under-privileged man, who had begged access to the bin that contained all the dust from the theatre's vacuum-cleaning system. This bin was the size of a washing machine bowl and this he emptied out on the concrete floor of the cellar to sift through with his fingers for cigarette-butts. He would then carefully place them to one side to open up and make a small pile of the tobacco; his next step was to remake this tobacco into cigarettes using Zig-Zag papers. When the job was finished, he told Dan he would sell them five for a penny, thus undercutting W.D. & H.O. Wills Woodbines which were the cheapest 'gaspers' on the market at that time, twopence for five.

Then at Smithfield he had experienced another slice of life in the raw in those days, when one could get a good meal of steak and kidney pie, mashed potatoes and peas for ninepence, pudding and custard for twopence, and a cup of tea for a penny, making a three-course meal for a shilling. However, he could only afford that luxury when his scraps of meat were unavailable and in this way he slowly gravitated to penury. He needed to move on and the ruin of his shoes was just the last straw that spurred him to buy the Journal of Commerce, and that happened on a Friday. It was customary on Fridays, in those days, for the shipping movements of all companies to be published for all to see, and under his old company, he saw that *Prince Rupert City* was due in Cardiff in two weeks time. Dan wondered why he should feel so excited and then, deep inside, he felt he must take a chance so he told the foreman he wouldn't be coming back next week. He spent the afternoon saying goodbye to his mates, Dodger in particular, who said he admired Dan's faith in thinking he would get a berth, and the aristocratic Roy, who offered to buy his bicycle.

Dan settled his account with his landlady and then went to spend a few days with his sister, now living and working near East Grinstead in Sussex. It would be two years before he saw her again, but, not knowing that, when he had told his hopes and plans she lent him two pounds to travel to Cardiff.

He was at the dockside when *Prince Rupert City* berthed, and his eyes ran over the familiar lines of his old ship. Seamen can have a real love affair with their ships and Dan's emotions ran high, but when he was able to go on board and see the First Mate, his hopes of getting a berth were dashed: no one was leaving. That was a bit of a blow, but he decided to go to the Head Office in Merthyr House; after all he was an ex-employee and had served his time with them.

The Marine Superintendent listened to Dan's appeal, fishing out of his filing system his record of apprenticeship, yes everything was okay there, and he went on to say how difficult he found it dealing with many others in Dan's situation. Could Dan call at his office tomorrow morning and he would by then tell him what the prospects were. The outcome of this second meeting was the offer of a job as 'Sailor', a rank in those days between an O.S. (ordinary seaman) and an A.B., enabling a saving of one pound per month to be made by the company. The Superintendent assured Dan the ship was to do a short voyage of about four months duration and he might then be able to restore him to his rightful rank of A.B. Dan felt obliged to accept the offer and thanked him. The ship would be *Sacramento Valley* and she would be signing on at Newport early next week. Dan was to report to Mr Thomas the Mate. After an uneasy weekend with Dan staying at a dosshouse in Tiger Bay to conserve his funds, he finally got to Newport Docks and got a very welcome and pleasant surprise. The First Mate was none other than Tudor Thomas, former Second Mate of *Canadian City* and the juniors' guardian angel: what joy surged through him. They sailed the following day as there was no outward cargo available for the ship, and they headed for Panama, bound for Seattle, Puget Sound ports and Pacific coast to load timber and canned goods for the United Kingdom. For Dan, it was good to feel the lift of the ocean under his feet again, to be housed and fed and enjoy the warmth of the tropics after the cold of Britain for eighteen months. The passage to Panama and up the west coast of North America was uneventful and the landscape scenery as familiar as to have almost a homely feeling. It was good to be back in these parts.

The next stage was to sail down the coast to the Columbia River, calling at most of the small riverbank ports all the ninety eight miles up to Portland, the capital of Oregon state. Dan enjoyed these calls, sometimes at little more than a wharf, because the people were so friendly. The husky fellows who worked the ship engaged in some sports which were new to Dan and most of his mates.

One of these was log-rolling, where two men, one at each end of a long, freely floating log and wearing spiked lumberjack boots, would try to spin the log, then stop suddenly or change the direction of the spin and so try to topple the other fellow into the river. It called for exceptional balance and skilful footwork. Another sport was when twenty or more hefty men gathered in the centre of a flat-topped barge, normally used for carrying long logs. At a signal they would push and shove and try to throw each other off the barge. The survivor of this tense and hectic struggle would be crowned King of the River and he would need all his strength, agility and cunning to overcome the opposition. One of these fellows, the winner of a series of contests, later became the world heavyweight all-in wrestling champion, so it was just as well that the ship's Romeos did not fall foul of these men or a new sport might have evolved, that of tossing Limeys into the river.

Since the ship was named after a prosperous fruit-growing valley and its main city, Sacramento, the owners thought it prudent to call at as many ports in the area as they could, to show the flag. So they visited Alameda and Oakland, San Francisco, San Pedro and San Diego, where they loaded packaged dried fruit. At San Francisco, the massive Bay Bridge was nearly completed by then, but the Golden Gate Bridge was just a planners dream.

On the passage to Panama, some of the lads figured out a plan to enter the 'tween decks in the middle of the night by means of a large ventilator to help themselves to tins of canned fruit, plus a few tins of Libby's evaporated milk: just the thing as a substitute for cream. They had heard that a number of extra cases of the canned fruit were always added by the shippers to compensate for pilferage en route to the importers, so why not get in first! They were very choosy, peaches or apricots being preferred to tinned apples or pears, and they were careful to wreck and sink the empty cans over the stern afterwards.

They had glorious weather all the way to Panama, through the Caribbean, and well into the Atlantic before they encountered a heavy swell from astern, which foreshadowed the approach of a storm. The barometer took a steep dive and the sky looked ominous. As the storm overtook *Sacramento Valley*, she was tossed like a toy on the heavy seas. The great danger in such conditions was for the ship to broach-to, that is, for an oncoming wave to hit her on the quarter and turn her sideways into the trough between the heavy rollers, causing the cargo to shift and bundle the ship over. This was particularly dangerous when a ship, like *Sacramento Valley*, had a maximum deck cargo of timber.

Dan, doing his two hour spell at the wheel, could see the strain on the Old Man's face as the ship surfed and wallowed in the conditions that called for the utmost concentration and skill in helmsmanship. As the ship approached the continental shelf and shallower water, the swell finally subsided. The tension on the bridge diminished and there was just the roaring of the breaking sea alongside. The storm had pushed them ahead of schedule, they picked up the London pilot at Dover a day early, and after the strain of the transatlantic crossing the passage around the coast was nothing.

Everyone was looking forward to going home, but first it was to Millwall Docks to discharge the lumber, then to Victoria Docks to unload the canned fruit and general cargo. It was a thrill, when the ship passed through the dock entrances, with the busy road traffic temporarily held up, to wave cheerily to the pale-faced Londoners and exchange banter with the girls. With the London consignment discharged, it was on to Liverpool, and then Sharpness, a small port right up the River Severn beyond Avonmouth, Newport and Chepstow. This choice of port would provide the crew with an experience some of them would never forget.

Head Office in Cardiff, ever alert to wresting the last ounce of economy out of the ship, had decided to pay off some catering staff and anyone else not essential to the safety of the ship, reckoning the trip down to Cardiff would take only a few hours. So at five o'clock on a dark, wintry morning, after most of the cargo had been discharged, the ship sailed at the top of the tide with a pilot on the bridge and cargo only in number one and number five holds – the extremities of the ship.

At six o'clock, when Dan went to relieve the man at the wheel for what should have been a straightforward completion of the voyage, he got a surprise. The normal procedure was for the helmsman being relieved to give the course to be steered, or the last order given, to the man taking over, and then to repeat this to the officer of the watch or pilot, as the case might be. This time he whispered, "I think we're aground!" To any seaman, this is a frightening statement. Both the Captain and First Mate were on the bridge with the pilot because of the shortness of the run and the misty conditions. Dan could see them anxiously conferring.

The First Mate, in an attempt to reduce the tension, joked, "At least I'll be able to get the boot-topping painted while we're high and dry!" but the pilot was not amused.

"It would be wiser to get a lifeboat swung out, Mister," he said.

The Severn is notorious for its shifting sandbanks and tidal currents and at daylight it was evident that the ship had slid imperceptibly to a halt at right angles to one of these ridges of sand.

Worse still, with the tide falling and only her midship section resting on the sand, the weight of the cargo at each end of the ship with nothing in between, put such a strain on the hull that it flattened. Rivets flew off like bullets and the shell plating amidships bulged and split open with a sickening crack. It was possible to step out of the engine-room through the split in the hull on to the sandbank and back again, a frightening experience, especially for engineers used to being cocooned in the bowels of the ship.

What happened over the next twenty-four hours turned out to be a farce, although it wasn't funny at the time. There were urgent consultations between the ship and her owners by radio, and it was decided that when the tide changed it would be too dangerous to stay on board *Sacramento Valley*. All hands were ordered to pack their gear, put on their go-ashore suits and be prepared to leave when a launch came from Chepstow. When it came, it brought the marine superintendent who closeted himself with the Captain while all the gear was loaded into the launch. The super finally emerged from the Captain's cabin to say that they couldn't leave the ship after all as that would be tantamount to deserting her to the claims of salvage operators.

He then left in the launch with the three officers' wives and all the luggage which everyone in their disappointment had forgotten about, while the crew prepared to lower the starboard lifeboat. The plan was that with everyone in the lifeboat it was to remain attached to the ship overnight, but not to stay alongside in case she turned on her side when the tide rose.

By then it was late afternoon and getting darker by the minute. It had also started to drizzle. Boarding the lifeboat from a dangling pilot ladder, dressed in their go-ashore suits, some with overcoats and trilby hats, was bad enough, but when they discovered the lifeboat was smothered in coal dust they realised their gear was going to be a write-off. The rain didn't improve matters, but like everybody else in those days, they just knuckled down under the adverse conditions and obeyed orders, sometimes rowing to keep the boat clear of the ship's side, or simply resting oars at the end of the boat rope from the fo'c'sle head.

During that long night, cold, wet, hungry and tossing up and down, they could see the ship's list had worsened, with all sorts of crashes and clatters to confirm the fact. About four in the morning their spirits were lifted when they saw two powerful salvage tugs approaching, sent from Avonmouth.

The shivering crew in the lifeboat were given steaming cups of tea and hefty meat sandwiches before being sent onboard the stricken ship, now heeling at a dangerous angle, to heave by hand the heavy, greasy steel-wire towing hawsers and make them fast on the fo'c'sle head. Then they had to secure the ship's main engines to the engine-room skylight by steel wires in case the holding down bolts had been sheared off by the grounding.

It was hoped that there would be enough water at high tide and reserve buoyancy in the ship to enable the tugs to pull the ship off the bank, out of the shipping channel and ashore again on the mud flats at the side of the river. The whole procedure was a success and the towing cables were cast off when it became clear that the ship had enough momentum to reach the mud flats. She then slid to a halt on the edge of the Gloucestershire fields.

The Captain thanked the crew for their efforts and suggested they all turn in, which they did, just as they were, still in their ruined shore-going clothes. When they woke hours later, their suitcases and kitbags had been returned to the ship and they could change into working gear. Dan, in his later and more affluent years, would look back and marvel that he and his shipmates would tolerate such conditions without special rates of pay, overtime or danger money, plus compensation for ruined clothes. At the time, it didn't even enter his head.

While on the mud at low tide, ship-repairers from Cardiff patched the ship's hull and made her reasonably watertight for the short run to Cardiff. Then the water inside was pumped out and once again, at the top of high water, the tugs returned to take her away. Safely in drydock she was re-patched to make her as seaworthy as possible for the next leg to Wallsend-on-Tyne. She had broken her back and would have to be cut in half and knit together again by the expert shipbuilders of the Tyneside shipyards. What skilled men they were, and absolutely vital in the years ahead.

Sacramento Valley was eventually reborn to give further faithful service to the company until she was torpedoed and sunk, by a German submarine off Cape Verde in 1941. A common fate for many of these fine ships and the men who sailed in them.

More Maritime Mishaps

Dan had been promised a job on his old ship *Prince Rupert City* when she arrived, so he had decided to stay in Cardiff on his return from Wallsend. He had been given his rightful status of A.B. for the slow trip of *Sacramento Valley* from Cardiff to the Tyne in tow of an ocean-going tug.

After a couple of weeks enjoying life ashore in South Wales, it was like old times boarding the PRC again, he was quite used to joining a ship under the tips; loading coal, with coal dust flying and lying inches thick over everything.

He wasn't, however, prepared for the sudden loud crash behind him as he crossed the midship deck. He leapt a foot in the air and when he turned he saw a large sling-load of drums of paint lying on the deck right where he had been a second before. Several of the drums had burst open while others were badly damaged, and white enamel paint was pouring over the coal dust making an unholy mess. No one had called "Stand from under!" the usual warning on ships, docks and warehouses all over the world which could have been a fatal lapse. Luckily, Dan had sighted a familiar face further along the deck and had hurried forward to greet Mac, a fellow apprentice when Dan had been senior on the ship over two years before. He explained why he had not gone on to get his Second Mate's certificate and was now 'before the mast' then lost no time changing into his working gear and joining Mac to catch up on his news.

He learned that the new Captain was a tough little man from North Wales, well-known for his pugnacity. He had been known to challenge his officers 'out on deck', that is, to a fight, if they disagreed with him. The First Mate was the opposite temperament and able to ride the Old Man's storms with an impassive calmness which infuriated the Captain all the more. Maybe the company had deliberately put them together, since both men were excellent in fulfilling company policy: economy.

After an uneventful twelve days passage, they were back in an Egyptian port to supplement the bunkering needs of the ships of the Royal Navy. The coal was discharged at Alexandria where the British Fleet maintained a high profile at that time, not only afloat but ashore too, on account of considerable civil strife. The PRC then sailed through the Suez Canal for Djibouti, the capital of French Somaliland at the south eastern end of the Red Sea, where they were to load common sea salt for Korea. The best part of their stay was swimming in the beautifully warm, clear sea water, where one could swim for hours without getting chilled, as the Third Engineer discovered after spitting out his false teeth and seeking to find them.

Of course, for the Somali firemen it was home, although divided by conquest into British, French and Italian parts. During this visit, a Moslem holy day was celebrated and the Somalis were such good and reliable workers that the Chief Engineer readily gave them permission to take part in the festivities. These simple, clean-living men, shiny-black, with perfect gleaming white teeth, who proudly proclaimed "Cardiff my home, South Shields my country," were heartlessly exploited by a certain class of women living like leeches in the ports of South Wales and north-east England out of which these men sailed. They were snared by these women into a form of marriage, solely to obtain an allotment from their wages every month, and it was common knowledge that many had more than one 'husband'.

Dan was often asked by these fine men to read to them the letters they received from their wives. The messages were usually blatant appeals for more money on some trivial excuse such as "to look as nice as Mrs So-and-so." Dan derived the utmost pleasure in advising the men of the deception and then on their behalf writing letters rejecting the requests. Although of a different race and colour, Dan felt an affinity with these fellows, perhaps because of the quality of their lifestyle, which he admired, though not their religion.

After a week of steady loading night and day, with the customary siesta of four hours from noon when only mad dogs and the British crew worked, the PRC was loaded down to her marks and ready to sail. During the week, news had been received of the death of Sir William Reardon Smith, the founder of the company, at the age of eighty-five. As a mark of respect for Sir William, the customary nine-inch wide blue band was painted right around the black hull of the ship, and while the weather was perfect for it, it was a painstaking task.

The ship sailed – steamed would be a more accurate term – out of the Straits of Bab el Mandeb (Arabic for Hell's Gates) into the Indian Ocean. The Horn of Africa, Cape Guarda-fui, was passed to starboard and later the island of Socotra. The beautiful tropical weather inspired Dan in his night watches, to imagine Arab dhows, laden with the riches of India and the Orient, heading for the markets of Zanzibar, and other East African ports.

Also at night, the watchkeepers used to signal other ships by Morse Code flashed on an Aldis lamp. The usual drill was: "What ship?" and then a reply would come, like: "*City of Benares*, Calcutta to Liverpool." The receiving ship would then offer similar information.

One night, while Dan was at the wheel from ten to midnight, he was thus entertained by the enthusiastic signalling of the Third Mate who sought to contact everything within range. There had been "*Sarpedon*, Yokohama to London,"

"*Rawalpindi*, Bombay to Penang,"

"*Glenbank*, Haiphong to Rotterdam" and more – good practice for all the watch as well as for the Third Mate.

At about eleven-thirty, a ship's masthead light and red sidelight suddenly appeared fine on the port bow. It seemed the approaching ship had been steaming blacked-out and had switched on her navigation lights to be seen in passing. The Third Mate signalled "What ship?" – pause – "What ship?" – pause – again and again without the customary response, so in disgust he sent a very rude message. Still no reply, so the Third finally put down the Aldis, reckoning the other ship must be a foreigner. As she was by that time, almost abeam, and he thought she would pass in silence, unknown. Just then however, the darkness was shattered not by a single Aldis lamp, but by every light an American warship could muster, and that was a lot! From masts, crosstrees, yardarms, funnel, deck-housing and even her profile, lights blazed in an extravaganza of illumination to signal, "*U.S.S. Houston*, message received and reciprocated. Goodnight!"

Then, from right abeam, a powerful searchlight swept the PRC fore and aft. This brought the peppery Old Man scurrying up to the bridge to ask, "What the bloody hell is going on, Mr Evans?"

The Third Mate answered calmly, "It's the *U.S.S. Houston* passing, sir."

The warship had now returned to her normal navigation lights and the Captain muttered "These bloody Yanks love to make a fuss, don't they!", causing the Third Mate to say meekly,

"Yes sir, they do." When the Old Man had had a good look round, checked the course and studied the weather to ensure there was nothing else likely to cause a disturbance, he returned to his cabin.

The beautiful hot sunny weather continued all the way to Sabang, the small bunkering port at the northern tip of the island of Sumatra, where the ship took on bunker coal. Deeply laden once more, the PRC steamed through the Straits of Malacca, round the Malayan archipelago at Singapore into the South China Sea, to head northwards towards Korea.

A few days later, they ran into a full-scale typhoon, a frightening experience with screaming winds whipping the sea into a fury, treating the PRC as if she were a half-tide rock and sweeping anything not securely lashed down over the side.

Nearing Korea they were directed by radio to proceed to Konan on the east coast, and there they spent the next three weeks discharging the salt on to the open wharf where the piles looked like pyramids shining white in the sun, and grew bigger as the days passed.

Korea, at that time, was primeval compared with modem Korea, and as there was little scope for recreation in Konan, Dan and some of the lads spent their free time playing soccer on the wharf. However, some fellows ventured into the town and visited a couple of unsavoury bars, a jaunt which probably led to the tragic events that subsequently developed.

Orders had been received to proceed to Vancouver to load grain for the United Kingdom. They were homeward bound. It was to be another voyage across the North Pacific, light ship, but this one was to be tragically different. The PRC was well on her way, a week out from Konan, when a junior engineer became sick, breaking out in nasty looking sores over his face, head and body. After consulting the Ship Captain's Medical Guide, it did not take the Captain long to diagnose smallpox. His immediate problem was to decide whether it was best to turn back to Japan against the prevailing winds and current, or to take a chance and carry on to Canada where he could be sure of adequate facilities to deal with the outbreak. He decided to go on to Vancouver and, although he was criticised for it later, it proved the better decision.

Although as Master he was responsible for the ship and crew under his command, he undertook to nurse the sick young man himself rather than expose anyone else to the risk of infection and death. Then the cabin boy succumbed to the disease, so the Captain had two sick people to care for. The patients had to be isolated immediately. There was no spare accommodation on a trampship but by doubling up in other cabins one side of the midship housing was made out of bounds and a small cabin next door to the bathplace was set aside as the sickbay with its portholes and ventilator secured and sealed. Before entering the sickbay the Captain, and the Steward, who had volunteered to help with the nursing, put on oilskins, seaboots and sou'westers. Then they drenched themselves all over with disinfectant, and gargled with a mouthful of neat rum before wrapping a towel impregnated with more disinfectant around their noses and mouths, leaving only slits through which to see. They applied medication to the sores, of their patients, changed the bandages, and emptied the toilet buckets. Then they left the cabin and changed their gear in the bathplace before emerging in their underwear to go to their separate quarters.

The young engineer, from a well-found home in Darlington, died, but the cabin boy from the slums of Cardiff withstood the deadly disease and survived. It was subsequently found that neither patient had been vaccinated as a child.

Those who were able to, gathered at a distance to witness the first burial at sea for most of them, and certainly for Dan and Mac. The Captain and Steward emerged from the isolation area carrying the body they had securely stitched into a cocoon of old tarpaulin canvas weighted with a couple of worn-out firebars.

The ship's engines were stopped momentarily for the little ceremony, then with the body lying on a hatchboard the Old Man ordered silence and all heads bowed and bared. Then in his strong Welsh accent he read the 23rd Psalm, tilted the hatchboard and the canvas coffin plunged feet-first into the cold waters of the North Pacific. It was a very sad event for them all, little did they know that the scene would be repeated in a few days time.

During the night following the burial, one of the other A.B.'s developed a high fever and showed the same fearful symptoms seen in the others, so he too was immediately isolated. He died two days later. For the second ceremony it was thought best not to congregate, so it was left to the two nurses to repeat the melancholy duty by themselves. Needless to say, everyone wondered who would be next.

Fortunately, with following winds and good clear weather, *Prince Rupert City* excelled herself, arriving off Vancouver Island in record time. The authorities had been alerted by radio and now, instead of flying the "G" requesting a pilot, the ship displayed the dreaded "L" flag announcing there was an infectious disease on board.

From the outer limits of the pilotage area the pilot launch hailed the ship by megaphone, instructing the Captain to follow it to the wharf at the quarantine station on an island in the Sound. The wharfside men taking the ship's mooring lines were dressed like the Captain and Steward had been, plus long gauntlets, no doubt regarding the ropes as contaminated as the rest of the ship. All their clothing was bright yellow.

As soon as the gangway had been lowered to the wharf, medicos and other quarantine staff streamed on board, first to take the cabin boy away, and then to organise the rest of the crew for the programme ahead. All hands now had to pack their belongings into their suitcases or kitbags, making sure not to include soap, or anything that would melt, and to leave out any leather or rubber items that would be damaged in the high pressure fumigating process.

Everyone had to strip off and put on a sort of medicated linen underwear and a crisp starchy clean dressing gown. They then went ashore, to be herded into one of the buildings in the quarantine complex.

In parties of six they were marshalled into smaller rooms where cabinets like vertical steel coffins awaited them. An attendant told them to take off their linen outfits, leave them in the containers provided, and step into the individual cabinets. The doors were locked behind them. It was just as well that they had been told what to expect or they might have died of shock. A fine warm spray of medicated water was directed on to their bodies from all angles. The spray got steadily hotter until it was almost scalding and there was no escape. Even the cabinet walls were too hot to lean against.

They were on the verge of shrieking when, mercifully, the spray stopped, and they were left to simmer down in the steam until finally the doors were opened and they stepped out into the warmed room looking more like lobsters fresh from the cooking-pot than human beings. After a thorough rubdown with large warm medicated towels they donned fresh suits of linen underwear, then dressing gowns, before being escorted into another warmed compartment. Here they remained until they regained normal body temperature, when every man was given a thorough medical examination.

Then they were ushered into a large dining hall where the tables were already laid and a delicious smell of cooked food greeted them. Not all the men who had left the ship were present; an engineer, two firemen, an apprentice and an A.B. seaman were detained until cleared by further examinations and declared free of the disease, but Mac accompanied Dan throughout the whole ordeal, a relief for both.

Big trays of tasty Canadian food were brought in and the hungry men could hardly wait to get started on it. Few of them had enjoyed such nutritious fare in their lives before, and certainly never on trampships. Being habitually underfed, they relished the feast, not caring whether the onlookers regarded them as being like pigs in a trough or not.

They were looked after for another three days under close medical observation while the ship herself was being subjected to an equally thorough fumigation with a special cyanide gas that penetrated every space within the sealed holds and accommodation of the ship. The smell of the cyanide remained with the ship for weeks after she was certified germ-free and returned to service, and those of the crew whose gear had also been fumigated found their clothing impregnated with it. To Dan's dismay a tin of solid brilliantine, which he had forgotten to remove from his suitcase, had melted in dull orange blotches all over his one and only suit, and had also forgotten to take out the belt from his sports trousers, with the result it was reduced to the size of a dog's collar.

From the quarantine station, and with a pilot on board, they proceeded through the picturesque Puget Sound to the grain terminals in Vancouver.

With seven men short, the company's agents advertised for replacements to work their passage to the United Kingdom for a shilling a day. There was a flood of applicants, there being massive unemployment in Canada at the time. For the newcomers, the trip down the West Coast was an exciting experience and some vowed to undertake a seagoing career as a result, but by the time the ship reached Avonmouth, most of them had changed their minds, reckoning they were not really suited for the semi-monastic existence of a seafarer.

One young fellow of seventeen did decide to accept the job of Deck Boy for the forthcoming voyage, and he, Charlie and Dan became good friends. Mac had finished his time as Apprentice and had left to go to Navigation school to study for his Second Mate's Certificate. Throughout the whole of the last voyage around the world Mac had written a page or two to his girlfriend Barbara in Newcastle every day, and was obviously 'cuckoo' about her. Before he left however, he told Dan he had just received a note from her to say she was going with someone else and did not want to see Mac again, a not uncommon experience for seafarers.

On completion of the discharge of the grain at Avonmouth, the ship crossed the Bristol Channel to Newport, Monmouthshire, to load coal for Alexandria. The trip to the Egyptian port and the subsequent discharge there was accomplished with only a few skirmishes ashore between the new white firemen, who had replaced the trouble-free Arabs, and the Egyptian police.

Then it was through the Suez Canal, down the Red Sea and into the Indian Ocean, preparing the holds to load bulk sea salt at Ras Hafun, a small harbour on the coast of Italian Somaliland, a change of cargo from glistening black to glittering white.

There was nothing to do ashore, but Dan and Charlie spent their off duty time exploring the sun-drenched, sun-bleached beaches strewn with driftwood and relics from wrecked ships, including skulls and human bones. They revelled in the warm clear water and sunned themselves nutbrown all over, while the others fished from the ship and supplemented the dull diet with what they caught.

The Chief Steward had managed to acquire a live goat, but during its brief life at sea it proved to be a menace, eating everything within reach, cardboard boxes, doormats, washing on the line, all was grist to its mill. Then came the day for it to be slaughtered and neither the Steward nor the Cook were prepared to tackle the job. A call went out for a volunteer and Chips, reluctantly, agreed to do it. He was the P.T. fanatic who had started off Dan and his mates three years ago, and was still as keen as ever. The animal, bleating pathetically, put up a tremendous resistance, and at one point tried to commit suicide by leaping over the ship's rails. Everyone felt they would gladly forego fresh meat and let the poor creature live, but the would-be killers were not to be denied – and a gruesomely lengthy process it proved to be. What took the Carpenter and his helpers ten minutes, a skilled butcher could have accomplished in a few seconds.

When the meat was cooked it was found to be stringy and tough, not the delicacy they expected, and most men were put off the goat's head soup when they saw its reproachful eyes floating around in it.

The fine weather run across the Indian Ocean passed quickly and as usual they called in at Sabang to top up with bunker coal to last until the ship reached Japan. Here, for reasons best known to themselves, the firemen went berserk when they got ashore, and got fighting drunk on the local grog. They proved to be too much for the four native policemen to handle, and defiantly rejected orders to return to the ship. The Captain regarded this as mutiny, flagrant disobedience of a lawful command, and, in consultation with the Chief Engineer decided to use the deck personnel to fire the ship for the passage to Japan, where new firemen could be engaged. Whereupon the Captain told the ship's agents in Sabang to have the men arrested for either mutiny or desertion when they sobered up, and the ship sailed without them.

Fortunately, the donkeyman (the equivalent of Bos'n in the engine-room) was still on board and he and the Chief Engineer demonstrated to the six chosen seamen, the art of firing the ship's furnaces. The aim was to have a bright, fiercely-burning fire with a crust of fresh coal on top to produce the maximum amount of heat without allowing any build-up of ash or clinker to lessen the draught or stifle the fire.

Full of confidence, Dan and Dave, a fellow A.B., started off with a flourish, but they soon realised it wasn't going to be as easy as they thought. First, they were in the Straits of Malacca with tropical temperatures on top of the stifling heat of the stokehold. Far worse was the fact that the coal just loaded was not good Welsh coal, but poor quality stuff from South Africa and instead of burning down to ash that could be easily removed, it set in lava-like clinker on the firebars and had to be broken off and cleared out so as not to impair the flow of the all-important draught. It would have been difficult for the regular firemen, but for the inexperienced new chums it was a crippling job.

Each man had three fires to attend, and one of these had to be cleaned out each watch after it had been allowed to die down a little. The heat in the stokehold was bad enough, but when a furnace door was opened and the red-hot embers drawn out on to the hot, steel-plated floor, with heavy eight-foot steel rakes, it was blistering. The clinker then had to be broken up with eight-foot steel pokers called slices, and this was the hardest job of all.

One of the several mishaps occurred when a young apprentice, with the best of intentions, threw a bucketful of sea water over the white hot clinkers just drawn from the fire and Dan's eyes, mouth and nostrils were enveloped in a cloud of scalding steam and ash.

With the firebox cleaned out, a new fire had to be started by transferring a few shovels full of live embers from one of the other fires. First class firemen could do that quickly, with little or no reduction in steam pressure, but the combination of poor coal and untrained firemen meant that the ship could only muster about five knots, less than half the normal speed.

Nevertheless, after rounding the Malayan peninsular into the South China Sea, the heat was less oppressive and as the acting firemen got better at their job the speed of *Prince Rupert City* improved. After twenty days, instead of the normal twelve, she arrived safely in Fushiki on the west coast of Japan where six Filipino firemen were waiting to relieve Dan and his mates, who were glad to return to their deck jobs.

Fushiki in those days was just a small fishing port. Dan, Dave, Charlie, Jack and Albert spent their evenings sampling *sukiyaki* and other appetising Japanese food in an eating house where their meals were served by table-mistresses who saw that their glasses were topped up, their cigarettes lit, and warmed-scented hand-towels were ever ready to wipe hands or face. The girls were charming, trained to serve and satisfy their men folk, but the Japanese men seemed to be harsh and curt in their responses, with none of the carefree banter of these seamen, relaxing after their recent hard work. For Dan in particular, it was good to be back in Japan, sampling their traditional warm hospitality once more, but with the discharge of their salt, the ship was on her way once more.

On their way to Cebu in the Philippine Islands to load sugar for New York, the ship steamed for about two hours through a mass of leaping dolphins as far as the eye could see. There must have been thousands of them. Then, a day out from Japan, the ship encountered the tail end of a typhoon and being empty of cargo, she was tossed around like a balloon. The new firemen found it difficult to keep their feet with the stokehold floor rising and falling so violently. Weather conditions on deck were tempestuous, but seafarers are used to gales, cyclones and hurricanes, and even waterspouts. Close acquaintance with these awesome manifestations encouraged a healthy respect for nature and the Creator, with genuine atheists few and far between. The winds and sea decreased as the disturbance passed, to continue on its rampaging path into the Pacific, and *Prince Rupert City* was left to wallow on her course to Cebu.

When Dan first saw that delightful island paradise, as it was before exploitation and the later devastation caused by World War II, he was captivated by its beauty. The abundance of luscious fruits for sale on stalls alongside the ship encouraged all hands to indulge in a feast of bananas, paw paws, mangoes and other exotic and unfamiliar fruit. The local people, especially the girls and young women, were entrancingly good-looking and their easy-going relaxed lifestyle appealed to Dan, who thought how good it would be to live there. The Philippine Islands were more or less an American colony, with most of the larger businesses owned and managed by Americans. These lived in luxury in and around the sprawling city of Manila, taking advantage of the cheap local labour.

That was also why a British trampship was used to carry their sugar to the United States. American ships, with expensive American crews, had priced themselves off the market. A similar situation occurred from the mid-1960s to the first class, efficient ships of the United Kingdom, France, the Netherlands, Scandinavia and Italy, when ships registered in Liberia or Monrovia or some other unlikely maritime nation employing cheap, unqualified labour, undercut them and put the fine ships on the scrap heap, and their well-trained crews were made redundant.

In Manila, with his mates, Dan decided to have a look at what was claimed to be the largest ballroom in the world. The Santa Ana Dance Palace was the size of a football field, with an orchestra at each end and the sides lined with hundreds of gorgeous dance hostesses in ankle length embroidered gowns with thigh-high slits. There was subdued lighting with shimmering coloured lights illuminating the dancers and it looked unbelievably beautiful.

Dan's party felt out of place since they were the only males in civilian suits. All the others wore the uniforms of the US Army, Navy or Air Force, they moved in clouds of expensive aftershave and deodorant, and carried wallets stuffed with US dollars. When the lads finally plucked up the courage to ask a hostess to dance they felt it prudent to wait until everyone else was dancing before they chose the left-behinds. They had seen too many brawls in the past to go looking for one. Nevertheless, they managed to get a few dances, handing a ticket to each partner which, at the end of the evening, would be cashed by the management as her wages. Dan was surprised to learn that some of the beautiful 'girls' were in fact young men and boys, but he never came to the point of discovering this as emphatically as others had done.

Once again, the ship was fully-loaded and set off on her Great Circle course across the Pacific to San Pedro, California for fuel oil to take her to New York. *Prince Rupert City* was converted to an oil-burning ship when fuel oil was cheaper than coal, and changed back again when it wasn't: just another cost-cutting procedure employed by the company.

Three days before arriving at San Pedro, Dan became ill with a fever and rash. He did not display the fearful symptoms of smallpox, cholera or other tropical illness, and both the Captain and First Mate were puzzled, even after studying *The Shipmaster's Medical Guide*, as to what the problem could be. They thought it best to isolate Dan and see what developed however when his condition continued to deteriorate, with a high temperature and spasms of violent shivering they suspected some form of malaria and alerted the port health authorities by radio.

In San Pedro, even the port doctor couldn't be sure what the problem was, but rather than risk an outbreak of a deadly disease at sea he ordered that Dan be put into hospital ashore for observation. If he got better in time he could rejoin the ship in New York. Captain Linden endorsed Dan's discharge book with an extra "V.G." to express his satisfaction with Dan's service while under his command, an endorsement that would prove a real blessing to Dan on more than one occasion in the years ahead.

Dan was only vaguely aware of his transfer from ship to hospital and even less aware that that would be the end of his association with the company he had started his apprenticeship with nearly eight years before. He would certainly have no idea, that *Prince Rupert City*, a ship he was very fond of, would meet the same fate as so many other merchant ships in the coming war when she was sunk by enemy aircraft off Cape Wrath, Scotland, in 1941.

With proper medical care in the isolation wing of the hospital in San Pedro, Dan steadily recovered from the undiagnosed ailment that had afflicted him. The doctor decided that he had probably been infected by some insect bite while ashore in either Japan or the Philippines and as a result had contracted a rare form of malaria and would not be able to rejoin his ship. Now here he was, paid off his ship and in hospital in the United States. In the hospital wing in which he had been placed, there were several other men with equally strange ailments, one a Danish seaman whose nose was being eaten away by a germ. He had been stowing away the ship's mooring lines and the rope rasped against his nose as he was coiling it in the rope locker. Whatever it was ailing Dan, it was neither painful nor disfiguring, and for this he was truly thankful.

Romance In San Pedro
And Rejection In Canada

When he recovered Dan was still kept in the hospital until the British Consul in Los Angeles decided what to do with him. Someone told Dan that he would probably be deported back to the United Kingdom as DBS (distressed British seaman) at a wage of a shilling a day. The idea was repugnant to Dan and he wondered what he could do to avoid such a fate.

All his personal gear had been locked away and all he had was the underwear he had on and a white towelling dressing-gown, because, it was explained, so many patients took the opportunity to disappear and illegally enter the United States. The west coast from California to Canada had absorbed thousands of seafarers, mostly Scandinavian, into the lumber camps, large construction jobs like the San Francisco harbour bridges and docks, and some to better paid ships, trading to Alaska.

Meanwhile, he made the best of things, enjoying the leisure and good food, the luxury of being able to sleep all night and get up at seven to a delicious American breakfast. During his wanderings around the hospital, he became friendly with a couple of elderly Japanese gentlemen who seemed to spend most of their time either bowing and chatting to one another or massaging their feet with perfumed oil. They spoke perfect English and encouraged Dan to learn Japanese, and by the time they left he had learned to count and to write their alphabet in *kata kana* and *hira gana*.

Dan had met Charlie's parents when they visited their son in Vancouver, and he knew that they owned a fruit farm at Penticton, BC He now decided to ask their help in getting into Canada so he wrote to them, explaining his predicament, asking if they would write him a letter offering him a job if he could make the trip up from San Pedro. He posted the letter and sat back to await developments.

One warm sunny afternoon, feeling rather bored, he was swinging in a hammock-seat under a tree in the hospital grounds watching visitors come and go. Suddenly, he saw a young woman stumble shakily down the steps, one hand holding the handrail and the other over her brow. Dan leapt forward, afraid she would fall, and steered her to the hammock-seat. Then he dashed away to get a glass of ice-water and as she sipped that, he fanned her with the magazine he had been reading. After a few minutes she said she felt much better, but Dan, anxious to enjoy her company for as long as possible, asked her name. She told him her name was Terese, adding that she was half-American, half-Mexican and at nineteen, the second eldest in a family of eight children. She explained that she had been visiting a friend who had just had an operation and the smell of ether was so strong she had been almost overcome.

Before she left she said she would see if he was around the next time she came to visit her friend, he assured her he would be, but was genuinely surprised the following afternoon to see Terese heading his way carrying a basket full of oranges and bananas, not for her friend, but for him. The other fellows in Dan's ward were green with envy when he unloaded the fruit on to his bed, but he hurried back to Terese with the empty basket in case anyone else muscled in.

The following evening, Terese visited him again, in an old high-sided Model T Ford. To Dan, she was as luscious as the fruit she brought: so emotional and excited about everything, waving her hands around as she spoke in her fascinating broken English. He was entranced, and it wasn't long before they started kissing and cuddling like young lovers.

Limited to the hospital grounds they had no privacy – it is not only evil-doers who prefer darkness to light – so they planned that Dan would sneak into Terese's car and lie low until she drove out past the gatekeepers. Dan felt very guilty the first time they did this, as indeed he would be with all forms of deception throughout his life, but it was the first of many romantic evenings of scenic drives, winding around the cliff face with glorious views across the ocean that pounded the rocks far below. At times it was nerve-wracking because of Terese's habit of taking her hands off the steering wheel even when rounding curves, but it seemed a power was watching over them to see that they came to no harm.

One evening, that power exercised a direct influence when Terese, who always did things suddenly, turned off into a railway siding, bumped to a halt and, switching off the engine and headlights, indicated she was ready to 'pitch woo' as the Americans say. Dan had a feeling that this sort of behaviour was not normal for Terese, she had probably got ideas from a True Romances magazine. As their lips met in a preliminary kiss, the distinctive "toot toot-ta toot" of an American locomotive almost froze them to their seats as they realised the car was parked right across the tracks... panic stations! Terese turned the ignition key but stalled the engine in her haste. They could hear the rumble of the train as they frantically released the handbrake and leapt out of the car to push it clear just seconds before a long goods train appeared round the bend. As it rumbled heavily past, Terese crossed herself and muttered a prayer of relief, and they hugged each other in thankfulness for their deliverance.

One evening, they went to an outdoor cinema, something quite new for Dan. There he was, still in underwear and a thin gown watching a picture about a torrid Mexican love affair that had gone wrong, with Terese loving every heartbreaking minute of it. Dan couldn't understand the dialogue but he clearly understood the unhappy lot of any suitor who found disfavour with a Mexican girl's family. He was pleased that, in spite of her strong physical attraction, he had resisted several tempting moments to take advantage of her. She was so unspoilt and trusting, a truly nice girl.

Getting back into the hospital undetected was becoming Dan's growing problem, there were too many absentees at the 10 p.m. check and a tightening of regulations was looming.

It had been four weeks since Dan had written to Charlie's parents at Penticton and he had almost forgotten about it, but one day he received the reply. His first reaction was a mild surprise that they were prepared to go along with his plan, even to the extent of enclosing a separate letter for the purpose of satisfying the Immigration officials.

The British Consul in Los Angeles had offered him two ways to leave the United States: by paying his own fare to New York to rejoin *Prince Rupert City* or by being deported DBS. Now, armed with his Canadian letter, Dan appealed to the consul to allow him to travel to Penticton to accept the work offered and start a new life. The Consul agreed, but only on the understanding that if he wasn't allowed into Canada, or if anything else went wrong, he returned to Los Angeles and reported to him in person. Dan gladly accepted the helpful proposal, and signed a clearance document to that effect. The Consul then advised the hospital authorities that, if he had a clean bill of health, they could release Mr Robson with his money and personal belongings. Dan's precious Discharge Book was handed over and he moved with all his gear to a boarding house run by a Swedish lady, Mrs Petersen. He booked his journey to Vancouver by Greyhound coach the next day, and then faced the problem of telling Terese that he was going.

He decided to take her to a dine and dance restaurant on the outskirts of San Pedro and to break the news there. She took it more calmly than Dan had imagined, knowing her excitable nature, she then told him her mother had prepared her for the probability of such an event. So, after a sometimes sad, but otherwise enjoyable evening they said goodbye with promises to write and keep in touch for ever more, each believing they would at the time.

The following morning Dan boarded the long-distance Greyhound and settled back in luxury. Their first major stop was San Francisco, then they crossed the harbour by vehicular ferry to drive off at Oakland on their way north to Oregon. The main highway from Oakland to Portland became the Redwood Highway, a picturesque route of fragrant pine forests but as the hours passed, Dan found his eyes were too tired to take much interest in the scenery, and he spent much of the time asleep. It was a long, tiring trip, punctuated by comfort-stops at which Dan revelled in the wonderful variety of American food at reasonable prices.

At Seattle he changed coaches for Vancouver and as they neared the Canadian border at White Rock, an elderly lady in the next seat asked him what his plans were. When he told her he was hoping to get work on a fruit farm she said he wouldn't stand a chance as there were so many unemployed Canadian workers and they would get preference.

"No," she said, "If you really want to get past the immigration people, it would be best to tell them you're just passing through Canada."

Dan knew the letter he carried was more a kindness than a genuine offer of employment, so he decided to take the old lady's advice. On disembarkation he got in line to file through the screening gates. Most of his fellow passengers, with their passports at the ready, passed through after only a fleeting glance from the official and then re-boarded the coach. When Dan offered his discharge book the official took one look at it and said, "Stand over there, please," and beckoned the remaining travellers through.

When they had all been processed the official turned to Dan and said, "Now what about you, why haven't you got a passport?"

Dan replied that British seamen regarded their discharge books as bona fide travel documents. "Well, we don't in Canada," he said. He then grilled Dan with all sorts of questions, halfway through signalling the coach driver to continue his journey. "And what are you proposing to do in Canada?" asked the official.

"Oh, I'm just on my way through" answered Dan.

"Oh yes... how much money have you?"

Dan said truthfully, "Forty-two dollars, sir."

"That won't get you very far, will it?" said the officer, warming to his work and filling in a foolscap form.

Dan hastily concocted a story about his sister in the UK sending him some money when he got to Montreal.

"Oh! Where are you going to stay in Montreal - where does your sister live – what is her occupation?" and so on and on, until Dan got more and more tangled up in his own story. Finally, looking Dan straight in the eye, the man said "Why don't you tell me the truth for a change instead of all these lies?"

By that time Dan was so tired that he answered, "Yes, I admit I have been lying. I was only following advice given to me on the coach before we arrived. In fact I have a letter here offering me work on a fruit farm in Penticton and I was going to use that."

"Can I see that?" said the official, and when he had finished reading it he said, "If you had given me this in the first place it might have made all the difference, but it's too late now, I've made out a deportation order in quadruplicate on these official numbered forms and I can't get them revoked without weeks of correspondence." He told Dan that he could challenge his ruling by writing to Ottawa, if he wished, but Dan wisely decided to let the matter drop.

It was getting dark by that time and the whole area was floodlit. A wide white-painted strip across the road separated Canada from the United States. Dan picked up his suitcase and trudged over to the American side and presented his deportation order to the nearest official. "How come you got this?" was the first question, and when Dan told him he said, "But you're a British citizen, aren't you?"

"Yes I am" said Dan.

The official looked puzzled and said, "Well, that's British Columbia over the road and that's where you should be – we don't want you here."

Dan, with a smirk, said, "I suggest you phone them over there and tell them that." The resulting discussion was quite entertaining but in the end the Canadians won the argument on the ground that since Dan had come from the American side he was their responsibility.

The American immigration officer explained that he would have to arrest Dan and put him in the detention centre, but Dan urged the man to let him go back to San Pedro where he could ship out. He was able to convince the officer that he had promised to report to the British Consul in Los Angeles if he was unable to enter Canada. "Okay, if we give you this chance it is only on condition that you report, not only to the British Consul, but also to the chief immigration officer at San Pedro. We shall inform him of this arrangement and if he doesn't hear from you within the week you will be on our wanted list." Dan thanked him for his kind consideration.

He was issued with a free travel warrant back to Seattle and sent to the waiting room to get a cup of coffee and something to eat while waiting for the next southbound coach. To while away the time, he returned to the immigration area and was surprised at the grilling that even incoming American citizens received. If someone said his home town was Phoenix, he might be asked on what street the Central Police Station was situated. It was most interesting to listen to these checks on the truthfulness of the traveller. One man was asked what he did for a living, and when he said he was a carpet layer, his interrogator said, "A carpet layer, eh? Do you ever pick them up again?"

When the man retorted "Oh no, I get my mate to do that" Dan felt like saying 'Well done!'

It was nearly midnight when the coach arrived and the small hours of the morning when it reached Seattle. Everything was closed down, and feeling like a derelict, Dan wrapped his overcoat around himself, curled up in a doorway with his head on his suitcase and tried to sleep.

At five o'clock he was aroused by cleaners, and after a visit to the ablution block for a shave and a shower, he had hot coffee, ham and eggs with buckwheat cakes in the cafeteria, to set him up for the long trip south. Once on the coach to Los Angeles, he settled down to enjoy the luxury of being a tourist, and resolved not to take advice from anyone, especially female passengers, young or old.

However, he did have an overnight stop in San Francisco after enjoying the delightful scenery en route through Oregon and northern California, with its regular stops for delicious American refreshments.

On arrival in Los Angeles he reported to the British Consul and then to the US immigration office in San Pedro as promised. The next step was to head for Mrs Petersen's boarding house where Dan learned about a Scandinavian seamen's club or union that, by arrangement with US immigration, controlled a register of men leaving or joining ships, provided they did not stay in the United States for more than sixty days. When Dan told the Scandinavians that the end of his sixty days was just a week away, those big-hearted fellows arranged for him to join their club and what's more they put him at the top of their roster. Dan was deeply grateful as he had no wish to be deported to the United Kingdom, D.B.S.

So when three days later, the Danish ship *Anna Maersk* called at San Pedro wanting an A.B. seaman, the Captain was obliged to accept Dan. As most Scandinavians speak English fluently, there were no language difficulties and Dan soon settled into his new environment on a faster, better class ship with better food, than he had hitherto experienced. There were two men to a cabin, and the crew were housed aft, which was a change. She was the first motorship Dan had served on, and after the silence of steamships Dan found the 'puff-puff, puff-puff,' quite comforting. She was spotlessly clean, as are most Scandinavian vessels, and carried six passengers. There was a marked improvement in the food, with a variety of cold meats and salads, something never seen on trampships, and another innovation: the watchkeepers were four hours on and eight off. Only officers had those conditions on trampships in Dan's time.

She was bound for Yokohama, Kobe, Shanghai, Hong Kong and Manila, with a cargo of general merchandise. Part of the cargo was a large consignment of garlic and the whole ship reeked, and unloading in Yokohama, another part of the cargo attracted everyone's attention when a few insecure bales of used silk stockings, loaded in New York, fell apart. The dockside gusts of wind blew the flimsy, rolled top stockings all over the ship catching on anything and everything. The randy Danes found the incident extremely erotic, not that they needed any help in that direction, and they couldn't get ashore quickly enough.

Dan found that his shipmates were allowed to draw every dollar that was due to them and they usually did. He, on the other hand, contemplating the opportunity to pay off the ship before she left the Far East again, volunteered for the unpopular job of night-watchman. His hardest task at night was struggling to help returning revellers up the gangway and safely into their bunks. Sometimes one or two would fall into the dock and have to be fished out, more dead than alive. After these nightly frolics continued at most of the Philippine ports, they arrived at Manila on the return leg of the voyage.

Dan called at the British Consulate to discuss the possibility of working ashore in that exotic place.

"Oh dear no, we couldn't possibly sanction any plan of that nature," said one of the officials in a superior Oxbridge accent, as though the Philippines belonged to Britain, regarding Dan as though he had just emerged from a sewer. Maybe his suit still reeked of garlic, thought Dan, wondering why the official's nostrils twitched and wrinkled.

Ah well, he knew that some people regarded merchant seamen as being on a par with the lower forms of marine growth, and treated them accordingly. Never mind, he would try in Hong Kong: they might be more approachable there.

On The Beach In Hong Kong

During the passage across the South China Sea from Manila to Hong Kong, Dan asked Captain Hansen if he could pay off. The Captain reluctantly agreed, provided the Hong Kong authorities had no objection and provided also that there was a replacement available. Dan was lucky; a Swedish A.B., recently released from hospital, was keen to return to sea, so he signed on as Dan paid off, and this seemed to him to be a really good omen.

'Well,' thought Dan as he stepped ashore at Kowloon, 'Here I am, free as a bird, just what I've wanted for a long time – the chance to create a prosperous future as others have done in this colourful country.'

He didn't know a soul and he wasn't sure where to go, but as soon as he came out of the dock gates he saw a large four-storey building right opposite, with YMCA in bold lettering across the front of it.

The well-spoken reception clerk offered him a single bedroom with full board on either a daily or weekly basis, so Dan settled for a week and paid in advance, much to the clerk's surprise. A houseboy escorted Dan up to the first floor and showed him a small bedroom adjacent to the washing and toilet facilities. The boy, in quite good English, explained the routine of the 'Y', told him what time meals were and handed him that morning's *South China Daily News*.

'This will do me,' thought Dan, feeling *pukka sahib* already, and seeing that it was almost lunchtime, he went downstairs to scan the newspaper. The headlines screamed of dastardly attacks the Japanese Army was making on Woosung and Dan recalled the horror of seeing high-explosive and incendiary bombs being dropped in earlier raids in the area. *Anna Maersk* had been anchored in the river just a few miles away, so the crew had had a ringside seat, and the callous inhumanity of it all, confirmed in their hearts the utter barbarity of war.

A gong announced lunch and several men converged on the dining room. Dan paused uncertainly at the door and one of the waiters showed him to a table with two vacant seats. During lunch Dan learned from his table companions that almost all those staying at the 'Y' were from the UK, in some kind of government service on three year contracts, with six months' leave on full pay on completion, and with the sea passage paid both ways. He wondered if there might be any crumbs under the rich man's table, but when he said he hoped to find work in Hong Kong, his table companions said it would be extremely difficult without the right contacts. Nevertheless, they agreed there was only one way to find out – to give it a go – and that's what Dan determined to do.

He studied the situations vacant columns and saw that an English teacher was required by the X.Y.Z. Language School. He crossed the harbour from Kowloon to Hong Kong and managed to see the principal, a well-spoken Chinese. All he asked was where Dan had been educated, so Dan simply said "London." He was told to start the following morning at nine o'clock and Dan returned to Kowloon believing he had made a breakthrough into the wonderful life of the Orient.

That evening at dinner, his companions couldn't believe it when he told them of his success. They congratulated him, probably thinking, 'This fellow is better qualified than we thought,' but the next morning at breakfast, a young man at a nearby table called out, "We didn't know you were a professor, Mr Robson."

Dan replied, "What do you mean? I'm certainly not a professor."

"Well, take a look at this" said the other fellow, handing him the morning newspaper. With boggling eyes, Dan read:

English, French, Chinese... London professor converses freely *sans* book. English subjects 9 to 10 a.m., 4 to 5 p.m. and 8 to 9 p.m. daily, five day a week.
Fees $6 per month.
Apply now at the X.Y.Z. Business School, Caine Road, Hong Kong.

Obviously, the X.Y.Z. school was not allowing grass to grow under its feet.

Dan hurried to the telephone and told the principal to cancel the arrangement, because there had been a misunderstanding: he wasn't a professor from London. The principal expressed dismay and couldn't see why Dan was concerned about such a trifle, since it was intended solely to impress would-be candidates, but Dan was adamant. He knew his own race would regard him as an impostor, and would have no difficulty in making his life in the colony distinctly uncomfortable.

His next effort was when he answered an advertisement for an agent on a commission basis, at the Boomerang Advertising Agency. Dan slowly climbed the stairs to the fifth floor of an office block in downtown Hong Kong, gathering his thoughts and planning his approach. Before entering the door of the agency he removed the chewing gum from his mouth and dropped it into a rubbish tray. A few seconds later he was ushered into the manager's office to be greeted by a middle-aged woman who said, "Well, thank God you're not a gum-chewing Yank!"

After scrutinising him thoroughly, she asked what experience he had had in advertising. When Dan truthfully replied, "None at all, I'm afraid ma'am" she said,

"Oh you don't want to be bloody well afraid, you'll never get anywhere being afraid: all you need is some bloody common sense and a bit of backbone, that's all I had when I started here, so do you want to give it a go, or not, it's up to you?"

She was as Aussie as Ayers Rock, and her friendly, open style was refreshing and appealed to Dan, so he said yes, he'd give it a go. She said she was Mrs Woods, and explained that she wanted someone to contact the last of her former customers, who had not as yet renewed their contracts. It was just a temporary job, she told him, but if he was lucky he could earn a few dollars to keep him going until something else showed up.

Armed with her list of addresses and trying to remember some of the sales patter she had suggested, Dan set out the following morning to call on the advertising managers of the listed companies. He didn't have much luck – in some places he didn't even get an interview – but one of the toughest, according to Mrs Woods, agreed to see him. The man's name was Mr McNab and Dan was determined not to be overawed, by the man's reputation.

So, when Mr McNab introduced himself, Dan shook the proffered hand and said, "That's an interesting name, I think I've seen that somewhere quite recently, but I can't recall where."

"If it was on the stern of a boat in Port Said, I can tell you right now, he's no relation!" quipped the Scot, beating Dan to the punch. They both laughed and the atmosphere eased to the extent that Dan was asked about his background, and how he came to be peddling advertising space. Mr McNab said that the whole shipbuilding fraternity of the Far East knew the reputation of his company, the Whangpoa Shipbuilding, Drydock, and Engineering Company, so there was little need for them to spend money on local advertising. However, he would sign two contracts for space on both the trams, and the Peak railway. Dan had the feeling it wasn't so much his salesmanship that did the trick, but a kind-hearted gesture to help a fellow countryman.

Dan was delighted at the unexpected outcome and Mrs Woods was astounded to see the contracts. In fact, that was the last success Dan had, and while his total commission for the two weeks only covered one week's board and lodging at the 'Y', it was better than nothing. That was the end of his second attempt to establish himself in Hong Kong.

Dan's table-companions admired his determination to try anything and told him that there was some very hush-hush work in progress on the opposite side of the island. Apparently, very few people, apart from those actually engaged on the project, and the most likely enemy – Japan – knew of the massive system of fortifications being constructed on the seaward side of Hong Kong. Dan, with the supreme innocence, ignorance and confidence of youth, decided to investigate; after all he had nothing to lose.

He boarded a bus to Aberdeen, and when he got to the terminus he saw a constant stream of lorries grinding up a long, winding road towards buildings on the skyline. It was a very hot day and as he started walking he was frequently smothered in the dust of passing vehicles. He hadn't gone far before a truck full of coolies drew up alongside and the Chinese driver, by sign language, invited Dan to join him in the cab. He probably thought Dan, dressed in khaki shirt and shorts, was one of the British surveyors or engineers engaged on the site.

Apparently, the sentries made the same assumption and waved the lorry through. When it stopped outside a cluster of huts Dan got down and strode purposefully towards one marked 'Project Engineer' and stepped through the open door. Three khaki-clad men with their backs towards him were closely studying what looked like architect's plans. They were so absorbed, that after a minute or two Dan gave a polite cough. It was as if a grenade had gone off, galvanising them into startled attention. They turned to glare at Dan, folding the plans so he couldn't see what they were.

One of them barked, "Who the hell are you?" and then before Dan could answer, "And how in hell did you get here, don't you know this is a no-go area?"

Dan answered calmly, "My name is Robson and I've come to see if there are any jobs available."

"Who told you to come here?" asked one of the other men. "And how did you get past the security guards at the gates?" Dan replied that no one had told him to come, it was his own idea, and as for getting through the gates he had simply come in with a truckload of coolies.

"With coolies in a truck!" the first man bellowed, "Which one?"

By that time Dan was past caring. "I can't tell you which one, it was a convoy."

One of the men then grabbed the nearest phone and roared into it: "Send a car... immediately!" Into another phone he said he wanted to see the duty security officer RIGHT AWAY, and Dan decided that that was one job he would rather not have just then.

An Army saloon car drew up outside with a Chinese driver who was curtly told to, "Take this gentleman to Aberdeen," and to Dan,

"Goodbye Mr Robson," in a tone which clearly implied, 'and I don't want to see you again!' It was an extra speedy end to his third attempt at finding work.

That night, his table companions reminded him they had said he wouldn't find it easy, but one fellow suggested he try for the Hong Kong Water Police, seeing that he had a maritime background.

'Why not,' thought Dan.

Crossing the harbour the following morning, he soon located the waterfront depot of the Water Police where he was interviewed by an Inspector. Dan took a liking to him right away. He was a down-to-earth man with greying hair, and a solidly built figure – the sort of man it would be comforting to have alongside you in a punch-up. Dan felt relaxed as he answered the Inspector's questions: how come he was in Hong Kong; had he deserted a ship; had he ever been in trouble with the police; was he medically fit; was he interested in sport.

His answers seemed to satisfy the Inspector, who drew out from a drawer an application form for Dan to fill out, and said that he would pass his application on to the Commissioner of Police who would make the final decision.

Pleased with the events of the morning, Dan went back to the 'Y' reasonably confident that at last he was on the right track. However, at lunch, when he told his story to the men in the dining room they said he had seen the wrong man, he should have gone direct to the Commissioner. They were so definite about it that Dan thought they must be right. So, without the buoyant spirits he had enjoyed in the morning, he re-crossed the harbour to see the Commissioner of Police in person.

This man was an entirely different type of person from the Inspector – younger, more of an academic, and probably a product of a top English university, judging by his speech and superior manner. He had hardly got beyond asking Dan the purpose of his visit, when there was a tap on the door and who should step into the room but the genial Inspector Dan had met in the morning. There was an awkward silence while the Inspector looked at Dan in surprise, and then at the Commissioner, who said, "Yes, Inspector?"

The Inspector seemed momentarily lost for words, but then said that among other matters, he had come to submit an application he had received that morning from this young man here, indicating Dan.

The Commissioner said, "Well, that's what he's doing here now?" and suddenly the warm, sunny atmosphere of the morning seemed to evaporate as a cloud covers the sun. The Inspector's glance at Dan was enough to make him wish a hole in the floor would swallow him up.

The two men looked at each other and then the Commissioner said to Dan, "This interview is now closed, and so is your application." Without another word he was shown the door.

That was Dan's fourth and final attempt to land a job in Hong Kong. To say he was shattered with disappointment would have been putting it mildly. Normally he didn't drink, but feeling dejected, he headed for the Peninsular Hotel and its renowned Circular Bar.

While sipping a gin sling, it dawned on him that it was his twenty-fifth birthday, a good excuse for a celebration. Just then, he was joined by a man called Aubrey whom he had met during his time with the advertising agency. He was a charming man, a cultured, well-spoken, well-educated Englishman, immaculately dressed, although his suit had seen better days, and in appearance he resembled film star David Niven.

Dan told him about his troubles, and then Aubrey confided that he lived on his wits, and that the Peninsular Hotel was one of his hunting grounds. All the time he was speaking, his eyes were watching who came into the bar. Listening to the fascinating stories of Aubrey's business deals, Dan wondered if it might be possible for him to join in these ventures, but he realised that he was just not in that fellow's class.

Dan learned that Aubrey lived with an attractive Chinese girl in Kowloon, not far from the 'Y', and that the young woman was the liaison officer in the head office of a large group of general merchants operating throughout the Far East.

'How very convenient for him,' thought Dan enviously. At that point, Aubrey spotted someone he wanted to see so, excusing himself, he crossed the bar to join a group of fellows and they were soon shaking hands, laughing and settling down at a table. 'It's all right for some,' thought Dan, but he was glad he had given in to the impulse to call at the hotel, as the interlude had taken his mind off the events of the day.

Dan had by then been in Hong Kong for a month without any real income other than the commission from the advertising agency, but he had written to his sister asking her to send some of his money to tide him over until he got work. His funds were getting very low, so when he saw a letter addressed to him on the rack in the hall, he opened it eagerly. There was no money order, only a letter which said in part, "No, I am not going to send you any money, it will only encourage you to be lazy and not look for work."

By coincidence, the topic of conversation at dinner that evening revolved around the predicament of some people unfortunate enough to run out of funds and become an embarrassment to His Majesty's Hong Kong Government!

After dinner, as Dan walked slowly along Salisbury Road towards the Ferry Wharf, wondering what he should do next, he saw an attractive Blue Funnel ship approaching her berth at Kowloon Docks, and he paused to study her fine lines, 'Beautiful ships,' he thought, enviously.

A strong impulse urged him to visit the ship and enquire if there were any shortages in the crew. Dan immediately dismissed the idea as being ridiculous: such well-run ships as the Blue Funnel Line would never be short-handed. It would be a complete waste of time, he reasoned.

"WASTE OF TIME, WASTE OF TIME, YOU'VE GOT ALL THE TIME IN THE WORLD, AND YOU CERTAINLY WILL BE WASTING IT IF YOU DON'T GO OVER THERE RIGHT AWAY, GO ON."

Dan was taken aback by this inner voice, and its imperative tone. Oh well, perhaps he should go; he really had nothing else to do anyway. Against what he thought was his better judgment, Dan turned back, and when he reached the dockside he could see the ship was *Memnon*. When the gangway was lowered and a quartermaster came down to secure the platform and its safety net, Dan asked him if by any chance there was anyone short.

"Well," said the quartermaster, "We put an A.B. ashore in Shanghai, but whether the Old Man will bother replacing him I don't know. We're homeward bound, you see." Dan could hardly believe his ears.

"Have I got it right, you're an A.B. short?" The quartermaster assured him that was correct, so Dan told him he was an A.B. on the beach and would try his luck for the job.

So, after all the officials left the Captain's cabin, Dan presented himself at his door to say politely, "I understand you're an A.B. short, sir."

"Yes, that's right," said the Captain, who looked as rugged as the Rock of Gibraltar.

"Well, sir, I'm an A.B. and I would like to apply for the job." The Captain, after a searching look, asked him whether he had a Discharge Book.

"Yes, sir, but not on me at the moment."

"Well if it's in order, come back at ten tomorrow morning and I'll sign you on. We sail at noon." To say that Dan fairly floated down from the Old Man's quarters and all the way back to the 'Y' would hardly be an exaggeration.

'Hallelujah!' said the inner voice, and Dan himself felt that something wonderful had happened so muttered, "Amen."

The next morning at breakfast, when there was a lull in the conversation for maximum impact, Dan announced that he was sailing at noon for London via Singapore, Penang, Aden, Suez, Malta, Marseilles and Casablanca. He should be home for Christmas, he added casually. A satisfyingly stunned silence greeted his news. It was Dan's turn to be self-satisfied, and he relished the moment.

Luckily, Dan had paid for his board and lodging a week in advance and he now asked for the unused balance to be given to the houseboys as a parting gift.

Then, boarding *Memnon*, he presented his discharge book to the Captain who scanned it carefully. He could see by the certificate of discharge from *Anna Maersk* that Dan was in Hong Kong legitimately and wasn't a deserter, and noted the endorsement by Captain Linden of *Prince Rupert City*, so he signed him on.

Dan felt like embracing that bluff old sea-dog after all the frustrations he had experienced, but contented himself with thanking the Captain fervently: he must be a blessing from God, he reckoned.

Dan saw immediately that *Memnon* was in a different class altogether from the tramps. She was superior even to *Anna Maersk*, faster and with excellent accommodation and food. On no ship had he ever heard of bacon and eggs and pikelets for breakfast: it was just a heavenly dream.

Pork was regularly on the lunch and dinner menus and by the time he got to London, he reckoned he had had more pig flesh than in the whole four years of his apprenticeship. He learned that Alfred Holt & Company, the owners of the Blue Funnel Line, had a large investment in agricultural enterprises in China, and with cheap Chinese labour, used those resources to the fullest commercial advantage. The only drawback was that the pigs were fed on discarded fish, which gave the meat a distinctly fishy flavour, but that was a mere detail unworthy of mention.

Blue funnel 'Memnon'.

The cruise liner.

Merchant shipping at KVG Docks, London, 1962.

*From the bridge of 'Queen Elizabeth', Empress Dock, Southampton
RMS 'Mauretania' departing on left.*

'Queen Mary' leaving Southampton.

The 'other end' about to cast off.

Pushing and pulling a big lady around.

Almost 'straightened up' and on her way.

Well known faces of yesteryear, Gary Cooper, Douglas Fairbanks Jnr.

Tommy Farr, British Heavyweight Champion en route to his memorable challenge to Joe Louis.

The 'Knife Edge' bow of the 'Queen Mary'.

By contrast the bow of the 'Karitane' at her fitting-out berth at Leith, 1939.

'Oriana' arriving at Auckland, N.Z. on her maiden voyage.

'Canberra' arriving on maiden voyage.

'Auckland Star' departing.

P & O 'Arcadia' departing.

Brand new 'Port Auckland' ready to berth on maiden voyage.

Chilean training ship 'Esmeralda' departing Auckland, 1960.

RMS 'Somerset' in the Panama Canal.

46 year old pilot vessel 'Waitemata' of Auckland.

The replacement vessel 'Akarana', 1960.

'Ruahine' approaching reef entrance into Papeete Harbour. Tahiti.

RMS 'Ruahine' transitting the Panama Canal.

A Trampship loading timber, Portland, Oregon, USA, 1930.

'Centaurus', Cowes.

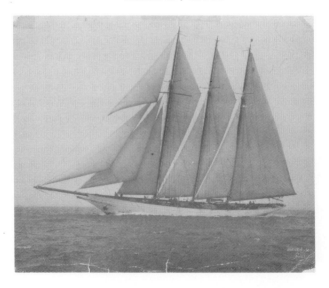

The trip home passed very quickly and enjoyably. Dan soon got used to the Merseyside dialect of his shipmates, a contented bunch of fellows who prized their jobs and though they called at romantic-sounding ports such as Penang, Port Swettenham and Casablanca, those fellows rarely went ashore, so there were never any hold-ups waiting for crew to return to the ship.

Dan felt fortunate at having got a toehold into the Blue Funnel Line, affectionately known as the 'Birkenhead Navy'. Everything seemed to be done from a well-established and tested routine.

In no time at all, it seemed to Dan, they were steaming up the Thames, and into Victoria Docks, where the crew were temporarily paid off and their places taken by cockney runners, an arrangement which allowed the deep-sea men to go home on leave while their ship was in home waters, and to rejoin her before she left again on her next voyage.

Bound For Australia

Thus ended Dan's dream of life ashore in the glamorous Orient. With hindsight, maybe it was just as well, for within a few years, the whole area was overrun by the Japanese army with very unhappy consequences for all Westerners.

Having used up all his money in Hong Kong, Dan couldn't afford to be out of work in London, so he re-engaged as a cockney runner. These men crewed the ship to Antwerp, Rotterdam, Bremen and Hamburg en route to her final discharge port of Glasgow. After discharging tea, rice, rubber and oriental spices at the continental ports, the passage round the north of Scotland in January was as stormy as they expected, the ship being buffeted by fierce westerly gales all the way. But the Blue Funnel ships were exceptionally well-built and could withstand such onslaughts, to the extent that they carried their own insurance. Dan knew the company took a great interest in the welfare of their Chinese employees and *Memnon* had Chinese firemen. He was however, not impressed when, during the height of the bad weather to the north of Scotland, he was told, in the middle of the night watch, "to have a good look around the foredeck for any Chinese terrified by the storm." With heavy seas being frequently shipped Dan was also scared that in his quest he too could easily be swept over the side.

In Glasgow, the ship's holds and 'tween decks were emptied and thoroughly cleaned out before loading the new cargo for the Far East – Singer sewing machines, shipped from right alongside the huge Singer factory at Shieldhall on the banks of the Clyde.

Memnon then sailed for Birkenhead, and here again the efficiency of the Alfred Holt organisation manifested itself, when all the ship's running gear, that is, all her cargo handling equipment, was removed from the ship to the rigging loft ashore and a freshly overhauled set rigged in its place. This reduced the possibility of accidents due to gear failure on the company's tight schedules, and the work in the rigging lofts was carried out by ex-seamen of the company who knew the ropes in more ways than one.

The founder of the company had built into its operation a strong sense of consideration for those engaged in its day to day work, with justice and fair play for all. The day before *Memnon* was due to sail again for Yokohama, she was rejoined by her usual foreign-going crew, refreshed from their spell at home, and the cockney runners returned to London.

Dan went to the Head Office in Liverpool to ask if he could be taken on to the regular crew list, and because he had already made his debut and had received a good report, he was accepted. After passing a stringent medical examination, he was told to report in ten days time to sign on *Orestes*, fresh out of drydock and loading at the Gladstone Docks for Australia.

Rather than hang around in Liverpool, he decided to visit Connie in Chichester for a few days, and then went on to Southampton to call on Brenda, but her parents told him she was now working in a village hotel just outside Winchester. So, boarding a Hants and Dorset bus that passed through the village it was not long before he located the typical English-style tavern, with impressive black beams against a white background with dormer windows peeping under the thatch. He entered the public bar, which was deserted except for the barmaid. He ordered a Watney's brown ale, which seemed as much in keeping with this rural pub as the gin sling had been in the Peninsular Hotel in Hong Kong, and asked if Brenda Turner worked there.

"Yes she does" said the girl, "But she's upstairs at the moment. I'll just nip up and tell her she's wanted."

She reappeared a couple of minutes later with Brenda, who seemed surprised to see Dan and drawing him aside she whispered that she had expected to see her new boyfriend, that she was preparing to quit the job and would he go round to the back of the hotel, and she would explain properly later. Dan drained his glass and then went dutifully around to the yard and stood opposite the back door, expecting her to come through.

He had been waiting about five minutes when the proprietor, seeing a stranger hanging around, came out to ask what he wanted.

At that precise moment a window above their heads opened, Brenda's voice called "Catch!" and down came her suitcase.

When the manager said "What on earth is going on?" Dan could only say, "I think Brenda is leaving, sir!"

The manager realised that Dan wasn't party to the scheme, but when Brenda appeared, he gave her a severe talking to. He said that to leave without giving notice and in such an underhand manner was enough justification for him to call the police to search her suitcase, and it would be no use asking him for a reference. Brenda, sulky and on the verge of tears, was wise enough to open her case for his inspection, which placated the man, who told them both to get moving.

They journeyed back to Southampton on the bus together and parted good friends, Dan hoping mischievously that the new boyfriend would be better behaved when invited into Brenda's front parlour.

Back in Merseyside, Dan lodged at the Liverpool Sailors' Home where he came to know several other fellows and their girlfriends, or Judys. These young women knew as much as, if not more than, their male friends about the relative merits of the different companies, the seaworthiness of various ships and the conditions on board – even about the domestic relationships of Captains, Chief Engineers or Chief Stewards and whether they were good husbands. The Judys also had an awesome vocabulary of swear words, and though outwardly tough and abusive could, when the occasion demanded it, show intense kindness and loyalty. These qualities came to the fore in the wartime bombing of Liverpool docks. Dan was amazed to learn that most of them were married to seafarers and he hoped that if he ever got to that stage, it would be to a girl not so knowledgeable of the shipping fraternity.

Orestes finished loading cargo for Adelaide, Melbourne, Hobart and Brisbane and duly sailed to Glasgow, then round the north of Scotland to Hamburg. Again, this passage was extremely rough, but instead of westerlies, they struck fierce north-easterly gales, so again they encountered bad weather.

In Hamburg, snow and ice combined to build a frozen mass twelve inches thick on exposed decks, but work continued with the ruddy-faced German cargomen seeming to revel in the sub-zero temperatures. Dan and his shipmates weren't so appreciative and suffered chilblains and frostbite; nevertheless, they felt it would be good to have a look at the bright lights of the downtown part of the city of Hamburg. As part of the viewing, they decided to pass through the special street initiated by Hitler's Third Reich in its war against diseases of any kind. There were huge gates across each roadway entrance and smaller side gates through which pedestrians passed, but the sight of so many women, both young and older for hire and on show in shop-windows, sickened and depressed them. They hurried on to San Pauli, the equivalent of London's West End, where they felt more at home, and enjoyed fun at the Hippodrome where patrons could imbibe the best German beer, and watch fellow patrons riding ponies round the circus ring below.

Later, they engaged a cab to return them to the docks where *Orestes* was berthed, trudging the last bit of the way through snow and ice. The ship sailed the following day and they were mighty thankful they were headed for more temperate climes.

Their next port of call was far more to their liking - Takoradi on the Gold Coast of West Africa. Here *Orestes* loaded bagged cocoa beans from large surf boats which were superbly handled by beautifully proportioned West Africans, with splendid physiques, heaving the bags into sling loads, their shining, sweaty bodies rippling with muscles. Loading was completed at Accra just along the coast, and since there was no air mail in those days, *Orestes* took on mail for Australia, New Zealand and the South Pacific.

They had warm flying-fish weather on the long passage southwards, round the Cape of Good Hope, across the Southern Ocean and the Australian Bight to Adelaide. Some of the crew played cricket in their off duty hours, deck versus engine-room or perhaps officers versus crew, and sometimes even a Test match, England versus Australia, for the Ashes – a cigarette tin full of galley ash.

The balls used for these games were made by wrapping a steel nut inside a wad of cotton waste, binding it with rope yarns to the size of a real cricket ball and then stitching the whole thing with sail twine into a reasonably smooth sphere the same weight as the real article. They needed a bucketful of these because, despite the best of intentions, a ball could easily be swiped over the side, the batsman ruled out and his score to that point wiped off the scoreboard.

Another diversion was an Australian family who boarded the ship at Accra. Most seafarers love children, so with the permission of the parents, they played games with them on home-made swings, seesaws and slides. The parents, William and Helen Trueman, had spent five years in Nigeria and were now returning home on furlough from the mission field. Dan couldn't understand why anyone would bother to do that sort of work far away from home, especially when he heard that they didn't even get paid, but depended on money given by their supporters back home.

The Truemans held a form of church service each weekend, a simple but reverent hour of hymn singing, Bible reading and prayers. Dan's duties only once prevented him from attending, his real motive being to encourage the missionaries, not because he felt in need of what the Lord was anxious to offer him. But he did ponder on the difference between this quiet, devoted couple and the noisy enthusiasm of those warm, hospitable people who had been so kind to him and Jim all those years ago. Why, he wondered, if they were of the same religion, did they behave so differently?

After rounding the Cape of Good Hope with moderate westerly winds and a following sea, they sped on towards Australia and one afternoon the watch-keepers sighted land low down on the horizon to port. It was Cape Leuwin, the south-western extremity of the continent. A few days later, they arrived at Adelaide, capital of South Australia. The Truemans were thrilled to be back and wasted no time going ashore to catch a train to Sydney, their home town and missionary base.

Dan, too, experienced a sense of exhilaration at being back in this 'land of the freed' – a reference to Australia's convict past. He was aware that it was largely due to the labour of the convicts that many of the docks, breakwaters, bridges and buildings had been built.

From Adelaide, the ship sailed for Hobart, Tasmania, known to all as the ABC country, for the apples, beer and cherries, (some said 'crumpet') all readily available in generous quantities.

Hobart was a delightful place, the scenery reminding Dan of parts of England. The girls were warm and friendly and once again he thought how good it would be to settle down ashore there; it was becoming a recurring complaint with him. In a few days, they were on their way to Brisbane, the Melbourne cargo having been transhipped from Hobart to maintain the ship's all-important schedule. The bulk of the cargo was for Brisbane anyway, so ample discharging time was allowed in case of waterfront strikes, stop-works and go-slows.

During that time, the refrigerated spaces were prepared to receive a full quota of frozen beef, mutton and lamb, and on the completion of discharge, *Orestes* shifted down-river to the huge Thomas Borthwick's works at Pinkenba, where the animals arrived to be slaughtered, frozen and despatched to the other side of the world. Dan remembered the name Borthwick from his Smithfield days, when he had to go to their store for loads of frozen pigs' heads to take to another in the market which made pork pies.

Although he wasn't keen to see the killing process, Dan and one of his mates thought that it would at least be educational to go through the slaughter house. First they watched the cattle, moving in single file towards a box-like structure into which they were prodded and the door was closed behind them. An electric light bulb was rigged so that as soon as the animal lifted its head to look at it, it was pole-axed, and as it collapsed, the floor was tilted, the side lifted up, and the beast slid out. Within seconds a slaughterman whipped a noose around its ankles, it was hoisted upside down, its throat was cut, then it was skinned and disembowelled, the chain moving along all the while. Even as they watched, the carcass was brought up against an electric band-saw which neatly halved the animal right down its spine. Further along the moving chain, these sides were halved again, transversely this time, so that the beast was now two forequarters and two hindquarters, the size and shape so familiar to Dan at Smithfield.

Next, the two mates went to the sheep chains where they were told that sheep were so stupid they were led by one of their own kind to their execution. Watching intently, Dan and Taff pondered on the black-hearted treachery of the leader who, when it reached the top of the ramp, was let into its own small pen, leaving the following sheep to face the butcher's knife. They wondered if the leading sheep felt guilty, or whether the doomed sheep were aware of the betrayal. Did the slaughtermen ever give the Judas sheep a taste of its own medicine?

"Too right!" they said. Dan and Taff actually felt sorry for the animals.

It is said that pigs are among the most intelligent of animals and understand what is going on around them, so they might well have some idea of what is in store when they are driven into abattoirs and smell blood.

There were blood-curdling shrieks and squeals as Dan and Taff entered the pig slaughtering department, where they saw struggling animals hanging upside down as they were moved along an overhead track to where a butcher with a razor-sharp knife was deftly slitting each pig's throat from ear to ear. For a split second, the pig was silent, then there was a short but ear piercing squeal until the pig reached the next stage where it was released from the track to drop into a big tank of boiling water. A minute later and it was tipped into a whirling, rack-like device which miraculously removed the bristles and hair from the pig's body, leaving it smooth and clean. By then Dan and Taff felt they had seen enough and reckoned they weren't cut out to be slaughtermen.

On leaving the works, they asked a man the best way to go into Brisbane that evening. He asked if they had a match so, thinking he wanted to light his cigarette, Taff reached into his pocket.

"No, I don't need one but you will" he said, and went on to explain. Pointing out a path across a nearby paddock, he told them that if they walked along there they would come to a railway line. At about seven that evening, a train should come round the bend there, and when they saw it coming, they should light a match and the train would stop.

Dan laughed incredulously, "We haven't come down in the last shower you know, mate! Pull the other leg!" But the man assured him he wasn't joking.

That evening, still suspicious, knowing that Aussies delighted in that sort of prank, Dan and a group of his friends decided to put the matter to the test and walked along the path to the railway line to wait for the train. Seeing it come round a distant bend, they lit their matches and sure enough, the train ground to a halt so they could clamber up into the nearest carriage. They couldn't imagine an English suburban engine-driver being so obliging, or being permitted to do so.

A hold-up somewhere along the supply line delayed the loading programme and enabled Dan and his shipmates to enjoy the sunshine and golden beaches of the area. Then, one day, they responded to an advertisement about a riding school. Dan hadn't been on a horse before and the two friends who went with him weren't much better, but with the owner's two daughters and a friend, they set out on six horses for an hour's ride.

Dan was in trouble almost from the start, when his mount broke into a spine-shaking jog-trot that nearly shook his head off his shoulders. Then to make matters worse, it blew out a big mouthful of chaff which wafted back into Dan's face causing him to lose his balance so that he swung down under the horse's neck. He was rescued from his undignified position by one of the girls who encouraged him to remount and try again. The evening proved so entertaining that a booking was made for the following Saturday afternoon.

When the time came and Dan saw the animal allotted to him, he decided it looked like a broken-backed cab-horse, so he asked the boss if he could have a better one. Without a word, the laconic Aussie brought up another, so tall that Dan almost needed a stepladder to get on its back. He was just about to ask Taff to take his photograph, when the boss gave the horse a slap on its rump and off it went, with Dan hanging onto the saddle for dear life. Dan had absolutely no control over the animal, which bolted down the busy road, turned across the traffic and thundered along a riverbank. Dan, still clutching the saddle, ducked down to avoid being swept off by low tree branches under which his horse was dashing with the sort of gusto Dan was in no condition to appreciate. Finally the animal pulled up beside a gate into a field and wouldn't budge. When the others arrived on the scene the owner said, "I knew he would bring you here, it's his paddock!" It was obvious that Dan was no John Wayne!

The horse spent the rest of the afternoon treating Dan in a cavalier fashion, having proved who was master. For example, when they stopped at a kiosk later, Dan stood holding the bridle with one hand while he licked an ice cream in the other. Suddenly, the horse planted a foreleg hoof on Dan's left instep, and when he tried to lift it off, without success, the boss said, "He only wants some of your ice cream."

"Go on!" said Dan, "Come off it, horses don't eat ice cream!"

"Try him and see!" was the answer. Since the horse had been breathing heavily all over it ever since he had bought it, Dan gingerly held out the ice cream to his lips. The next instant the whole thing had disappeared, with just the tip of the cone left in his fingers. "See?" said the boss.

For Taff, coming from a farm in Wales, it was like home – so much so that he fell in love with the eldest of the four daughters. They got engaged and he vowed to pack up the sea at the end of the voyage and emigrate to Brisbane. For Dan, however, it was a different story. He hadn't the slightest wish to marry and settle down, but in Sydney, he was handed a slice of romance on a plate.

He, with some of his mates, visited a Catholic Hospitality club for seafarers, run on relaxed lines with hostesses and gramophone music, for dancing. One of the girls especially appealed to Dan, and by the end of the evening he and Linda had arranged to meet outside. She said she had to go to a nightclub to give a message to her flatmate and he could go with her if he liked.

Thinking that would be a new experience, Dan went with her, but found the smoke-filled place so unattractive he told her he would have one drink and go, he never could drink much, it made him sick. She insisted on getting his lager, and while at the bar he saw her down a couple of whiskies with her friends behind the bar. Returning his glass, she downed a couple more, and it was close to midnight before Dan was able to wrench her away from it all. But, once outside in the cool night air, Linda became abusive, telling him in no uncertain terms that is, in lurid Aussie expletives, that he could pee off as far as she was concerned, what was he hanging around her for anyway?

"Get lost," she commanded, kicking off her high-heeled shoes, "I'm going to walk home." If Dan hadn't picked them up she would have left them there in the gutter.

He felt he couldn't possibly leave her out on the street in the middle of the night in her condition so he hailed a passing taxi. At that point she collapsed onto the pavement and the taxi driver said, "I'm not going to take her in that state unless you come too, mate, I don't want her spilling out in my cab!" Feeling he might as well be hung for a sheep as for a lamb, Dan lifted her and eased her into the back seat: luckily she had told him where she lived earlier in the evening.

Arriving at Double Bay, Dan asked the driver to wait while he took her up to her flat. He got the man to hold her upright so he could get her over his shoulder, but no sooner had he taken her weight with her stomach over his shoulder, than she threw up all down the back of his raincoat. Once inside the building, into a lift and up to her floor, she was able to find her key so Dan could open her door and take her inside. There he wiped her face and mouth with a towel, laid her on a settee, then he beat a hasty retreat. It was two-thirty in the morning, when he got back on board.

The following afternoon, it was a Saturday, the Quartermaster on gangway duty, told Dan he was wanted on the telephone. There he heard a gentle female voice ask, "Is that Dan?"

"Yes," said Dan.

"Well it's Linda here, and I want to apologise for my awful behaviour last night. Please forgive me, and I'll make up for it if you'd like to come and see me again. You could come this afternoon if you haven't anything better to do."

Dan thought briefly about the sleep he had promised himself to have that afternoon to make up for the night before, but just as quickly reckoned he could always get more sleep at sea, and that invitations like this didn't come every day.

"That's really kind of you, Linda. I'll get cleaned up and come over later in the afternoon."

"Good," said Linda, "I'll be waiting for you."

'My word,' thought Dan, 'That sounds encouraging,' and when he told his mates he had a date, they thought so too.

At about three-thirty, looking and smelling spruce, he presented himself at Linda's door. When she opened it, she looked as pretty as a picture in a very attractive frock but with bare legs and feet. Dan settled down in an armchair while she brought him a drink, refusing one herself saying that she'd had too much the night before. She apologised again for behaving badly and thanked him for refusing to leave her in the street: she was so different and so keen to make amends that when she invited Dan to join her on the couch he responded eagerly. She was such an attractive 'spider' and he such a willing 'fly', and that was the beginning of a warm, exciting and memorable weekend.

The following afternoon when they were walking in the Domain, viewing the beautiful harbour from Mrs Macquarrie's Chair, she confided that she had a regular boyfriend in the Royal Australian Navy but that if Dan had any pangs of guilt about being a party to her unfaithfulness to forget it, because she was sure he would be playing around with the local girls in Darwin where he was stationed.

Dan didn't feel too guilty, and he felt even better when she said that she was free and independent, with a well-paid job in the city. To prove it, she offered to treat him to dinner that evening at Usher's Hotel. They enjoyed a splendid meal with all the trimmings, and a final cuddle afterwards at the flat, and that was that – the fifty-hour flirtation was over when they parted at midnight.

Orestes was well-filled on leaving Sydney, so there was only finishing off to do in Melbourne; picking up mail and topping up her fuel tanks to last to Las Palmas. The long trip from Australia to Liverpool, via Las Palmas and the continental ports of Le Havre, Antwerp and Bremen, passed without incident.

Human nature being what it is, Dan found that now he had achieved a place on the roster of the Birkenhead Navy, and could settle comfortably in a first class shipping company, something moved him on. He knew the Pacific Steam Navigation Company's *Reina del Pacifico* was about to begin a cruise around South America and tried to get a job on her, but too many others had the same idea. He was disappointed, too, when he tried for *Empress of Britain* and her popular round-the-world cruise, so he decided to try his luck in his old home port of Southampton.

The celebrated world cruise liner *Franconia* was laid up, undergoing her annual refit, so there was nothing doing there. He therefore booked into the newly opened Jellicoe Rest in Orchard Place, a clean and comfortable residence for seamen. He wasn't sure what he really wanted to do.

R.M.S. Queen Mary

With large passenger ships sailing every day, Dan's best chance was as a pier-head jumper – someone who filled a vacancy at the last moment. He went to the Board of Trade shipping office in Canute Road to see what the prospects were. There were only a few men there, and as he moved towards the counter a voice came over the tannoy to announce that an A.B. was required to stand-by the *Queen Mary*, sailing at 6 p.m., thus it so happened that being first at the counter, Dan got the job.

By five-thirty that evening, he was an A.B. seaman on the world's largest and fastest passenger liner, the pride of the British Merchant Navy. It was a thrill for him to see and hear the crowds on the quayside waving and cheering their friends lining the ship's rails, the atmosphere filled with excitement as the tugs manoeuvred the huge vessel out of her berth and into Southampton Water.

With regal dignity, she steamed towards the Isle of Wight, Spithead and Nab Tower en route to the English Channel. Dan had not yet been assigned to a watch, so all he could do was watch the familiar coastline slip by, but soon he was collected by 'Cracker' Ford, one of the Bos'n's mates, who showed him to the seamen's quarters.

Dan's bunk had a dunlopillo mattress and two pillows, and he was issued with freshly laundered sheets, pillow cases, blankets and towels, which made him think his lot was getting better day by day. He was also given a blue jersey with 'CUNARD' stamped across the chest and a round sailor's hat, both of which had to be worn whenever he was on deck.

He was off watch until their arrival in Cherbourg in three hours' time so he decided to explore. He had been warned to used his chinstrap out on deck or he would lose his cap, but he was unprepared for the strength of the wind on the for'ard well-deck and he nearly lost his footing. With a surge of pride he saw they were racing past the Nab Tower, with the Isle of Wight receding in the background, the main engines were throbbing with all the power necessary to streak across the Channel and reach Cherbourg on time. His boyhood dream had come true.

When the gong sounded for dinner, he found the crew's messroom, like everything else, was bigger and better than any he had hitherto seen. He joined a queue which filed past big hot-presses on which were trays piled high with sliced beef, chops, vegetables, boiled or chipped potatoes, plates of buttered bread and plenty of dessert. 'This is fantastic,' thought Dan, as he hadn't had much food since leaving *Orestes* three days before, so he made the best of everything.

During the general conversation, he learned that the Deck department, with one hundred and ten men, was the smallest. There were twelve men in each of the three working watches, six special lookout men, six quartermasters and many others assigned to different duties. He was on the graveyard watch – midnight to four am and midday to 4 p.m. In between, they could do as they pleased – sleep, read, write or even visit The Pig and Whistle, the crew's pub at the after end of the ship, a long but pleasant walk for sailors living at the bow.

One old seaman nearing retirement had been given the cosy job of sweeping the working alleyway, the ship's main thoroughfare from bow to stern through the innards of the vessel. Old Ben would start off after breakfast with his broom, light his clay pipe and slowly proceed with his task, aiming to reach The Pig and Whistle by lunchtime. There he would collect his standing order – a pint of ale and a thick corned beef sandwich – sit in his favourite spot and contentedly dispose of both before beginning his slow, steady return trip for'ard, timing his arrival for 5 p.m.

It was amazing how many different trades people were employed in, providing the best possible service for the two thousand passengers. Apart from the more obvious ones, there were printers, policemen (masters at arms), masseurs, health therapists, chemists, florists, photographers and many, many more – just about every trade found in the average large town.

New to Dan was the large number of female crew members – stewardesses, nurses, nannies, hairdressers, beauticians and so on, going about their business as though in a city job. There were married couples serving on board, a practice not officially approved by the Cunard Line. There was even a kosher kitchen to cater for the large numbers of Jewish travellers.

Dan found that *Queen Mary* had charisma, a loveable personality that made a great impact on all those lucky enough to be associated with her. She was a favourite ship for thousands of transatlantic passengers, many of whom formed a *Queen Mary* fan club. She was rather like a really beautiful woman; it was so easy to succumb to her charm.

While most of the passengers were embarked at Southampton there were some who found it more convenient to join the ship at Cherbourg. There was no transatlantic air travel in those days so the big liners of Britain, France, Belgium, Holland, Germany and the Scandinavian countries vied with one another for the lucrative trade, and operated fleets of attractive-looking, efficiently run ships. From Mediterranean ports, first class Italian, Greek and Spanish liners also challenged for a slice of the trade, all of them beautiful ships.

As they approached Cherbourg on Dan's first trip, the Bos'n aroused the watch to go to their respective stations, some to the fo'c'sle head for anchoring duties, others to the doors in the ship's side, where baggage and mail were taken aboard from the tenders. The French seamen on these vessels, keen to finish the job, threw the baggage down the chutes helter-skelter, often with a hatbox or small suitcase between two large cabin trunks. The resulting smash would be 'listed' by the officer in charge, and the work hurried along. Dan was put to work with eleven other men carrying passengers' baggage from one of the side doors to the chute into the baggage room, and when it was all taken on board, the massive ship-side steel doors were secured.

By the time the ship left Cherbourg, it was after midnight so Dan's watch began its normal duties which, that night, was to wash down the length of the working alleyway with a hose and brooms, a job that took three hours. Even such a menial task as that had to be done according to Cunard practice. The hose-man (the diver, a senior A.B.), was followed by his understudy (the kink), then the ordinary broom-hands, followed by the most junior member of the party, the scupper-rat, whose job it was to see that the scuppers were free of anything likely to hinder the draining away of the water.

All the decks were scrubbed every night between midnight and seven, and for those passenger decks to be as dry as possible, two squeegee-men had to follow the broom hands. It was hungry work, and between three and four in the morning, the night stewards, seeing the last of the passengers drift away to bed, passed on the leftover turkey, ham, chicken or tongue sandwiches and other titbits to the wash-down gang. Dan had certainly improved his lot from his days in the trampships, a transition from workhouse to palace.

With *Queen Mary*'s speed being in excess of thirty knots there were notices around the ship advising people not to throw anything overboard as it was likely to be blown back on board. One night 'Cracker' Ford was supervising the washing down of the promenade deck when he suddenly found his face covered by a pair of lady's silk knickers, obviously thrown out of a First Class porthole, they were still warm, he said. He stuffed them hastily into the pocket of his uniform jacket to a chorus of jokes and laughter, the gang reminding him to make sure he got rid of them before he went home to his wife.

The arrival of *Queen Mary* at New York always received the maximum publicity anyway, but in addition, there were often film stars, top politicians, foreign princes or other notable people to interest newspapermen. The ship would steam majestically up the Hudson River to Pier Ninety and, when abreast of it, turn slowly to glide into her berth with the tugs pushing and pulling. With great precision she would then be secured in position so that the special electrically operated gangways could be placed in the side doors to allow passengers to disembark. This enabled the travellers to proceed to the customs and immigration area within a few minutes of arrival.

Dan's work so far was so easy and entertaining on this glamorous liner that he found it hard to believe he would get paid for it. The normal schedule saw *Queen Mary* sailing from Southampton at noon every other Wednesday, to arrive at New York the following Monday at 8 am, and to sail again for home two days later, at noon Wednesday.

Dan found that, as in the theatre and Smithfield market, there were always people ready to cheat or steal, while others, by their willingness to do extra work, earned bonuses for themselves. The cabin stewards looking after first class passengers could usually count on substantial tips at the end of every trip, so they saved themselves the drudgery of spring-cleaning by paying seamen to do it. Some men would do laundry for those too lazy to do their own.

One day, Dan saw a notice on the board inviting anyone willing to take part in boxing contests for the entertainment of passengers to report to the gymnasium. Dan found several volunteers already there, and the instructor paired the men off according to their size and weight, issued sparring gloves and gave each pair a trial bout to see how they shaped up.

For publicity's sake on the programme, Dan was labelled 'Tiger' Robson, while his opponent was tagged 'Wild Bull' Edwards, maybe on account of his ungainly shape which, Dan carefully noted, included long arms.

As an inducement to put up a good show, the volunteers were promised an equal share of the collection that would be invited from the spectators at the end of each session. However, by common assent, these small sums were donated to a Seamens' charity. The ring was located on the after end of the top promenade deck outside the Verandah Grill, with seating all round, and the fights were of three two-minute rounds. Sporting business men couldn't resist the temptation to pick the winner, but the gym instructor declared every bout a draw to discourage betting, and possible 'wheeling, dealing'. Dan often found two minutes more than enough, trying to avoid the exuberant swings of the "Wild Bull," but the boxing provided good entertainment for those passengers keen to watch. The only blood spilt was when a boxer was too slow removing his nose from a hefty blow, but there was no hostility between the combatants who regarded it as a bit of fun and healthy exercise.

While in New York, Dan and another A.B. were selected for the job of painting each side of the bow where the anchor's mud had made a mess of the gleaming black paintwork. Dan and Mike were both ex-trampship men used to stage-work on ship's sides, but they found that the flare of *Queen Mary*'s bow demanded the added skills of both gymnast and trapeze artist.

On a narrow plank suspended from the rails above and pulled into the ship's side so they could paint, they were in a precarious position which was appreciated by thousands of waterfront visitors taking photographs of the ship from all angles. Sometimes Mike and Dan showed off in front of the crowds and, in so doing, risked falling off into the filthy flotsam that covered the water like a dirty carpet, thirty feet below. Once or twice they had narrow escapes through playing to the gallery.

Queen Mary, like all the regular liners out of Southampton, was regarded as a married man's ship, hundreds of families in the area being dependent on her for their livelihood. Young, single women were very conscious of the possibilities and were always on the lookout for likely partners. There were also women who made themselves available on a more casual basis, as they have done through the ages, in the taverns in the dockland part of town.

Not being a drinking man, Dan rarely came across those, but he did have a brief flirtation with a girl named Daisy whom he met at a Town Hall dance. She was an assistant at Woolworths, and she told him that in order to supplement her wages, she used to slip the odd sixpence in her shoe or, before the advent of cash registers, help her friends by handing them change for half a crown when they had tendered only a shilling. That common ailment again, but it didn't seem to hinder the financial growth of the multi-million dollar business.

Dan was not above acting dishonestly, and while he didn't have the nerve to steal directly, he sometimes took advantage of stolen goods offered for sale, which was just as bad, if not worse. Once, two of his shipmates, while loading baggage at Cherbourg, whisked away an expensive-looking suitcase, ripped it open with their sheath knives, to remove its contents into one sack, and into another, the sliced-up case itself. Both sacks were then collected by a third member 'innocently' picking up the rubbish bags for disposal. This was all so swiftly done, and according to plan, that one could hardly believe that it had happened.

Taking advantage of this enterprise, Dan bought a beautiful black silk dance frock for five pounds. He could have got it for three if he had been willing to take it ashore himself, but he knew his knees would have knocked so loudly passing through security that he would have been an easy catch. The regulars had all the wheels well greased.

He gave the dress to Daisy, she was delighted with it, but she was smart enough to know it would look out of place on her, so she sold it, and with the proceeds bought a frock better suited to her style, plus some extras as well. She expected Dan to make some demand on her in return for the frock and was quite nonplussed when he didn't. For some reason he could never figure out, Dan backed off as though he had seen a red light. His interest in Daisy simply died.

There were many occasions of danger and excitement that made Dan's time on *Queen Mary* memorable; times when superb skill, nerve and seamanship won the day. For example, there was the tangling of the massive anchor chains, when both her anchors had to be used to hold her in a fierce northerly gale at Cherbourg. This was revealed when the time came to heave them in at departure, in the fierce weather prevailing, the untangling was a hazardous job with cables so heavy, but the skill and experience of the officers and men, used to these big ships, finally won the battle.

Then there was the berthing of the ship in New York when the pilots and tug-crews were on strike. This manoeuvre became the focus of attention for all the striking waterfront workers who were hoping and expecting that the difficulties would be such that the attempt would be abandoned, or at least, that sufficient damage would be done to ship and wharf to discourage any further attempts.

At one stage, just as *Queen Mary* had glided alongside perfectly, with the mooring lines run out, she started to drift across the basin towards an Italian liner, *Conte di Savoia*. When the mooring lines couldn't stop her and broke in the process, heavy 'insurance' wires were hastily employed in their place and finally succeeded in heaving the ship back to her berth. The cause for this unexpected sideways movement was found to be the slow turning of the propellers of another liner on the other side of the wharf supposedly testing her engines, but many suspected it was done to sabotage a successful manoeuvre. The Cunard Line, and New York newspapers, were loud in their praise of Captain Irving, his officers and crew in completing the job. Dan and some of his mates even figured in newspaper photographs holding the broken ends of the seven-inch mooring lines, and this in turn resulted in a flood of 'fanny mail' from New York females.

At a later date, Dan was given the chance of becoming one of the six special lookout men, and since this released him from the chain-gang scrubbing decks and so on, he took it. The hardest part of his new job was climbing up the hundred and four rungs of the steel ladder inside the huge foremast, but the view from the crow's nest, high above the decks and bridge, was worth it. He spent two hours of his watch up there, and the other two hours on the monkey island, the uppermost part of the bridge. From both positions he was required to report to the officer of the watch, all shipping or anything else that came into view seawards, so he had to be alert at all times.

The crow's nest was made of steel, encircling the tubular steel mast, with a canopy overhead and a steel floor. The forepart had a plate glass window which provided a view from right ahead to just abaft the beam on both sides. The inside of the nest was lined with blankets to make it as snug as a jenny-wren's nest, there were two small electric heaters, a windscreen wiper, a telephone to the bridge and a seat for the man on watch, and they were all essential, especially in wintertime crossing the North Atlantic in bad weather.

It was a real thrill to be up there, to look down and see the bow cleaving through the water like a knife, reaching for the horizon ahead like a jet aircraft speeding to take off. To other ships she must have presented a magnificent picture of power, speed and beauty as she raced past and Dan could imagine many cameras taking snapshots of the occasion. Judging by the respectable graffiti scratched on the paintwork inside the nest, many well-known people had made the climb, one such, being Gracie Fields, a star singer and actress of those days.

It was during Dan's time on board, that *Queen Mary* recaptured the 'Blue Riband' for Britain from the giant French liner *Normandie*. This maritime honour had been contested for many years among the ships on the transatlantic run, and the famous Cunard liner *Mauretania* had held the speed record for twenty-two years. She was a coal-burner at that, with skilled and dedicated British firemen doing the stoking, plus the very best Welsh coal, of course.

According to the rules it had to be announced beforehand that an attempt on the record was about to be made. That was partly for publicity reasons but mainly to prevent a record being claimed afterwards because of a flukey set of fortunate circumstances. *Queen Mary*, on this occasion, obliged by breaking the record both eastbound and then westbound when, with favourable conditions, she crossed in three days, twenty-three hours and fifty-seven minutes, the first merchant ship to cross the Atlantic in under four days.

A few weeks after this triumphant 'Blue Riband' run another exhilarating event took place. Just before two o'clock one morning, in thick fog, Dan was sent to the bow, or the eyes of the ship, because it was sometimes possible to see under the fog. As well, the fog signals of other ships could better be heard from that vantage point. While Dan was pondering on where he would finish up if they met the *Normandie* bow on, he heard the deep-throated blast of a big ship over on the port side. He was amazed to see a ghostly mass of lights less than a mile abaft the beam. He reported it to the bridge but they said they had been watching it for some time. Soon afterwards, Dan was relieved, so he made his way up to monkey island, the uppermost part of the bridge and there, he was told the lights belonged to the German liner *Bremen* and that she was slowly overtaking *Queen Mary* although both were moving at greatly reduced speed.

This must have nettled the Captain and his officers as the rivalry then, just before the outbreak of war, was intense with much *braggadocio* from both sides. With his bird's eye view, Dan could see the Captain conferring with his senior officers and, as soon as the Bremen's lights disappeared into the fog on the port bow, a slight alteration of course was made to starboard, and Dan could tell by the throb of the engines that an increase in speed had been ordered. That was before radar revolutionised navigation in nil or poor visibility. Within minutes of the change of course, the ship emerged from the fog into perfectly clear conditions and the Captain wasted no time in ringing "full speed," telling the Senior Engineer on watch down below of the situation to get his maximum cooperation. *Queen Mary* leapt forward like a greyhound let off its leash, and with *Bremen* still in the fogbank over to port and out of sight, she headed for Cherbourg with a bone in her teeth. She arrived triumphantly on schedule and was about to sail again when the Bremen arrived at last. The officers and crew of *Queen Mary* relished the moment, their German counterparts must have scratched their heads.

Another indication of her speed was her ability, at the height of the tourist season, to land passengers at Plymouth at 6 am, cross the Channel to disembark continental passengers at Cherbourg at noon, and reach Southampton at 6 p.m. There was also the tragic mishap during the war when the cruiser escorting *Queen Mary* misjudged her speed when zigzagging and was sliced in half, with heavy loss of life.

Dan had also seen what her weight alone could do, even without any noticeable forward movement, when, coming out of drydock and turning into her berth at Empress Dock, her stem touched the strongly constructed knuckle of the wharf and ploughed into it as a steel ploughshare would into soft soil.

The excitement and drama of sailing time was always a real fanfare performance, with the seamen standing-by the mooring lines fore and aft. At ten minutes to the hour, a prolonged blast on the ship's sirens was given as the signal to take in some of the lines that secured the ship to the wharf. There was another warning blast five minutes before departure, so that right on the hour, with every line on board and tugs in position, three short blasts were sounded to indicate the Queen was on the move astern.

The siren blasts, when unexpected and heard for the first time, were a real shock. The ear-drum crushing sound made an explosive impact on people's bowels, and Dan had often seen pipes drop from smokers' lips, ladies clutching their breasts, and children shrieking with their hands over their ears. Indeed, *Queen Mary*'s sirens were so powerful that when she set off on her maiden voyage – an occasion that was broadcast worldwide – the blast had enough resonance over the radio waves to shatter a glass standing on top of a piano in Sydney, Australia.

Towards the end of 1938, Dan's closest friend on board asked him to be best man at his wedding. Dan had never been to a wedding before, but he managed not to lose the ring and all went according to plan. He found it was customary for the best man to escort the leading bridesmaid, and although he had never met Anne before he found the duty a pleasure. If Dan had been looking for a wife, she would have been an ideal prospect, but he was romantic enough to believe that there was more to marriage than practical and financial gain, and in any case, he was not yet thinking of settling down.

During the last two trips of the year, Andy, a young New Zealander, had joined the crew, Dan met him in the messroom and they chummed up right away. One day, Andy told Dan that before leaving Wellington he had been offered the opportunity to be an A.B. on a brand-new ship due to sail from Leith sometime in

February 1939. She had been built for the Union Steamship Company of New Zealand for their trans-Tasman trade. Would Dan like to take his place? Andy was having such a good time in the Old Country he would like to stay on for a while, and if Dan agreed he would let the company know of the proposed change. 'Well,' thought Dan, 'If I'm ever to visit New Zealand it may as well be now.'

On the last westbound sailing of 1938, filled to capacity as she had been for months with masses of continentals fleeing the coming holocaust, *Queen Mary* ran full tilt into one of the most severe storms of her career. Steaming into the massive seas it was not long before her speed had to be drastically reduced; she wasn't only burying her bow deeply into the seas but the heavy spray slammed against the bridge and even to the crow's nest.

The Captain deemed it prudent to reduce speed even more when men working in the capstan flat, under the fo'c'sle head deck, reported severe damage. As big and powerful as she was, *Queen Mary* was no match for the mighty forces of nature and her speed was further reduced to leave her adequate steerage-way until the weather improved.

The damage done under her fo'c'sle head was more extensive than at first thought. Temporary repairs had to be carried out in New York to enable her to return to Southampton safely. Then, during her annual refit, in the New Year, full repairs with added strengthening in the bow would be expertly carried out while in King George V drydock, which had been specially built to accommodate the world's largest liners. *Queen Mary* paid off on 21st December, 1938. Most of the crew went home for a well-earned respite, and Dan went to spend Christmas with his sister at their old friends' home in Chichester, not dreaming it would be twenty-three years before they would meet again. In the years he had attempted to settle ashore, Connie had tried to live as handy as she could to her extra-mobile brother, but they were never together for long: it seemed as though they were destined to live miles apart.

Early in the New Year, Dan travelled up to London for an interview with Angus McKenzie, the chief officer of the new ship. He took an instant liking to Mr McKenzie, just as he had for Tudor Thomas all those years before. The chief officer studied Dan's Indentures and Discharge Book very carefully and asked how he had heard of the job. When Dan explained about meeting Andy, Mr McKenzie said, "It sounds almost providential to me." Dan agreed, although he didn't realise the truth of the statement.

He was accepted and the chief officer joked, "*Karitane* isn't as big as *Queen Mary* you know, but she's a fine little ship." Dan was issued with a free travel warrant to Leith, and as he left the office he felt the old surge of excitement at impending adventure.

A New Life Down-Under

Angus McKenzie's remark about the meeting with Andy Thompson being almost providential was much nearer the mark than either man realised.

Dan saw his new ship *Karitane* for the first time, brand-new alongside the fitting-out berth. She seemed small compared with his last ship, but she was a neat, compact vessel with excellent crew accommodation amidships, as opposed to the regular for'ard or aft. She was made to earn her living right from the start. She was moved to the coal loading staithes to load coal for Port Said, something Dan thought he had left behind, and he was further surprised when he heard that after Port Said they were to load phosphate at Safaga for Australia!

He found that the food was better than the norm, though not quite up to *Queen Mary*'s standards, and the men were housed two to a cabin, apparently the usual pattern for most New Zealand ships. He also learned that this company was the largest shipping company in Australasia, with almost a hundred ships under its management, so it seemed there would be plenty of scope for further employment.

According to maritime awards, the company had to provide its officers and crew with all their bedding as well as soap and towels, and took advantage of the maiden voyage to ship to New Zealand a large quantity of these items direct from the manufacturers. In order to avoid customs duty, *Karitane*'s Captain had been instructed to see that all hands were given a fresh supply of sheets, pillow cases and towels daily so that none of the goods would be unused on arrival. The crew found it distinctly uncomfortable breaking-in starchy new sheets every day, so instead, they just crumpled and soiled them in other ways.

Like most New Zealanders, Dan's new shipmates loved nicknames, and they soon picked one for Dan - *Queen Mary* - which caused heads to turn when called out in a busy street. His friend

Andy Thompson had been known as the 'Millionaire Playboy' because of his dapper appearance with teddy bear coat and jaunty hat. Later, Dan met an old seaman whose face looked like a crumpled brown paper bag. He was known as 'Miss New Zealand' because he had once unwittingly inserted his face between a photographer's camera and that pretty young woman. The large front page picture in the next day's newspaper showed Albert's homely mug grinning above a caption that read 'Miss New Zealand'.

The maiden voyage of *Karitane* was straightforward, with none of the teething troubles that sometimes plague a new ship, and although the passage from Leith to the Mediterranean was stormy, the little vessel coped well. Dan was, of course, on a well-worn track, but to most of his shipmates it was new territory, especially Safaga where they loaded phosphate for Wallaroo. The passage between the two places was ideal, with the warm sunshine much appreciated after the chill of Europe, and *Karitane* behaved beautifully in the big sea and swell of the Australian Bight.

Wallaroo was well-known to the old square-rigged sailing ships, a port where they loaded their cargoes of wheat for the grain races and, in earlier years, it had been a favourite place to jump ship and head for the goldfields, or the fast-growing cities of Melbourne or Sydney.

Hundreds of Japanese ships had used the port in the preceding months, prompting one female hotel proprietor to be convinced of the impending invasion of Australia by the Japanese via Wallaroo, and probably through her hotel. When a dance was held at the Town Hall it was not to be missed, and Dan was surprised at the Aussie males' peculiar habit of leaving their partners to go and play cards with their mates in another room, leaving the women to dance together, or with any visitors that happened to be there. He and his shipmates had a really good time with so many nice girls to choose from, but when the local lads returned, some of them were the worse for grog and looking for a fight. Dan was not intimidated by them, he had survived several bare-fist affrays by now, both ashore and afloat.

Apart from that, his sport of boxing had given him a measure of confidence and on top of that he had learned a couple of useful tricks for use in a tight corner, from an ex-New York policeman, serving on *Queen Mary*. So now he was calm and confident in the knowledge that he could cope with any of those fellows, man to man if they chose to have a go, but strangely, they seemed to get the message and looked elsewhere.

The trip from South Australia to Wellington seemed just a hop. As soon as they had berthed and were clear of Customs and Immigration, an elderly Seamen's Union official, a Polish man, came on board to ask if the crew had any complaints. When he was told that there was nothing they could complain about, he went off mumbling, "If ve haf no tropples ve MAKE tropples." He seemed a very disappointed old man.

All hands were signed off at the Wellington shipping office. They had been engaged on the understanding there would be no repatriation, so Dan was as free as a bird in the new and exciting country of New Zealand.

Over the years, Dan had kept in touch with his Kiwi friend of the Smithfield days and had told him he was coming to New Zealand. So, as soon as the pay off and farewells were completed, he went to the railway station to book a seat on that night's Limited to Auckland, and sent a telegram to Owen to let him know he was coming. That evening, he boarded the train and located his seat, and before long the elderly couple across the aisle began to talk to him, they could see he was a 'new chum'. They had been seeing off friends on their way to England, so they were eager to hear the latest about the Old Country and the possibility of war.

The compartment gradually filled up with people, most of whom seemed in very good spirits. One young man was taking swigs from a bottle of Johnny Walker and Dan wondered how long he could keep that up. Soon the youth became abusive, and unruly when the guard was called, he too was cursed with filthy language. By arrangement, the train was stopped at the next station and the drinker, by then foaming at the mouth, was yanked off the train by a very large policeman, his big talk and bravado having drained away.

The peace that followed was disturbed only by the rush for refreshments at the next station. It seemed that everyone was dying of hunger, judging by the stampede, and when it seemed Dan was the only one not going, he followed the others, returning five minutes later armed like his travelling companions with a meat pie and a cup of tea. He was now joined by a lady taking the seat next to his, her name was Nancy she said and her husband was a dairy farmer near a place called Te Aroha. She was a very pleasant, well-informed and friendly person, so she soon explained where her town was situated and points of interest round about. In this way, the night passed quickly and Dan was sorry when she disembarked at a station called Frankton Junction.

Owen was on the platform when the Limited pulled into Auckland next morning. He was easy to pick out from the crowd with his rich auburn hair. They drove home to meet his wife Olive, who gave Dan a cheery welcome and provided a hearty breakfast. Although Olive and Owen had offered to accommodate Dan until he got himself established, he decided to stay at the Sailors' Home down on the harbour front.

He had been favourably impressed with everything he had seen so far and the immigration policy at the time was quite open and ready to accept him on a permanent basis. He tried to join the New Zealand Seamen's Union, but was told there was a long waiting list, although he could put his name down in case there was an improvement later.

There was virtually full employment in New Zealand at that time so he was able to get a job as a general hand at a large department store in Queen Street, in downtown Auckland. This made him ineligible to stay at the Sailors' Home, so he found a bedsitter within walking distance of the store.

When he started work at eight o'clock the following Monday morning, everyone was friendly and helpful as though they had known him for years. Dan was particularly pleased to note the absence of any class distinction – senior staff members and even the owner seemed willing to pass the time of day. He was also impressed by the number of sales girls whose parents dropped them off from expensive looking cars.

Dan was put in a gang of six, engaged in cleaning and maintenance work around the six floors of the store. That was all right, but one task nearly scared him out of his wits, that was vacuuming the floor of the glass showroom. The tiers of wine goblets and vases delicately balanced on cabinet shelves horrified him, he felt like the proverbial bull in a china shop, as he threaded his way between the showcases loaded with crystal and glass, towing the corrugated hose which did its best to catch the corners of the cases.

In the course of this work, he came across a smart little blonde whose cheeky remarks caught his attention. She started it by saying, "Hello bright eyes, where have you suddenly sprung from?" Each time he passed through her section she had something smart to say, and he was intrigued by her ability to keep one jump ahead of him all the time, no matter what he said.

One occasion when he saw she was cleaning the hot water boiler, just for something to say, he remarked, "I see you are cleaning out your flue," quick as a flash she said,

"I would want something better than this to do that," holding up the wispy brush for inspection.

On his first Saturday morning, she asked him whether he would like to go for a walk with her around the Domain on Sunday afternoon. Dan, never having met a girl quite so forward as this one, agreed. They took a tram to the Domain and then walked all over that beautiful park with Michelle chatting away as if she had known him all her life. When, tired from walking, they finally sat upon a park bench she suddenly asked him, "Excuse me, but do you wear 'long-johns', you know, long underpants?"

Dan laughed and answered, "No, of course not - why do you ask?"

"Oh, I just couldn't marry a man who wore long-johns," she said.

Dan was flabbergasted. 'So this is New Zealand,' he thought, 'Plenty of wild life here!'

Marlene, Dianne, and Linda had not been exactly shy, and the Judys of Liverpool were jack-blunt and outspoken, but Michelle matched them all. She seemed to delight in heading off what she thought he might be thinking.

That first evening on their way back to the Ferry Wharf, she said casually, "I won't ask you home this evening, you won't be able to do anything - I'm not well, you know what I mean!" giving him a meaningful look.

Dan, embarrassed, could only mutter, "Oh!" She was clearly well-versed in dealing with men, and he decided then and there he wasn't going to be one of them. It was just as well she was leaving the department store for more lucrative work, as she had confided while walking in the Domain. They never met again, though he caught a glimpse of her once during the war surrounded by a group of laughing GIs no doubt giving them 'the treatment'.

During lunch in the staff cafeteria the following Monday, Dan was asked how he was getting on and what he thought of New Zealand. He was happy to say he thought Auckland was a beautiful city and looked like a place he could easily settle down in, little dreaming those were prophetic words. Without naming names he jokingly referred to his experience with Michelle, and one of the girls present said vehemently that he wasn't to think all New Zealand girls were like that. Another woman said she could introduce him to some really nice girls. Dan declined the offer saying, a little pompously, that he could look after himself, he always had and always would select his own girlfriends. He asked the woman why she was concerned about him, so she said that a new chum, like him, could easily become prey to one of the 'town bikes'. He was surprised by her bluntness but appreciated her concern, and solely to humour her, he agreed to meet one of these nice friends of hers, but only on the understanding it was a 'one-off' occasion.

Later, Dan agreed to meet this lady at 7.30 p.m. the following Saturday at the entrance to the St James Theatre, to be introduced to one of the young women she had in mind. He had never had a blind date before and wasn't particularly keen about this one. He wasn't to know that the young woman was equally reluctant and had backed out at the last minute.

'The best laid schemes o' mice an' men gang aft a-gley' said the Scottish baird, Robbie Burns.

However, the girl's kind-hearted sister, feeling sorry for the unknown fellow, volunteered to take her place. Right from his first sight of Jessie, Dan knew that she was his true mate, and he never changed his mind about that over their long married life. Jessie, of course, had no idea of a permanent relationship – she was only filling the gap for her sister.

They enjoyed the film, *The Citadel*, and had coffee afterwards, then Dan escorted Jessie home to say goodnight at the garden gate. That was the start of a courtship during which Dan, with his past experiences of girlfriends, could assess the genuine character of Jessie. She was a real gem; there was none of the silly play-acting of which he had grown so tired, they were soul-compatible, and he felt that was all-important, though he wouldn't have been able to explain why. Jessie must have seen something about Dan to be prepared to continue their friendship, so they met whenever they could.

It was now June 1939, and war clouds were gathering over Europe, with Hitler's Third Reich brandishing its awesome military might and terrorising surrounding nations. On the opposite side of the world, New Zealanders could only read about it in the newspapers and listen to the overseas broadcasts of the BBC, so life went on unchanged.

About that time, Dan was needed as a temporary liftman. The lifts were old-fashioned, manually controlled ones which called for considerable judgment and skill to bring the floor of the lift in line with the floor outside. It was more difficult with the varying passenger loads and only experience enabled a liftman to provide a smooth service. Dan wasn't helped by well-meant advice to go up a bit, or down a bit, and thought it was just as well the lift couldn't go sideways.

He had to memorise the patter for each of the six floors: "First floor – dress materials, silks, patterns, embroideries. Second floor – furniture showroom, furnishings, lampshades, mats, rugs..." What with the balancing act at each floor, Dan found it difficult to get the patter finished before arriving at the appropriate floor, and he found it doubly so with a lift full of busy women, all talking. He got confused and sometimes swooped past a floor, only to hear a woman call out that she wanted to get off there. At first he was so anxious to please that he would nip down to the floor he had missed, or back up to one if they had been descending, but his indicator light showed the head liftman on the ground floor what was happening and that earned him a mild rebuke. He must not act like a yo-yo, but once started either up or down he was to keep going, the customers were not seeking a life on the ocean wave... and so on.

In his early days, he noticed that regular customers would try to pick one of the other lifts, and realised it was only the innocent, the reckless or the adventurous that came into his lift. He was a threat for pregnant women or anyone recovering from an internal operation, and following an extra rapid descent with sudden halt, his passengers often ended up in a squatting position. Customers and management were remarkably forbearing, thought Dan, and he often felt he deserved the sack.

When the Second World War broke out, Dan's thoughts immediately reverted to the sea and ships, and although his courtship of Jessie was proceeding happily, he felt his place was the Merchant Navy. Once when the British liner *Dominion Monarch* was in port, Dan 'stood-by' her in case an A.B. was required, but she sailed not needing him. He next tried for the Federal liner *Cumberland* and failing to find a vacancy there, applied to the New Zealand Navy, only to be told that, being a Merchant Navy man, he should remain there. He was blissfully ignorant of the fact he was not controller of his own destiny, but his course would be revealed in due time.

Next, he received a letter which was to set the seal on his future. It was from the New Zealand Seamen's Union to the effect that if he was still interested in joining the union he should call at their office as soon as possible. He had forgotten his application five months previously and now, after three setbacks, he felt this was a Godsend. How right he was, without realising it, it crossed his mind that if he was employed on New Zealand ships he would be able to keep in touch with his beloved Jessie, and maybe someday marry her!

To commence his New Zealand service, he was lucky enough to be selected to fill a vacancy on the trans-Tasman liner *Awatea* employed on what was known as the horseshoe run – Auckland to Sydney, Sydney to Wellington, back to Sydney, and then back to Auckland.

The ship itself, although the pride and glory of New Zealand ships, was just a miniature *Queen Mary* to Dan, and though the fastest ship crossing the Tasman at the time, she was not nearly as fast as her larger counterpart. Her master, Captain Davey, was a very popular man with the travelling public because, having a flair for publicity, he promoted an image of himself as a swashbuckling Skipper. But despite the good conditions and excellent run, which would have made her an ideal married man's ship, the Awatea was not a happy ship – the union delegate was always looking for something to complain about.

Dan signed off the *Awatea* in December 1939, just in time to spend Christmas with Jessie at her parents' home in Auckland. Between trips, they had got engaged, Dan having proposed in the romantic setting of Kohimarama beach.

Early in the new year he was back at sea in a different ship, Auckland to Dunedin via all the major ports in between. Again, he was impressed with the very good conditions on those ships and amazed at the relaxed way in which they were operated. Girlfriends of the crew could come aboard and travel up and down the coast with them, and when Dan expressed surprise, it was explained that the Captain and the company chose to turn a blind eye as they knew that forbidding the practice would cause more trouble than it was worth. On one occasion, when joining a new ship, Dan went into the crew accommodation and passing the open door of the bathroom glanced in and got a shock, a young woman having a shower with a sou'wester her only covering.

"Oh hello," she gaily called, liberally lathering herself with her scented soap, "Have you just joined? I'll catch up with you later." Dan wasn't sure whether it was a threat or a promise. The company seemed to be at the mercy of a few irresponsible union officials whose pet slogan was, "stick 'er up," meaning, prevent the ship from sailing at the time planned. Dan found the happy-go-lucky spirit of adventure was absent on those comfortable, well-found, well-fed ships, and in its place was a discontented urge to get more and more out of the ship owner, gloat over their power, and just cruise from one booze-up to the next.

Joining another of the company's ships, he was promoted to replace the Bos'n who was leaving, and this gave Dan responsibility for dealing with the men, and also gave him a cabin of his own. This made it easier for him to study, and revive his original aim of becoming a master mariner.

This ship was engaged in the trans-Tasman trade, loading steel goods in Newcastle and Port Kembla for New Zealand ports. It was 1940/41, when there were not only German surface raiders and minelayers around, but also Japanese submarines. Deeply laden with such a deadweight cargo as steel, just one shell below the waterline would have been sufficient to sink the ship like a lump of lead.

An added spur to his new-found ambition was when the new Third Mate, who joined the ship in Newcastle turned out to be none other than Charlie, the young Canadian he had befriended those years before on *Prince Rupert City*. Now here he was, higher up the ladder than Dan! It was just the impetus Dan needed, so after a couple more voyages to save the money, he left the ship to go to the School of Navigation in Auckland to prepare for his Second Mate's Foreign-Going certificate – nine years behind time.

A Step In The Right Direction

With his good grounding at the Sea Training School, and Jessie's patience as he endlessly recited the 'Rule of the Road at Sea' and the 'Knowledge of Principles', Dan passed the five day examination without undue stress.   They had a modest celebration and then capped it all by getting married at the Pitt Street Methodist Church. Then, after a brief but delightful honeymoon in New Plymouth, Dan, armed with his brand new certificate, resigned from the Seamen's Union and joined the Officers' Guild.

The Guild told him of a job on a vessel at King's Wharf, and Dan decided to investigate right away.   After being interviewed, Dan signed on as Second Mate of the auxiliary schooner *Piri*, owned and operated by Imperial Chemical Industries and commanded by Captain H. Lane.   She was only 155 tons, but she was a strongly built vessel with a loaded freeboard of only fifteen inches – quite a change from *Queen Mary*.   *Piri*'s cargo, mercury in heavy containers, was for Melbourne, which pleased Dan because such voyages were classed as foreign-going and would qualify for his next certificate.

There were five officers including the Captain, an elderly man with an air of ruggedness and vitality.   Dan had his own very small cabin down aft in the officers' quarters, and there was a miniature dining saloon.   Dan wondered whether he would get used to such confined space, but found, like everyone else, that the space seemed to get roomier as he adapted himself to it.

As *Piri* wasn't sailing until the next day Dan was able to settle in with his gear and then spend the night at home with Jessie.   Partings are always emotional for newly weds, but in wartime there was that added uncertainty about when, if ever, they would meet again. Saying goodbye was quite a wrench for both of them.

It was wintertime, and as *Piri* pitched and plunged her way out of the Hauraki Gulf, it wasn't long before Dan was heaving his heart out, 'feeding the fishes'. On the other hand, Captain Lane was enjoying every minute of being at sea again. He loved to see the sails set whenever possible, and while they had little effect other than to steady the ship and take the weight off the engine, it was a tonic for the Old Man. He was indeed a true seaman, the ocean was his life, the ship his home, and Dan came to regard him, respectfully, as a human albatross; he was so much part of his element.

There were two engineers in charge of the diesel engine, a Cook/Steward, and four A.B. seamen for'ard, a total crew of ten men. The seamen were ex-scow men used to discomforts and cramped quarters. They told Dan it gave them a sense of adventure that was missing on the bigger, more comfortable ships with the constant wrangling for better conditions.

Both the Captain and Mr Matheson, the Mate, made no attempt to hide the fact that they were avid readers of the Bible, and Dan often heard them discussing religious matters. Learning that *Piri* was usually employed carrying cargoes of high explosives, which, in wartime, was an extra-hazardous occupation, Dan wondered if they were preparing themselves for speedy promotion to heavenly places.

The two engineers on the other hand were very worldly fellows and when they went ashore they wore more gold braid than their *Queen Mary* counterparts. Of the four A.B.s, the oldest was a real old shellback who had served on square-rigged sailing ships and could spin some hair-raising yarns. Once, having gashed the ball of his left thumb, he calmly stitched the wound together with ordinary needle and thread, and it took a lot of convincing from the Mate before he agreed to have it bandaged.

Piri was so lively that it took Dan a few days to get his sea legs, and in rough conditions, higher bunkboards and straps were needed to keep him safely in his bunk. The Chief Engineer, a robust fellow, was frequently thrown out of his to crash to the deck of his cabin. At mealtimes, the Cook needed the skills of a high-wire performer, a juggler and acrobat, but for everyone, one essential activity was often the trickiest – going to the toilet. Dan learned the technique: hand-pump out most of the water in the bowl, and also out of the overhead cistern before sitting down, or else there was a strong likelihood of a cold shower from above when rolling one way, and a cold sluicing of the posterior, when rolling back. Neither particularly welcome in wintertime.

That first trans-Tasman trip in *Piri* was one Dan would not easily forget, with the little ship blacked-out, and screaming winds hell-bent on destroying everything in their path. On watch, he often had to twist one leg through the mainsail sheets to keep his feet. The man at the wheel would be concentrating on aligning the compass course point with the lubber-line on the inside of the compass bowl. In decent weather this was a simple matter, but with the violent gyrations of *Piri,* the helmsman would frequently report that he had lost the lubber-line. That was something new to Dan, who found that the only way to return the lubber-line to its proper place was to turn the compass bowl both ways at the same time. To relieve the strain on the helmsman's arms, there was a specially designed grommet to hold the spokes each side of the wheel and so ease the constant jerking.

Captain Lane was fully qualified to do his own piloting at all the ports *Piri* visited, and Dan found it interesting to watch the Old Man navigate the River Yarra to berth in Melbourne, within walking distance of the city. After discharging her cargo at the riverside wharf, *Piri* shifted to the explosives anchorage off Point Cook, south of Williamstown and well away from populated areas. There she loaded tons of gelignite and other high explosives for the mines and quarries of West Australia and, in a specially constructed locker, the detonators to match.

Heading westward heavily laden the little vessel had to contend with the huge swells of the Australian Bight and it took her two weeks to cover the distance. On one of these westbound passages, those on board *Piri* were treated to an unforgettable sight, whereas their vessel rode over the huge swells, they were overtaken by a convoy of famous troop-laden liners, burying their bows into the seas in thrilling fashion. Dan recognised the Cunard's *Aquitania*, and *Mauretania*, and the French liner, *Ile De France* while the escorting cruiser was making 'heavy weather' trying to maintain her position at high speed. On arrival at Fremantle, they saw the cruiser getting her de-gausing gear repaired, it had been wrapped around the forepart of her bridge by the bad weather, the troopships continued without stopping to their Middle East destinations another escort having been arranged. The explosives were off-loaded at the Woodman's Point depot south of Fremantle, and then she moved up to the Swan River to load in that busy port and later, Bunbury, timber for Melbourne.

On the return trip, *Piri* rode the swell whenever she could, to surf along at great speed. After an exciting ride, with the swell passing underneath, she would slide down the backs of the monsters and Dan was fascinated to see the log-line assuming the curve of the trough between them and the next oncoming beauty, with the rotator clearly visible, spinning down the face of it. On *Piri,* Dan was not only at sea, he was in it as well, watching the beauty and grace of the albatrosses as they glided effortlessly alongside.

Musing on the power and beauty of the ocean, that trip Dan remembered the remarkable story of a seaman in a windjammer, shortening sail on a topsail yard during a gale, falling into the mountainous seas, and being given up for lost. However, a few hours later the steamer *Northumberland* came across the man still struggling in the sea and with superb seamanship, considering the dreadful weather conditions, managed to pick him up. *Northumberland* arrived in Sydney ahead of the windjammer, and the story has it that the seaman was on the wharf when his ship berthed. It is hoped he wasn't logged for being absent without leave!

Back in Melbourne, *Piri* discharged her timber and loaded explosives for Greymouth and Westport, small gold quarrying and coalmining ports on the west coast of the South Island of New Zealand. On her way home, on a calm, moonless night, the ship had just passed Wilson's Promontory, a focal navigation point in Bass Strait, when the lookout sighted some shaded lights over to starboard. The Old Man and Dan had a good look at them through binoculars and agreed that the stranger looked suspiciously like a minelayer.

Concerned lest *Piri* be seen, when a single rifle shot could blow both ships into eternity, Captain Lane altered course and crept away. The other vessel, absorbed in her task, apparently didn't notice, and continued her nefarious work. At daybreak the following morning, scanning the horizon carefully first, Captain Lane broke radio silence to report the sighting. Subsequent events proved his judgment correct as several ships fell victim to mines laid in that area. It was common knowledge later, that the alert siren recalling the crew of a warship following *Piri*'s report, caused an elderly lady to die of heart failure in the Auckland Naval Base Area.

On another occasion, homeward bound, emerging from Bass Strait into the Tasman Sea, the tailshaft broke, rendering the engine useless. The Old Man, being the sailor he was, opted to carry on across the Tasman under sail alone, but fortunately the Mate, Mr Matheson, persuaded him not to risk it. They would be more of a sitting duck than ever if a surface raider or submarine showed up, so radio silence was again broken to report their plight.

A tug was summoned to tow *Piri* back to Melbourne, then all sail was set with a view to reducing the distance the tug would have to come. Then Captain Lane decided to see if the propeller had dropped off the broken shaft, and wearing only his bathing shorts, with a line around his waist, he dived over the stern and swam below to investigate. A short while later, clambering aboard, blue with cold, he announced that the propeller and broken stump of shaft had dropped back against the rudder post. He thought it might drop off altogether when they got under way, and since it might be impossible to get a replacement in wartime it ought to be secured. Feeling that the Old Man was risking his life for them all, Dan volunteered to go down and help him secure the propeller, although Mr Matheson respectfully asked the Old Man if the wretched prop was worth risking two lives.

This part of the world was, and still is, notorious for its man-eating sharks, 'grey nurse' and 'white pointer' being just two of the monsters. Both Captain and Mate, very conscious of the efficacy of prayer, bowed their heads to make a simple plea for the protection of the two divers.

Dan was almost paralysed when his warm body encountered the bitterly cold early spring waters of Bass Strait. Armed with wire rope, he and the Captain tried to secure the propeller from each side, but with the rise and fall of the ship in the swell they found it virtually impossible, and with bursting lungs they spurted to the surface. After three attempts Captain Lane signalled that it was too difficult and too dangerous to continue.

The Cook was standing by with hot soup, but the Mate got in first with a tot of rum to help restore their circulation. Dan was quite moved to see that the Mate had also taken the precaution of standing by the stern rail with a loaded rifle in case sharks put in an appearance.

They hadn't, but even as they spoke, a shoal of barracuda flashed past just where they had been. To Dan they meant little, but Mr Matheson said that the voracious fish, with wide jaws and razor-sharp teeth, would have torn them both to shreds in no time. Dan shuddered at the thought.

Piri made good progress under sail with the north-easterly breeze and was within sight of Wilson's Promontory lighthouse by the time the tug arrived. The sails were stowed when the towline was secured for the humiliating tow back to the explosives anchorage in Port Phillip Bay. The men on *Piri* smiled to themselves when they heard the tug wouldn't leave the bay until her crew had successfully negotiated danger money for the job.

With so many other ships awaiting repairs, it was six weeks before *Piri* could get the work done. While they waited, Dan was able to study for his next certificate and write weekly letters to his beloved Jessie.

At weekends, he and his A.B. friend Henry travelled by train to Melbourne, partly to watch the American servicemen captivating the local Aussie girls, or vice versa, and the common scene of servicemen brawling outside the pubs, but mainly to see the latest films.

On Sunday afternoons, they took a tram from Flinders Street to St Kilda, to the amusement park, which did a roaring trade with the GIs and their girlfriends, or the beach at Port Phillip Bay, where they knew of a first-class fish restaurant.

Two months passed before *Piri* left the drydock and headed once again for the Point Cook anchorage. For the second time, the New Zealand bound cargo was loaded and securely stowed, complete with its detonators. On receiving his Sailing Orders at the Navy Office, Captain Lane was told to stay alert for mines in area XY, and to be particularly vigilant when crossing area Z where they might sight a convoy of troopships heading south to avoid Bass Strait. Captain Lane decided to double up the watches.

In spite of some fog, always a hazard in close waters before the advent of radar, *Piri* managed to keep clear of shipping through the danger area XY and clear Bass Strait.

They reached area Z as night was falling and around one in the morning, with no moon, the Mate and Dan, their eyes straining into the darkness and their nerves on edge, almost froze with horror when a very large ship, just a black shape against the darkness, passed so close astern of them that her wash brought all hands on deck in alarm.   A minute or so later another large black shape streaked across ahead of them, and by that time no one was down below on *Piri*.

At daybreak the horizon was as bald as a billiard ball and just as shiny, with the sun peeping over the rim.   How much better, everyone thought, if they could have seen what must have been a magnificent sight of those fine troopships in daylight, at full speed en route to the Middle East.

The rest of the trip passed quickly and without incident, and after completing the discharge of her cargo at the explosives anchorage of an island in the Hauraki Gulf, they pressed on into Auckland Harbour. By the time they made fast at King's Wharf at the end of that voyage, his fourth on *Piri*, Dan had served on her for just over a year.

South Sea Islands

It was now 1943 and the war in the South Pacific had reached a dramatic stage. The Japanese, having pushed as far south as New Guinea, were threatening the mainland of Australia. Desperate air and sea battles were being fought in the Coral Sea. Japanese midget submarines had penetrated Sydney harbour defences, with a view to sink *Queen Mary* and other large troopships.

Piri was withdrawn from service for a while, so Dan was fortunate enough to be able to fill a vacancy as Third Mate on *Trienza*. She was a motor ship, bigger than the tramps he had served in, but not quite as big as *Memnon* or *Orestes*. Her name was a combination of tri (three), e for England, nz for New Zealand, and a for Australia. She was the height of luxury compared to *Piri*. Dan's cabin was spacious and just one flight of stairs down from the bridge. Even more satisfying was an efficient team of Indian Stewards who attended to the officers' needs and cleaned their cabins.

Trienza was the last of a fleet of six ships carrying phosphate from Nauru and Ocean Islands to Australia and New Zealand, the others having been sunk and their crews taken captive when both Nauru and Ocean were shelled and their installations destroyed. She was owned and operated by the British Phosphate Commissioners of Melbourne. One other ship, the Norwegian freighter *Arcadia*, cooperated with *Trienza* to keep the fertiliser needs of Australia and New Zealand satisfied with phosphate from the French island of Makatea, one hundred and twenty-five miles north east of Tahiti.

On their departure from Auckland, when Captain McInnes, a bright young Scotsman, opened his orders, he was instructed to follow a zigzag route to the Cook Islands picking up labourers, with their wives and children, from Rarotonga, Atiu, Aitutaki, Mauke and Mitiero and Tahiti, to disembark them at Makatea. A group of carpenters were on board to construct sleeping shelters, washplaces and toilets for the deck passengers en route to Makatea. Those cheerful people came aboard from the beaches in a variety of boats to the ship lying-off outside the reef. They were laughing, joking and singing, and carried their possessions in cleverly woven palm-frond baskets and although they came from different islands, they all seemed to accept each other like members of one big family.

A few days after leaving the Cook Islands, *Trienza* called at Papeete, the main port and capital of Tahiti, to discharge mail and some refrigerated cargo. It was a Sunday morning and the Cook Islanders on board were dressed in their Sunday best, with smart island-made straw hats perched primly on their heads. They were joyfully singing old-time Gospel songs accompanied by guitars, harmonising and clapping, and by the time the ship berthed crowds of Tahitians were on the wharf, attracted by the singing. Later, local French officials, after sampling the Old Man's Scotch, granted the Cook Islanders permission to go ashore.

They flooded down the gangways still singing, laughing and waving. They were welcomed by the Tahitians who draped sweet-smelling leis around their necks, and with true Polynesian hospitality invited them to their homes. Some six hours later when they were due back on board, several were adrift and the local gendarmes were alerted to round them up. They were a sorry sight. Unused to the lavish hospitality of the Tahitians, they had been overwhelmed by fruit punches, and possibly some other concoctions, which had eventually knocked them out. Many who were dragged on board dived straight overboard again and swam ashore, only to be re-arrested, returned to the ship and locked up. Everyone seemed to succumb to the special allure of Tahiti, and for the locals, the drama surrounding the departure of ships provided regular instalments of their best entertainment.

As Third Officer, Dan had occasions to visit the local Lloyds agent, a fine elderly Englishman called Mr Sharood who had married the beautiful daughter of a top Tahitian family, and had lived in Tahiti for over thirty years. Meeting that man proved a blessing to Dan because on subsequent visits he was always invited to the spacious, comfortable family home overlooking the harbour.

Leaving Papeete on this occasion for the Cook Islanders and their hosts ashore, was a fervent hotchpotch of emotions, singing, shouting, laughing, crying, waving and dancing, but by the time the ship passed through the reef entrance, the commotion ceased and peace finally reigned.

At Makatea, company launches removed all the Cook Islanders to their encampments on the island and loading commenced soon after. When weather permitted the ship could be loaded in five days, but in adverse conditions, loading could take as long as two weeks or more. On this occasion, with no delays or hold-ups, the ship was fully-loaded in four and a half days, then returned to Papeete to pick up a contingent of Tahitian soldiers who were to reinforce French Army personnel safeguarding New Caledonia from the Japanese threat. They were a happy-go-lucky group, with a relaxed view of life, feeding on the army rations they had brought with them and sleeping on top of the hatches at night. Dan was told by one of them, in broken English, that of all the punishments the Army could apply, the one they most feared was having their hair shaved off. Their hair was in some way linked to their sex appeal and that was sacrosanct. Luckily for Dan, the cargo was to be discharged at Auckland and he was able to spend a few days at home with his dear Jessie. It would be eight months before he would see her again, but he was unaware of that at the time.

By that time, he had completed the necessary service to enable him to sit for his First Mate's examination. Having studied consistently at sea, he would need only a few weeks at Navigation School to put the finishing touches to his preparation. In Melbourne he would also need to find lodgings not too far from the city, but with thousands of well-heeled Americans on rest and recreation leave he realised it wouldn't be easy. Dan was on good terms with Sid Baker, the company's night-watchman in Melbourne, and felt he would be a good man to solve the problem.

Melbourne was *Trienza*'s home port, so all her regular officers went home on leave, leaving Dan as the ship-keeping officer. Dan asked Sid if he knew of any likely places, and Sid said he would ask his wife, who knew more about such things than he. Mrs Baker said she could let Dan have a small bedroom and provide full board, she would also look after his washing and ironing. 'My word,' thought Dan, 'That's fantastic good luck!' So after ship-keeping for the three weeks, *Trienza* was in port, Dan took up residence with the Bakers and the ship sailed.

The neat, homely cottage at Bailey was only a few minutes by electric train from Flinders Street in the heart of the city, and when Dan met Sid's wife it was a case of love at first sight; she was a dear, motherly old soul and to her Dan was just another son. Like her husband, she was a typically blunt, no-frills Aussie, embarrassingly frank at times, but with a heart of gold and a great sense of humour. Dan could attend school, work in his bedroom and share meals with the old couple and their daughter-in-law, who spent her days with them and her nights with her grandmother.

This attractive young woman was introduced to Dan as 'Shirl' – a typical Aussie abbreviation – and when Dan called her Shirley, Mum Baker jokingly told him, "We don't want any of that la-di-da stuff here, she's Shirl to us!" It was a pleasure for Dan to have feminine company in the evenings, playing cards in front of a cosy fire, and when his companions pulled his leg about Jessie being left in Auckland with so many Americans on the loose there, Dan pointed out that Shirl was in the same situation.

Again, he passed his examination, but only after a struggle with his two favourite subjects, Meteorology, and Ship Construction, the other subjects he managed without trouble. He was jubilant, especially as Captain Hone, the examiner, was feared as being a very difficult man to satisfy, and Dan certainly found him hard to please in the orals, but to do it at the first attempt was quite an achievement. Dan wrote to Jessie right away, and the following day reported his success to the British Phosphate Commissioners, asking to be regarded as available for return to duty.

To celebrate, Dan invited Mr and Mrs Baker and Shirl to an evening meal at a city restaurant, but the old couple declined, adding that dining out was no longer their cup of tea. Shirl however, was keen to have an evening out and, after making sure it was okay with Sid and Elsa, Dan enjoyed her bright and breezy company.

For the remaining three weeks of his stay with the Bakers, Dan and Shirl went to cinema shows, a boxing tournament and two Australian Rules football games. Shirl was an ardent supporter of the South Melbourne team and her strident encouragement was a novel experience for Dan. He laughed when she mischievously claimed that 'Big Jack', her star performer, could put his boots under her bed any night!

On one occasion, while Shirl was vociferously giving her support to a good move by her 'star', Dan turned his head around to see the owner of another hearty female voice right in his ear. A pair of lovely eyes looked back and Dan noticed that in one of them a smut had landed, whereupon Dan, with the corner of his clean white handkerchief volunteered to remove it.

He was in the midst of doing this when Shirl looked around, and with an astonished voice said to Dan, "Hey, who are you with, me or her?" giving the other girl a hard look, and then laughing she said, "Make up your mind." Hastily, Dan assured her he was wholly with her.

It was good for Dan to have feminine company, but perhaps it was just as well that Shirl's husband came home unexpectedly on final leave just then, and a few days later, Dan received his orders to rejoin *Trienza* as Second Officer when she arrived back in Melbourne. Everything was working out extremely well.

At this stage, having previously received instruction in the use of A.A. weaponry while serving on *Piri*, Dan was now sent for further training at the D.E.M.S[1] Gunnery school at Flinders Naval Base. This was quite an exciting departure from his normal daily life, having firing practice with the rapid-fire Oerlikon guns, sometimes arousing the scornful invective of the ex-R.N. Instructor who appeared to enjoy his superiority over a class of trainee Merchant navy officers.

Dan, and some of his fellow class-mates, though introduced into the basic principles involved of operating larger guns of the type mounted on the poop-deck, (specially strengthened for the purpose) of selected merchant ships, was relieved to learn that, with the installation of these guns, a properly-trained naval gun crew was provided.

Becoming Second Officer was promotion in both rank and pay, a step up the ladder. A new Captain was in command when *Trienza* sailed again, under sealed orders as was customary in wartime. When the Captain opened his orders after dropping the pilot, he snorted with disgust as he handed them to Dan who was to lay off the courses on the appropriate charts. They were to proceed to Papeete via an extra long route, considered the safest at that time,

---

[1] D.E.M.S. the initials of Defensively-Equipped Merchant Ships

into notoriously cold and tempestuous weather. The track they were to follow was down the western coast of Tasmania to latitude 50 degrees, thence eastwards to longitude 150 degrees west, then due north to the vicinity of the Friendly Islands. Long after the war was over it was revealed that that area was a favourite rendezvous for German raiders and Japanese supply ships. Was *Trienza* sent that way to tempt them to reveal their presence? However, the voyage passed with only the occasional sighting of smoke on the horizon, which could have been anything, and they reached their destination safely.

Since Tahitian women love ships, it was usually hard to keep them from boarding. Not so with *Trienza*. Her Captain, determined not to allow females on HIS ship, kept her at anchor in mid-harbour with her officers keeping their normal sea-watches. This was perfectly correct, and a prudent procedure in wartime and in the midst of the hurricane season. It was due to the latter fact that *Arcadia*, unable to load at Makatea, had returned to the relative safety of Papeete.

Seeing *Trienza* at anchor, her Master also decided to follow suit, but to placate his Scandinavian crew, he allowed them to bring girls on board as the best way to keep his men happy and at hand. The problem for Captain Larsen was that more and more girls joined those already on board. For *Trienza*'s Australian officers, watching the goings-on across the water and the washing of skimpy female underwear fluttering in the daily breeze, was rather disconcerting. Added to this, delectable Tahitian girls with waist-long black hair paddled around *Trienza* in their canoes, inviting the officers to meet them at Quinn's, a well-known waterfront tavern, when off duty. It was the same old problem that had given Captains Cook and Bligh so much trouble years before, and long before taverns like Quinn's existed. There's something mystical about Tahiti, so the Old Man relented to the extent that off duty personnel were allowed to go ashore between their duty periods.

However, Dan invited two of his married fellow officers to visit Mr Sharood in his home. Papa Sharood had a large family of daughters, but no sons, and Mama had passed on, Dan thought the old fellow enjoyed having male company, while for him it was a providential escape from the snares of Papeete. On *Arcadia* though, the Captain's original good intent boomeranged, women of all ages and sizes now overran the ship, and in the end drove the crew ashore to get away from them. They just wanted a quiet drink on their own.

Though fights were fairly commonplace along the waterfront at Papeete, Dan once came across one of the most terrifying fights he had ever seen – and it was between two girls. It happened on the terrace outside Quinn's, when some heated words caused two girls to fly at each other, disregarding the crowded tables in between, and amidst the crash of broken glass, with teeth bared and with all the viciousness of wild cats, they bit, scratched and gouged each other. It took six men to pull them apart, they were so entangled. "Hell hath no fury..." pondered Dan.

Trienza sailed for Makatea a few days later to load her usual cargo and embark the Harbourmaster of Makatea and his wife. They then returned to Papeete to pick up four dour-looking French Army officers, and a very attractive French woman. The Captain relished the company of the two ladies, so he got the Chief Steward to organise a table for himself, the Harbourmaster, and the two ladies, while his officers looked on with jealous disapproval from afar.

A day or two later, Dan, in his Second Mate's role of ship's doctor, was asked by the harbourmaster for a mild laxative for his wife. After consulting *The Shipmaster's Medical Guide* Dan gave him two small tablets, adding, "That should soften things up a bit. Tomorrow morning I'll give her something as a follow-up." However, when he went on watch at midnight he found the harbourmaster waiting for him.

"Heaven knows what you gave my wife, he said, but she hasn't been able to leave the toilet since she took those tablets."

Flushed with success Dan answered, "Oh good, I'm so pleased we've got things moving. I'll finish her off with some Black Draught in the morning."

The harbourmaster laughed grimly. "Oh no you won't. You'd better keep out of her sight or she'll finish you off!"

Dan's thoughts of becoming a successful ship's medic were thus dashed, just when he was hoping Monique, the French lady might need attention. Instead, all he got was the messy job of treating a huge boil on the Fourth Engineer's bottom, 'What a pity,' he thought as each day he applied poultices to bring it to a head.

It was eight months since he had seen Jessie, so Dan was looking forward to their arrival at Auckland. He had a small suitcase packed ready, but an unpleasant surprise was in store. When the ship finished berthing at King's Wharf, Dan was told to go to the Captain's cabin right away. There, the Old Man announced: "I've just received orders from head office that you're to be transferred to *Triona* at Western Wharf. She's sailing at 10 p.m., so you'd better get your gear packed and hire a taxi to get there."

Dan couldn't believe his ears. It was 7 p.m. and he wouldn't have time to go home at all. It took him just two seconds to say, "No sir, I'm sorry, but I'm not prepared to be shunted around like that. I'm not a sack of coal and that's that!"

In the stunned silence that followed, the Chief Engineer, who was also present, and a great friend of Dan's, said "Take it easy, Dan, I know it's tough luck, but think of your future with the company." Just then the Chief Officer arrived and the Captain explained the situation.

"Why not make the transfer when we meet up with the *Triona* at Makatea?" said the Chief Officer.

The Captain turned to Dan, "Would that suit you better, Mister?" and Dan said quickly,

"Oh yes, sir, that would be fine!" His good friend the Mate had solved the tricky problem in a flash.

Since Auckland was Dan's home port he was excused all normal duties and so he was able to enjoy a brief holiday with Jessie and her family. The time flew and before he knew it Dan was on his way to Makatea where he was transferred on arrival to *Triona* within an hour of her departure. Dan had to get used to a new Captain and officers, and of course another Indian crew, but like all seafarers, that ability was second nature.

Triona stood for three (tri) places: the islands of Ocean and Nauru, and Australia. She was the replacement for the previous *Triona* which had been sunk by German raiders off the islands with the Triaster, the Triadic and the Vinni in 1940.

Soon after emerging from the blue skies and tranquillity of the tropics, *Triona* ran full tilt into a really bad westerly gale, incurring considerable structural damage and losing a strongly built life-raft overboard. She arrived at Lyttelton looking the worse for wear. It was still wartime and a charming group of young women came on board to invite the officers to their homes as part of the local hospitality. It was all above board and very much appreciated, the ladies being well-accustomed to entertaining visiting seafarers.

On completion of discharge of the Lyttelton phosphate, *Triona* headed for Dunedin to discharge the remainder, and when Dan and his Mates went uptown from Ravensbourne they were surprised to see so many American servicemen there, as usual, making a great impact on the local girls. The girls favoured American servicemen partly because they spent their money more freely, and partly because they were said to be more gentlemanly than their Aussie or Kiwi counterparts. The local men were more cynical. Once, during a concert at the Town Hall, a lady came onto the stage to announce that a special club for US personnel only, would shortly be opened. One of Dan's Aussie companions called out in a loud voice, "Yes, a PUDDING club!" to great laughter from all round.

Triona made two more trips to the South Island before heading for Melbourne and as there was no passenger accommodation Dan could only exercise his doctoring role on the Indian crew. These Lascars used to come to Dan holding their stomachs, rolling their eyes, their faces contorted with agony, to ask for Epsom Salts to relieve their constipation. While he wondered why they should be so regularly afflicted, Dan dispensed sachets of salts. Then he found out that those wise guys saved up the packets to sell in Calcutta, so he decided on another remedy. He told them there were no more salts so he would give them castor oil instead. One Indian said he would take it down to his quarters to drink, but Dan said "No, you must drink it here" and poured out half a tumblerful. The smell made Dan's stomach turn over but the Indian drained the tumbler without batting an eyelid, then had the nerve to say, "More, sahib, not enough for me." Dan wondered who was bluffing who, but poured out a full tumbler and handed it back. After a moment's hesitation the man poured it down his throat, then made his way aft a little quicker than when he came. That was the end of the run on laxatives.

Five months later, the ship returned to Melbourne and shortly after their arrival the marine superintendent came on board to say that all officers below the rank of Captain and Chief Engineer were no longer required, as the original officers were again available for service. They had been prisoners of war, now returned to Australia and eager to resume their nautical careers. So much for his future in the company, thought Dan.

Nevertheless, he was grateful to the British Phosphate Commissioners for providing him with employment on such comfortable ships and enabling him to accumulate almost enough sea time to go for his master's certificate. When paying off at the Melbourne shipping office, one of the officials asked if he would accept a Third Officer's job on a troopship soon to sail from Sydney for the islands. Dan needed four more months to complete his qualifying time and also concluded that a troopship would be a fairly large vessel, so a drop in rank from second to third officer could be regarded as equalised.

He was able to pen a few lines to his beloved Jessie to keep her informed of his movements. The war with Japan was still very much in progress, but the one in Europe was nearing its end, with the Allies pushing the enemy back on all fronts.

Australia's most prestigious train at that time was *The Spirit of Progress* and travelling on it from Spencer Street station to Sydney, Dan had plenty of time to reflect on his good fortune. He was beginning to realise how incredibly lucky he was, one thing following another in smooth succession it was marvellous.

Dan reported to the Office of War Transport as soon as he arrived in Sydney and was taken by car to Pyrmont where he saw his new ship for the first time. She had graceful lines and, pre-war, had once been a fast, popular Italian liner from Mediterranean ports to Australia. She must have been a very comfortable vessel to travel in, with elegant furniture and ornate carvings to satisfy the tastes of her Italian clientele. She had been appropriated by the Australian Government when Italy joined Germany in the war, put into service as a troopship and renamed *Reynella* after the famous wine-producing district in South Australia. On this particular trip she was to take Army equipment, and specialist personnel to various outposts at the rear of the war zone, in what had been formerly the Dutch East Indies.

Reynella was twice the size of *Triona* and Dan had to become familiar with the labyrinth of her layout. She carried a Fourth Officer, so he was not back at the bottom. All the officers were Aussies, but the Captain was a New Zealander and something of a martinet. He tended to favour Dan as a fellow Kiwi because of his home address, which earned Dan the nickname of 'Blue-eye'. However, they all worked well together as a team, supervising the loading of Australian beer, cigarettes, tobacco and chocolate – all highly susceptible to pilferage. *Reynella* also had a full cargo of building equipment, medical supplies and tinned food, and after loading she sailed with a Great Barrier Reef pilot as well as a Sydney harbour pilot on her bridge.

A few days later, they were threading their way through the reefs, islets and outcrops of coral that make up the fascinating Great Barrier Reef en route to Torres Strait. Then, at Thursday Island, a launch transferred their pilot to a southbound ship and they proceeded towards Darwin. The heavy damage done, earlier on to that northerly outpost of Australia by Japanese bombers, was evident everywhere and some of the machinery required to rebuild was off-loaded from *Reynella*. They filled up with more Australian beer, destined for released prisoners of war, who were seemingly dying of thirst for Australian beer!

Leaving Darwin behind, the ship pressed cautiously on through the islands of the Timor and Banda Seas and past the fabulous Moluccas where Dan had once dreamed of being a pearldiver. The ravages of war were everywhere – wrecked guns, aircraft, jeeps and assault landing barges – although the lush jungle growth would soon completely conceal them.

At night, without coastal navigational aids or ship's radar, it was a nerve-wracking exercise to follow the assumed mine-free route laid down by the naval authorities. The Captain, a meticulous navigator himself, was supported by the experienced chief and second officers and Dan learned much from them. In daytime, the tension lessened, good visibility brought confidence, and in due time they reached Morotai, the northernmost island of the Halmahera group.

At the small settlement of Aru, the hard work of discharging half *Reynella*'s cargo was done by Japanese PoWs under the watchful eyes of Australian soldiers who were quite prepared to hand out the same sort of harsh treatment they had been subjected to. The Japanese accepted their fate and certainly didn't expect any favours.

Reynella's next port of call was Zamboanga, on the island of Mindanao in the southern Philippines, to off-load mail and beer for the men stationed there. On again through the Basilan Strait, Sulu Sea and Balabac Strait to reach Labuan where the ship was completely emptied out, again by the hard-working Japanese. Then the specialist personnel began to build tiers of bunks in the holds for the returning Aussie troops.

Those fellows had suffered all sorts of hardships and discomfort but after sailing from Labuan they still had to suffer; their toes were being nibbled by rats as they slept. The rats were bad enough in the officers' quarters, where they could be heard squealing and fighting behind the panelling, and here and there had chewed through the back of a chest of drawers to get at chocolate. Dan had often banged on the panelling alongside his bunk to frighten them away but they answered back with the rat equivalent of a raspberry. At night down on the galley deck where food was stored, the tiled floor was sometimes covered with the vermin. The troops, apart from killing them when they came within reach, could do little until they reached Australia. That wasn't very satisfactory for the men in the holds, but at least they could use their wits to combat the pests, and it helped to pass the time.

Apart from the rats, a happy mood prevailed as the troops rejoiced in the fact that they had survived the war and would soon be home. One man had a narrow escape even at that stage. Strictly against shipboard rules, he had jumped up to sit with his back to the sea on the shiny, varnished top rail of the quarterdeck. Next thing, he disappeared backwards overboard. The cry "Man overboard!" alerted the officer of the watch, a lifebuoy was thrown into the sea and the ship immediately started to turn round.

It takes a long time for a big ship at full speed to turn, but meanwhile the accident boat crew, with Dan in charge, got ready to be lowered into the sea as soon as they got near the man in the water. Hundreds of pairs of eyes kept the bobbing head in sight and eventually he was plucked from the sea. Like all his comrades his torso, before he fell into the water, was sunburnt to a rich nut colour, but when he was pulled out he was like chalk, grey with fear. He was lucky to have missed the port propeller when he fell, and then not to have fallen prey to the sharks and other grisly creatures that lurk in the Arafura Sea.

There were no further incidents to slow down *Reynella*'s progress and when the Barrier Reef pilot boarded at Thursday Island, he was given a rapturous welcome and cheered as though he had won the war single-handed. A few days later, they berthed at Brisbane where the wharves were crowded to give the returning servicemen a rousing Australian reception. There were wild scenes and Dan was thrilled to witness all the excitement, and unmitigated rapturous joy.

When all the Army equipment had been discharged, the officers and crew were accommodated ashore so that the ship could be fumigated. By the time she was declared safe to re-board, a few days later, over two thousand dead rats had been removed. *Reynella* went on to Sydney, the home port of his fellow officers, so again, Dan was ship-keeping officer while in port.

He was amused one evening while sitting in the ship's office reading the Sydney Morning Herald when a civilian came to ask if there were any rats still on board. Before Dan could reply there was a screech and a squeal from behind the panelling. "Do you need any further evidence than that?" asked Dan of the startled man, who then introduced himself as a Health Department officer. Clearly, another fumigation was necessary as already planned for the following day. For Dan it meant standing-by in a nearby hotel, and this was very pleasant because he had little to do and was on full pay.

At the shipping office, when paying off *Reynella*, Dan turned down the offer of another ship because he wanted to return to Auckland to sit for his master's certificate. In that event, the official said he could arrange for his repatriation; a troopship bound for Wellington would be calling at Melbourne the following week, how would that suit him? "That's absolutely marvellous!" said Dan. The obliging official wrote out a repatriation warrant to cover the rail journey to Melbourne and the Tasman crossing to Wellington. 'Wonderful,' thought Dan, 'How providential.'

Arriving at Melbourne's Spencer Street station Dan took a taxi to Port Melbourne and the Bakers' home in Albert Street. After a most enjoyable weekend reunion with his old friends, Sid Baker, who knew those things, announced the arrival of Dan's troopship the following day. At Station Pier Dan saw the familiar contours of a sleek Union Castle liner. The wartime grey paint couldn't disguise her lovely lines and to Dan it was like meeting an old friend now in uniform. When he reported on board he found her to be *Stirling Castle*, formerly a regular mail and passenger liner on the fast service from Southampton to South Africa.

It was a pleasant three day hop across the Tasman to Wellington and Dan enjoyed meeting the servicemen going home. Mostly they were New Zealanders, including Maoris, but there was a sprinkling of Tongans, Fijians and wounded Tahitian soldiers who put a brave face on their injuries, waving the stump of an arm or leg when the other Islanders strummed hula music on their guitars.

One afternoon, Dan was walking along the alleyway below-decks towards the baggage room, when who should he see coming towards him but the familiar figure of his old boxing opponent of *Queen Mary* days. The 'Wild Bull' recognised him immediately – after all, they had studied each other's faces often enough during their bouts, but this time, instead of shaping-up as they used to, they shook hands warmly. Later, over a drink in the crew bar, they swapped yarns. He, too, had improved his lot, now in the role of baggage master.

As *Stirling Castle* glided smoothly into her berth at Wellington, the wharves were crowded with cheering throngs, supported by a military band playing 'Maori Battalion'. It was all very stirring, but Dan would not feel completely at home until at last he met his dear Jessie. She was the same as ever, and was given a week's holiday from her job to celebrate Dan's safe return.

A Further Step On The Ladder

Dan went to the Navigation School in Auckland and six weeks later he passed the examinations for his master's foreign-going certificate. He and Jessie celebrated at a restaurant and the next day they went to Rotorua for the weekend to enjoy the warm mineral baths, explore the thermal wonderland, the trout pools and the beautiful lakes.

On returning from their holiday, Dan called at the Merchant Navy Officers' Guild, mainly to see if his subscriptions were up to date, and learned that a Second Mate was required for *Matai*. Although Dan knew nothing about the ship, to him, this was a direct invitation – he was more likely to be impulsive than dilatory. When he was introduced to *Matai*'s Master, Captain Webling, he was accepted and without further ado, signed on.

Matai belonged to the Marine Department and before the war she had been the Government lighthouse tender, servicing the many navigational aids around the coast of New Zealand and off-lying islands. She looked smart and reminded Dan of the lovely steam yachts at Cowes. She had served with the Royal New Zealand Navy in the South Pacific, but had now been returned for peacetime use.

Captain Webling and the Chief Officer were a great couple to serve under and all three men worked happily as a team. *Matai*'s first task was to dump tons of old ammunition from army stores in the Wellington area to sites in Cook Strait where depths of over five hundred fathoms were considered safe for the purpose. The manhandling of the heavy metal cases was done by army personnel and all that Dan had to do, apart from watch-keeping duties, was record the exact positions of the dumping spots, so that shipping could be notified, in current editions of Notices to Mariners.

If he had not been drawn into this pleasant local job, Dan, armed with his master's certificate, could have risen to the top of his profession quite rapidly. At that particular time, just after the end of the war and on into the next decade, opportunities for promotion were just the opposite to what they had been in the early 1930s. Then, redundant ship's captains had taken on lower deck positions, but now, and for a few years to come, there were instances of Chief Officers of large ships holding only a First or Second Mate's certificate.

Matai's next assignment was a couple of trips from Auckland to Norfolk Island with stores and motor fuel. Dan knew that some of the Bounty mutineers had been sent to Kingston, the penal settlement on Norfolk, and was keen to explore the place where there had been so much agony, cruelty and despair in its early days.

If misery and hopelessness can create an atmosphere that can linger for years, it had done so at Kingston, where a moaning wind through the pines reminded visitors of the anguish of guard and prisoner alike. Dan saw tombstones with the well-known names of Quintall, Adams and others of the Bounty story, and the hollow tree where legend had it, an escaped convict was able to avoid recapture for seven years. He also saw the bridge, reputed to be the grave of a particularly vicious guard who was caught unawares, chopped up by the convicts' shovels and mixed in with the stones and mortar of the bridge.

Following completion of these trips, *Matai* was to go to Timaru in the South Island and tow a hopper barge to Lyttelton, and there to add an oil barge and tow both to Auckland. That job would have been no problem for a well-equipped ocean-going tug, but *Matai* was in no way suitable, and would need good weather, good luck and good seamanship to succeed.

All went well, until abeam of Gisborne on the east coast of the North Island, when they were overtaken by a gale, a real 'southerly buster'. The tow-line parted during the night and by daylight there was no sign of either barge. With a screaming wind, heavy seas, spume and spray, visibility was limited even in daylight, and though the day was spent searching back and forth in a grid pattern there was no sign of the truants. At dusk, Captain Webling decided to give up and head into Gisborne to have *Matai*'s towing gear repaired. Everyone thought the barges had either crashed into one another and sunk, or that they had wrapped themselves around the low-lying Ariel Reef and become wrecks. A warning to shipping in the area was broadcast.

After the gale had passed, the weather improved rapidly and *Matai* resumed her voyage to Auckland, albeit rather shamefaced at losing her tows. However, the following morning, much to everyone's amazement, they sighted their charges still tethered together, rising and falling daintily in the heavy swell just south of East Cape, as though to say, where have you been? Dan calculated that the barges had travelled about eighty miles on their own, so Captain Webling had every reason to be thankful it had not been a northerly blow, but a fair southerly one. Of course, the Auckland newspapers made a big story of it: success, despite trials, complete with photographs of *Matai* and her erring barges sedately in line astern, now behaving themselves.

Even after that lesson, the naval authorities, no doubt short of suitable vessels for the task, gave *Matai* another, and possibly an even more hazardous assignment: towing two minesweepers to Sydney from Auckland Naval Base at Devonport.

Providing extra heavy towing gear, they had suggested taking the two in tandem until Captain Webling pointed out they would probably lose both. Respecting Captain Webling's long experience and judgment, it was agreed on one only at a time.

All went well until midway across the Tasman, when they ran into a deep depression with all the bad weather associated with it. Luckily the Pahau wasn't manned, for she broke adrift, her anchor cable, being used as part of the towing gear, snapped in her hawsepipe, leaving the whole length of remaining towing wire and cable, hanging down from *Matai*'s stern. In the appalling conditions, it was an extremely difficult and dangerous job to get the gear back on board, releasing it aft and trying to heave it up through the hawsepipe for'ard. When the drum of the windlass crumpled under the strain, the whole lot went snaking overboard at great speed. The Skipper was determined not to lose his tow and managed to keep her in sight, and with just enough speed to give steerage way, he did, until the weather moderated and preparations to board her were made.

The surf boat was launched and a heavy insurance wire was shackled on to the end of the remaining anchor cable of the minesweeper which was then slacked back until about sixty feet was hanging beyond the hawsepipe. Then her windlass was screwed up, and the towing gear firmly secured, before the men who had boarded the minesweeper got back to the surf boat and returned to *Matai*. Carefully, Captain Webling resumed the tow, and the remaining three hundred miles into Sydney harbour were safely navigated. Once inside the harbour limits, a naval tug made fast alongside the Pahau for her last few miles to Garden Island dockyard.

Again, it was headline news in the local newspapers, and marine artists made some extra income for themselves by recapturing the adventure on canvas; selling their first copies to *Matai*'s crew. Back in Wellington once more, *Matai* resumed dumping ammunition until the work ran out, after which she was laid up for Christmas. Dan returned to Auckland with Captain Webling's promise to let him know in the New Year about *Matai*'s future programme.

Though Dan had no idea of it, a new phase in his life was about to begin: he would not be returning to his 'plum' job on *Matai*.

The Best Of Two Worlds

While he was enjoying home life with Jessie and her parents, and knowing that an addition to the family was expected in April, Dan's adventurous spirit was temporarily converted to a more domesticated one and he began to think how nice it would be to stay ashore.

One day, on the spur of the moment, he called in at the Harbourmaster's office to see about getting a start in the Harbour Board. He met Mr Sid George, the H.M.'s pleasant and helpful secretary, who gave him an idea of the scope available to someone with a Master Mariner's certificate. Later, Dan was interviewed by the Harbourmaster, Captain Hogan, who showed a friendly interest, but said the only job he could offer at that time was relieving signalman at the Mount Victoria signal station. Dan, never one to dilly-dally, asked to be considered for the signalman's job, then hurried home with a buoyant heart to relate the news to Jessie, and collect his papers.

He had no need to worry: Sid George was moved to favour this young man's application and was simply playing his part in unfolding the next phase in Dan's life-plan. Dan's impetuous decision to try his luck, even though he was returning to the bottom of the ladder, was a wise one, as it gave him a toehold into the best of two worlds, nautical and shore, and was to provide him with the longest term of employment in one job in his life.

He thoroughly enjoyed the month he spent on shift work at the top of Mount Victoria. The signal station, with a glorious 360° panoramic view over Auckland, the whole Waitemata Harbour and the Hauraki Gulf from whence most shipping approached the port. The station was connected by radiotelephone and conventional phones to the Harbourmaster's office, the pilots and the pilot boat. The hardest part of the job was the walk up the steep roadway to get there, before it was made available to cars.

At the end of a month, Captain Hogan advised Dan that they needed a Mate for *William C. Daldy*, the larger of the two Harbour Board tugs – was he interested? All Dan's earlier ambitions of becoming Captain Robson of some ship in a good company had evaporated now that he was sampling married life in a nice home, so he said, "Yes, please sir," and became an understudy to Captain Bill Wright, regarded at that time as the best tug Skipper in New Zealand. Dan still couldn't bring himself to believe that his welfare was not solely his problem and just felt he was remarkably lucky.

There was much for Dan to learn before he could become relieving Skipper of the second and smaller of the two tugs, *Te Awhina*. Both jobs provided excitement and thrills when helping the harbour pilots to berth ships in the swirling tidal currents running across the line of the wharves. Prior to this, as an officer he hadn't had to do any real physical work, but as Mate on the tug, he was expected to handle the heavy tow ropes, which revitalised his muscles and made him feel all the better for it.

Dan and Jessie had been able to buy an attractive house in Prospect Terrace in the North Shore suburb of Milford, with a glorious view up the Hauraki Gulf to the Coromandel Peninsular. They had a grandstand view of all the shipping entering and leaving the port of Auckland, an ideal spot for an ex-seafarer to settle down ashore.

They enjoyed planning the furnishing of their first home and usually all was harmony, but one day Jessie asked Dan to pick up some curtain material she had ordered. The same afternoon *Matai* arrived in Auckland, and Dan decided he would just pop on board to say hello to his old shipmates. Captain Webling and the First Mate, delighted to see him again, produced a bottle of whisky. Despite Dan's protestations, they urged him to have just one for old times' sake and poured what to Dan seemed a very generous tot. Apart from the occasional glass of beer, Dan had never been able to take spirits, his stomach seemed to reject any excess of either, but here he was, cornered by two seasoned hosts set on having a good time. In between tots he kept thinking of his promise to take home the curtain material, so when a truck driver came to get the Mate's signature for some stores he had just delivered, Dan begged a lift. The driver agreed, but told Dan he would have to sit on the back of the truck as he already had two passengers in the cab.

Thanking his hosts and grabbing his small Gladstone bag, Dan unsteadily followed the driver and scrambled into the back while the driver fitted the tail-gate to make sure he didn't fall off. Dan was vaguely aware that sacks of flour had been unloaded and that he, in his pinstripe suit, was sitting on the spilt contents, and every time the truck stopped or started in the busy traffic he rolled around the deck because he had nothing to hold on to. By the time he was dropped off at George Court's, he looked like the Abominable Snowman.

With as much dignity as he could muster, he wobbled into the shop, found the right department and paid for the material, then he hurried to catch a tram to the lower end of Queen Street. As the tram rolled and swayed down the hill Dan, who had drunk several whiskeys, realised that the contents of his stomach were on the move and, in the nick of time, managed to open his small Gladstone bag to receive its delivery.

The sound was heard all along the tram and brought the conductress scurrying along, but Dan, ever gallant, reassured her with, "It's all right, my dear, it's in the bag!" She was very relieved and able to laugh at the reference to the popular weekly radio show of that name. Fortunately the curtain material was wrapped in a roll too long to go into his bag! Dan was late getting home and Jessie was shocked at his appearance, but he delivered the material and when he lay down on the settee before dinner he passed out.

She told him later that, seeing him like that, she wondered if he was showing his true colours now that they were on their own. By the following morning Dan had learned his lesson, his head felt like a forty-four gallon drum full of scrap iron being shaken every time he moved.

"NO," he assured Jessie, "Never again," would he be so foolish.

They were no sooner settled in their nice seaside home, with a bonny little daughter, Suzanne, to cheer their hearts and sometimes keep them awake at night, than Dan was offered the post of Skipper of the pilot boat *Waitemata*. A Harbour Board house was provided at a peppercorn rental on the pilot station at Cheltenham, handy to the defence wharf at North Head where *Waitemata* was normally berthed. That was the bottom rung of the ladder to the top of the tree – Harbourmaster – and Dan felt he must accept the job. He also wondered if he would ever get off the lower rungs of the success ladder, but he was enjoying the comforts of domesticity so much, he reckoned it was worth foregoing his earlier ambitions.

Neither he nor Jessie wanted to leave their home, but they realised their prospects would be better if they did. So they let the Milford property and moved to Takarunga Road, where they became one of the five families living on the pilot station. Each house was fitted with an intercom system, as well as external phones which they found to be both essential for the job, and very convenient.

The pilot boat was a sturdy little vessel, powered by a diesel engine, with a crew of three – Skipper, Engineer and Deckhand – and was such an excellent sea-boat that there was never any weather too bad for her to do her work. There were, however, many times, in storms, when to go alongside a ship out in the Gulf was an extremely hazardous affair. One of the dangers, with a rise and fall of ten to fifteen feet, was to get the pilot safely on to the rope ladder hanging down the ship's side and away from it again without catching the ladder with the boat's belting, bringing ladder and pilot crashing down. That never happened during Dan's fourteen years as Skipper, but in bad weather the possibility was always there.

He was proud of the fact that no one during his term of service, in all sorts of weather, was hurt, either boarding or disembarking. His particular delight was taking a pilot off a departing ship doing about ten knots when, at the same speed, he would approach the ladder close enough for the pilot to just step on board, without touching the bigger ship. That job as master of the pilot boat was the most congenial Dan had ever had, being in close touch with the sea and ships and yet home with wife and daughter. When not working, the pilot boat crew went home until needed again, and they could spend time with hobbies, gardening, studying or whatever appealed to them. Living together consistently for the first time since their marriage, Dan and Jessie became better acquainted with each other and found how well-suited they were, despite the fact that Jessie's background was quite different from Dan's.

She had been brought up in a good Methodist tradition, had been a member of the Pitt Street Church and choir, and a Girl Guide Captain. She was a keen Christian and while she never pressured Dan, she tried in her gentle way to get him to go with her and Suzanne to the Devonport Methodist church. He always teasingly said that it was only sinners that needed to go to church. In fact, at that time, he seemed to lean in the opposite direction, making home-brew, and organising Sunday afternoon table tennis parties on the back lawn with their neighbours, the pilot staff.

That must have been a worrying time for Jessie, but she believed the Scriptures and the first six verses in chapter three of Peter's first epistle, where he states that a wife with a quiet and gentle spirit, can win salvation for her husband without uttering a word. Jessie prayed that would one day happen, and of course it did in due time. Unknown to Dan, Jessie or anyone else, a Christian family in a two-storey house overlooking the lawn where the Sunday afternoon parties were held, also prayed for Dan's conversion and deliverance from his obvious worldliness. When it eventually happened, the same family were among the first to congratulate him and welcome him into the Lord's worldwide family.

With the success of the Sunday afternoon parties, Dan negotiated with the young proprietor of the Cheltenham Tea Kiosk to hold regular social evenings there with concerts, dancing and alcohol, all in accordance with local bye-laws and police requirements. The Cheltenham Social Club thus became a popular local attraction, and the young proprietor later progressed to become one of Auckland's leading restaurateurs.

Having accumulated rents from the Milford property, Dan could afford to buy a lovely two-storey, cedar weatherboard house at Narrow Neck, overlooking the main shipping channel and Rangitoto Island. He sold the Milford house and leased the Narrow Neck house to an elderly couple at a reasonable rent; they kept the lawns in order, and Dan did any maintenance work that became necessary. That happy relationship lasted five years, with Dan feeling that he was preparing the place for his retirement. Also, with retirement in mind, he and Jessie bought a beautiful section near Taipa, in the far north of the island, where the Taipa River runs into a picturesque bay with golden sands on both sides of the estuary.

During Dan's years of service on *Waitemata* there were several big occasions. One was the Royal Tour, with Queen Elizabeth and Prince Philip arriving on the Shaw Savill liner *Gothic*. *Waitemata* was dressed overall with flags, and the Harbourmaster performed the pilotage, but as *Gothic* was a regular visitor to New Zealand ports he had probably handled her many times before that royal occasion. Other notable arrivals were *Oriana* and *Canberra* on their maiden voyages, the square-rigged *Pamir* and a three-masted barquentine the *Esmeralda*, a Chilean Navy cadet ship. Another departure from the norm was the arrival of a British trampship which was crewed by young women, though the Deck and Engineer Officers were males. Later, still a further development was meeting a qualified female Captain with male officers and Chinese crew. What next? Some ship owners are operating large container ships with fewer than ten personnel, and aim to reduce even that skeleton number.

There were also some maritime mishaps which were part and parcel of the everyday handling of ships, and frequently there was storm damage, such as when the harbour dredge capsized off Cheltenham beach. The righting of that useful vessel took several weeks and provided a centre of attraction for the local residents.

A Change Of Lifestyle

Some pilots were born ship-handlers, but others found it a strain every time they stepped on board. Dan often noticed the build-up of tension before the job and the relief when it was completed. He could also see that by the time he had passed through the intermediate steps to become a pilot himself, he too might lack the nerve to do the work without undue strain.

He therefore nestled deeper into his own cosy role, where in many respects, he felt like a yacht owner without having to foot the bill. All he had to do was write out a chit for rope, shackles, equipment of all sorts, repairs, painting, dry-docking and it was all done by arrangement with the Harbourmaster. In that pleasant easy-going way the years rolled by, he could relax and carry on to retirement. He could see why the Harbour Board was regarded by some as an old men's home.

One of the pilots, Captain 'Rah' Smith, was regarded as a very religious man and everyone was careful not to offend, with bad language or indecent jokes when he was aboard. Sometimes, Mrs Smith and their grown-up daughters would come with him, or a group of Maori girls from the hostel that was part of the Christian outreach from their home church in Ellerslie. There would then be a truly joyous singing of hymns and Christian songs, with guitar accompaniment, and everyone who heard them was impressed with the lovely rhythmic tunes.

Dan, in his ignorance, wondered if such singing and laughter was in keeping with Christianity, but came to know it was certainly appropriate, it was his conception of religion that was out of touch. Nevertheless, those outings made an impact on his dormant spirit, and when Mrs Smith and her husband took the opportunity to 'witness' to Dan, sometimes directly by explaining a verse in the Gospel, he got an insight into what they believed in so strongly.

Dan began to look forward to the visits of the Smith family, having the utmost respect and admiration for Captain Smith as an excellent pilot, but also the straightforward, unaffected way he combined his work with his religion. On top of that, he was a very practical man, as evidenced by work-hardened hands with a few missing fingers, his circular saw getting the blame.

Jessie was interested to hear Dan's reports of the Bible discussions and when he said that at last he saw what they were getting at, she resisted the temptation to say, "I told you so." She was in fact excited at the interest Dan was showing in scriptural topics, and confided in Mrs Smith how much she appreciated the effort they were putting into bringing him into the Light of Salvation.

It just so happened that the 1959 Billy Graham Crusade to New Zealand was due, and while Dan showed no interest in it whatsoever, he couldn't help hearing the Smiths as they enthusiastically discussed their plans for taking part. Something in Dan reacted negatively to the whole idea, and he tried to fob off the efforts of Jessie and the Smiths to get him to attend. Underneath his assumed indifference, however, he planned to go along just to see what all the hullabaloo was about, putting on a long suffering air of martyrdom as a cover.

At Carlaw Park, he was amazed to see so many people milling through the gates; anybody would think they were going to a football match, thought Dan. At the same time he realised, as he and Jessie were jammed in the crowd, that even if he wanted to, he couldn't change his mind, there would be no chance of moving against that human tide. He also noticed that the atmosphere was different; he could hear music in the distance and the sound of massed singing. It could be more interesting than he had thought.

They were eventually squeezed into a space where the seating was simple planks on low log supports. Everyone seemed in an incredibly jovial mood, and when the whole crowd stood to sing, 'How Great Thou Art' and 'Amazing Grace', Dan, despite his plan to appear untouched, was strangely moved and thought the words were wonderfully meaningful. The preacher claimed that Jesus was sent to earth on God's behalf to save sinners, and that it did not matter how much we had sinned, He could wipe our slates clean and make us as if we had never sinned at all. This seemed almost too good to be true. The preacher read many verses from the scriptures to support his claim, furthermore he went on to say that all we had to do was accept this wonderful offer, because we could not get it any other way than through Jesus.

'Well,' thought Dan, 'I know I am a sinner for sure, so I qualify for this gift of salvation: how wonderful, how marvellous.' He really had laid hold of God's message. He was enveloped in a sense of peace and joy, such as he had never experienced before, and although he did not know anything about it at the time, he was 'born-again' by God's Holy Spirit entering his human spirit. He was carried away by a sense of peace and joy, a feeling that continued throughout Billy Graham's message – so much so, that when the appeal came to make a decision for Christ, he would have missed its significance had it not been for a dear old lady seated next to him. She gave him a terrific nudge in the ribs and in a stentorian voice, quite out of keeping with her frail form, she shouted, "Go on, young man, what are you waiting for?" Dan rose to his feet and went forward, and as he passed, he saw she wore a faded Salvation Army uniform, and she roared, "Hallelujah," in an exhilarating manner to stimulate his spirit.

When Dan walked forward with many others that night, it seemed a dream, then he became conscious of a young man at his elbow muttering unintelligible phrases. Dan wondered who he was and why he was disturbing his peace, but as he noticed others paired in a similar manner, he realised the young man was a member of the organisation, fulfilling his duty.

Dan was led into a tent where he was asked if he sincerely wished to grow in the Lord now that he had mouthed the sinner's prayer, repented of his past sins and received Jesus into his heart? Dan found himself eager to respond and say "Yes!" very firmly. He felt that was a turning point, he had had enough dithering in the past, and was keen to enjoy the born-again experience that Billy Graham had described. From that moment, he knew he was a new man in Christ, a brand new creation indeed. He cooperated with the counsellors, supplying them with his name and address, and then hurried back to Jessie. She was still where he had left her, but the Salvation Army lady had gone, as had most of the crowd. Jessie said she had thanked the old lady for her action, tantamount to nudging her husband into the Kingdom of God, and that had pleased the dear old soul greatly.

The following day was a Sunday, and Dan, meditating on the significance of his commitment, felt a new kind of joy. He broke the news to a neighbour on the other side of the road whom he knew to be a regular churchgoer, but he got a shock when the man showed no interest at all, saying he thought such Crusades were emotional publicity stunts designed to raise money. A cold, lifeless, stony response designed to dampen the ardour of any new Christian.

Later in the day, his confidence was restored when the eldest daughter of the family in the two-storey house next door called at Dan and Jessie's door. That in itself was remarkable for a very conservative family, but she said, "We, that is, my family, are so pleased to hear that you have been saved, we have been praying for your salvation for a long time, you know."

Dan could only mutter, "No, I didn't know, but thanks anyway." He was bewildered that anyone, especially anyone as remote as those folk, would bother to pray for him or anyone else. He found out later that one of the counsellors at Carlaw Park was a member of that family, and had recognised Dan when he made his commitment. He also found that the family was intimately involved in a section of the Christian church known as the Close Brethren – lovely people though usually very reserved and uncommunicative.

Another surprise came when the same family invited Dan and Jessie to an all-day seminar on Queen's Birthday Monday at a large hall in Auckland. Jessie was anxious to encourage her husband as much as she could, and as he was keen to see what the meeting was about, they accepted.

It was quite different from those meetings Dan had attended at Houston and other places in the Gulf. This was a sedate affair, with the whole day spent studying the Bible, and while Dan didn't know 1 John from John 1, he found it all fascinating. He was further impressed with the orderly manner in which the discussions and even the meal breaks were organised. These people seemed to know the Bible off by heart and sought to extract deep meanings from the readings. A panel of elders dealt with any unresolved questions, and Dan was impressed with the humble manner in which they all summed up and delivered their findings. Dan and Jessie were treated as part of the family and Dan learned a lot from that experience.

A complete change came over his life after going forward that night to receive Jesus Christ as his Saviour and Lord. He discovered a hunger for studying the Scriptures which he had never had before, though he had been obliged to read them as a boy at home and at school. He started memorising Bible verses to get those jewels of wisdom firmly into his mind. He found they were so true – "old things pass away, all things are become new" – in that swearing dropped away overnight, so did his fiery short temper, and since he lost interest in making home-brew, his desire for the worldly pleasures of the Club waned too. He handed over control to his deputy, and some of his associates reckoned that his next step was a monastery or a mental home, such opinions and comments leaving Dan blissfully unconcerned.

He knew he had found a pearl of great price, what else mattered? There were no more table tennis/home-brew parties on Sundays – Dan needed to feel squeaky-clean, and if he heard of an evangelical meeting anywhere on his off duty days, he was off like a shot. In his innocence and ignorance, he went forward at any altar calls to be doubly sure that he had left nothing undone. He was just like many other new-born Christians, zealous in stressing to all the vital necessity of their own salvation, which, of course, had the effect of driving some further into their rejection of the Truth. He had yet to learn not to make the mistake many new Christians make of spiritually mugging people.

Now when the Smiths came for a trip, especially when they brought a group of Maori girls, it became a joyous occasion with plenty of singing, laughter and rejoicing, which Dan encouraged as a witness to the engineer and deckhand. The visitors now regarded him as one of the family, referring to him as "brother," and they explained that they were "Open Brethren," not the same as "Close Brethren" though with the same basic beliefs. It puzzled him, until he learned of the different viewpoints separating the various denominations.

Even at that early stage in his Christian walk, he felt it was somehow distasteful to the head of the Church, the Lord Jesus Christ, for anyone to align themselves to one particular section of His family to the exclusion of all the others. That attitude, which other brothers and sisters regarded as peculiar, remained with him for the rest of his life.

As the eyes of his understanding opened, it was revealed to him that all born-again believers ARE ONE BODY and united in the New Covenant, though they persist in labelling themselves with various denominational names.

The Uprooting

Life in the pilot service stayed much the same; although some people steered clear of Dan, others were curious about what had happened to him, as he reconsidered his plans for the future.

With the best of motives, Dan was about to make the common mistake of so many newly-saved people, in looking for full time Christian service in one form or another. In gratitude for their transformed lives, they earnestly seek to please their Saviour by so doing, but if it is not God's will that they should do these things, then they should remain where they are, until called by Him.

Dan wondered if he should study to play some active part in church life, feeling he was wasting precious time where he was. He chose not to see the example set by Captain Smith, who devoted his off duty time to Christian work, yet earned his and his family's livelihood, in the secular job in which he excelled. Not being gifted with Smithy's talents, he would have to think of something else. It occurred to Dan that he might be able to become a Missioner in a seamen's welfare organisation, so he contacted the Superintendent of the British Sailors' Society at their Mission on the Auckland waterfront.

He found Mr McLean was not only a dedicated born-again Christian, but also an ardent soul seeker for the Lord among seafarers. Mac gave Dan a warm welcome and invited him to visit the club so that he could see what went on. Dan liked the fatherly man, the goodwill was mutual and they got along very well together. To judge his sincerity, Mac invited Dan to give his testimony in various suburban churches and chapels to raise money for a new and bigger Mission on the waterfront. Dan's colleagues in the pilot service were now, more than ever, convinced that he was going round the bend. They felt he should think more of Jessie and Suzanne, now aged fourteen, so he compromised, with one of his days off for them, and the other for Mac and the Mission. He didn't realise it, but by engaging in the Mission work, he was loosening his roots in the Harbour Board and preparing for a change.

Those close to him in the Pilot Service could see the change in him, and the senior pilot, Captain Carter, a particularly close friend, was concerned that he might give up his good job. He pointed out that at the age of fifty it would be unwise for Dan to throw away his security for a dream. Dan could see his point of view, but when his spiritual guide, Captain Smith, said more or less the same thing, Dan was quick to quote the Scriptures he had learned from Smithy himself, namely, "Jesus said, Fear not, for I am with you" and, "If we have faith we have no need to fear." Through his association with Mac, Dan met the overseer of the British Sailors' Society's work in New Zealand, the gentlemanly Revd Raymond Phillips. That fine, godly man expressed his willingness to help Dan get established as an assistant Missioner, but there were no openings anywhere in New Zealand at the time. Dan, wondering whether it would be wiser to stay in his present job until he could step straight into an opening, nevertheless took the plunge and sent in his letter of resignation. He told Revd Phillips that he had a strong urge to return to his homeland to see what was available there in some maritime venture, so Mr Phillips compiled for him some letters of introduction.

With some understandable reluctance from Jessie and Suzanne, they sold their lovely house at Narrow Neck, and booked a three-berth cabin on the liner *Southern Cross* leaving Wellington at the end of January 1962. At that point, Dan heard that he had won a building society ballot, which meant an interest-free loan of two thousand pounds. He opted for the alternative – two hundred pounds in cash – and withdrew his deposit, having to show their Shaw Savill bookings first. That bonus, which almost covered the cost of their fares, seemed to Dan, a nod of approval, a real blessing of the Lord.

It was only natural that even in the glow of impending departure, there should be a certain amount of misgiving and sadness, when their friends said goodbye at the Auckland railway station. There was no stepping back, the break was made, and after an overnight stay in Wellington, they boarded *Southern Cross*. The unknown future lay ahead, but in between lay Sydney, Melbourne, Fremantle, Durban, Cape Town, Las Palmas, Vigo and Southampton.

Dan was really looking forward to being at sea again, especially now he had his wife and daughter with him. From their very comfortable, well-positioned cabin on the Promenade deck, they would sally forth to enjoy shipboard life and seek fellowship with the other passengers. It was wonderful. In Sydney, he was able to renew his former friendship with his Canadian friend Charlie, now with wife and family, and at Melbourne he introduced Jessie and Suzy to his old friends Mother Baker and Shirl – Sid had passed on years before. In Fremantle, they saw where the little *Piri* berthed after discharging her explosives at Woodman's Point, and they did a scenic coach tour of Perth.

Crossing the Indian Ocean, the usual sports fixtures were organised, and with so many nationalities among the passengers they were able to hold a mini-Empire Games, with contests as keenly fought as though gold medals were at stake. One boxing bout was a surprise to many, a rather effeminate steward nicknamed Marilyn, was matched with a rugged looking Kiwi, but Marilyn wasn't only a first class steward, he was also a first rate boxer, and made his opponent look like a novice, a fact the New Zealander gracefully acknowledged. This same fellow, Marilyn, had won a commendation from the Mayor of Sydney for diving into the harbour at night when he saw a child fall overboard from the ferry on which he was travelling. His unhesitating response won the praise of the ferry passengers, and to those who knew this, it confirmed the truth of the old adage, "You can't judge a book by its cover."

Apart from all the entertainment, Dan was even more interested in seeking out fellow Christians among the passengers, sometimes by noting the titles of books they were reading, he was eager to get advice on the furtherance of his quest for service. He located several missionary families returning to their fields of service in Africa, and he was especially interested in hearing their testimonies. He encouraged them to organise meetings for the benefit of interested passengers, and even disinterested ones attended to hear the Gospel that changes lives and causes some, to become missionaries.

At Durban, with his family, Dan went sightseeing, and while impressed with the beauty of the city and surrounding countryside, they were very conscious of an underlying air of hatred, suspicion and sorrow.

In Cape Town, Jessie went shopping while Dan and Suzy took the cable car to the top of Table Mountain, which was a thrill of a lifetime, suspended as they were at times over deep ravines and jagged rocks in a seemingly fragile gondola. They enjoyed the spectacular views from the summit and saw in the distance their ship *Southern Cross* like a toy in the docks. Later, as they left the harbour, Dan was thrilled to see the familiar, elegant lines of *Stirling Castle*, now back in her peacetime colours, another instance of a seaman's love affair with the contour of a favourite ship.

Las Palmas, and Vigo came and went with just brief shopping trips ashore, then the end of warm sunny weather, and they were in the cold grey waters of the English Channel with the icy winds of early March to welcome them.

After twenty-three years, Dan was back in his native land, much better off in every respect than when he had left it. He was spiritually born-again, he had a lovely wife and daughter, a Master Mariner's foreign-going certificate and a healthier bank balance. Jessie had left the United Kingdom as a little girl in 1923, so everything was new to her.

Dan's sister Connie, her husband and family, were waiting to greet them behind the barriers at Southampton, and it took two cars to take them all, plus the luggage, to Little Chalfont in Buckinghamshire. It was wonderful to see the English countryside in its wintry setting, the leafless trees with their delicate branches coated with hoarfrost, all shrouded in a still and silent grey mist.

Dan's brother-in-law, Stan, insisted on making a couple of comfort stops on the way, and Dan found those old pubs with their warm and friendly atmosphere, very different from the 'watering holes' of Australia and New Zealand. He realised that what drew the regulars, was not so much the alcohol, but the companionship. Dan sampled a Watney's brown ale, an old favourite, while Jessie had a sherry and Suzanne a lemonade.

During their first week in Little Chalfont, snow covered everything. Dan and family were enchanted with it. He showed them some of the sights of London, including the Tower, and introduced them to English pork pies, Chelsea buns and other delicacies, at Lyon's Corner House in the Strand.

Later, when they visited Dan's birthplace at High Wycombe, they tasted lardy cake, a Buckinghamshire speciality, it was thrilling to be back;

Breathes there any man, with soul so dead
Who never to himself hath said,
This is my own, my native land.[2]

The time came when Dan remembered what he had come to Britain for, not a leisurely holiday, but the call to Christian service. Armed with his letters of introduction, he sallied forth, feeling fairly confident that the Lord would lead him into the right place. He was naïve, unaware of being presumptuous and likely to barge in where angels fear to tread.

He visited the offices of all the seamen's welfare organisations he could find and even went to addresses outside London, but everywhere met the same polite statement that there were no vacancies as the demand for their work was shrinking. He remembered the story of Gladys Aylward and the fantastic missionary work she accomplished in China despite being considered unsuitable and unwanted. It was, in a way, comforting to know that rejection was as commonplace when seeking Christian work as with secular, but depressing all the same.

Someone suggested the Sea Training School at Dover, so in the Morris Traveller he had bought, Dan set off with Jessie and Suzanne one Monday morning, only to be told when they got there, that there was nothing doing. With this failure at Dover, Dan had the distinct impression that he was out from under the cosy protective covering he had enjoyed in the Harbour Board, and the continuing idea of it, in the letters of introduction. How right he was, "Back to square one."

Some wise mortal said, 'Man's extremity is God's opportunity,' and the truth of that was about to be demonstrated in Dan's case, as indeed it had been in Hong Kong those years before.

They decided to stay overnight in Dover, and take a leisurely jaunt along the south coast to Southampton. En route, Dan could show his wife and daughter the scenes of his boyhood at Brighton

---

[2] Canto 6, st. 1 by Sir Walter Scott

and Chichester. They stopped at Arundel to let Suzy see the fairy story castle, home of the Duke of Norfolk, then Goodwood House, the home of the Duke of Richmond, nestling at the foot of the South Downs. In Chichester, Dan took them to his old home, the Market Restaurant, which had lost none of its charm, and The Golden Fleece next door.

They stayed at the Dolphin Hotel overnight, where their little Morris Traveller looked somewhat out of place among the classier cars parked in the courtyard. Then they continued on to Southampton thirty miles away, the following morning.

When they arrived at Southampton, they all noticed an inexplicable lift of their spirits. They booked into a modest hotel in Brunswick Place and Dan bought a copy of the local paper which he found to be full of interest: shipping movements, situations vacant, houses for sale – all relevant to his present situation. Dan had been away from Southampton for twenty-three years, a war had intervened, parts of the city he had known had been obliterated by bombing and now rebuilt. He didn't know anyone he could go to for advice, but of course he did know One, who was not only acquainted with the present, but with the past and future too, so he appealed to Him now in prayer.

He admitted to the Lord, as if He didn't know, that he had done his best to find some form of Christian service, but without success. His own efforts had failed, would He please take over?

The next morning, Dan got the bright idea of calling at the Merchant Navy Officers' Association. He had no difficulty finding the place, and he told one of the girls in the front office that he was looking for a job. He was ushered into the office of Captain Jackson, the secretary, whose first question was, "Are you a member of the Association?"

Dan wasn't, so Captain Jackson said that, if he needed their help he would have to join, and suggested that he complete an application form which the girls in the outer office would give him. Dan was rather taken aback by the comfortless reception, but thanked the man and left his office. He was back in England!

Made To Measure?

Before he could ask the girls for an application form, they asked him in a whisper how he had got on. When he told them, they said, "Didn't he say anything about a job going here?" Dan, bewildered, said no, and they chorused, "Why not have a try for it?"

"I would if I knew what it was and how to apply," said Dan.

They explained that Captain Jackson was a sick man and was being retired before time. His second-in-command was moving up, but that would leave the post of assistant secretary vacant, and if Dan was interested, he should apply to Head Office at Oceanair House in London right away.

Over a cup of tea in a café, the family decided Dan should give it a go, that things looked promising. Jessie and Suzy liked what they had seen of Southampton, and felt they could settle down there quite happily.

When they got back to Little Chalfont and related the story to Connie and Stan, they found it hard to imagine why those girls in the office should be so helpful to a stranger, it was most uncharacteristic of the conservative English nature.

The following Monday at Oceanair House, Dan asked to see the secretary of the Association. He was first taken to meet Miss Preston, Captain Tennant's secretary, who gave Dan a searching scrutiny. Dan had the feeling he had been read like a book from cover to cover, but they got into a harmonious and frank discussion which seemed to auger well, and after only a few minutes he was shown into the secretary's office.

Captain Douglas Tennant was a fine man in his mid-fifties with a warm, friendly personality that impressed Dan right away. He came straight to the point: why was Dan seeking employment in the M.N.O.A? Was he tired of going to sea? Where had he been serving up to now?

Then, after a glance at the application form, "I see you're from New Zealand. Why did you leave that lovely country to come here?" Dan felt he couldn't discuss his Christian aspirations, so he simply said he had always been interested in the welfare of seafarers and had, in fact, at one stage, been an official in the Auckland Harbour Board Employees' Union.

That was like the magic key to the door, and Captain Tennant suddenly seemed to take more interest, but continued studying the Application Form, deep in thought. Then he stunned Dan by saying, "If we do consider you for a post in the Association, would you be prepared to go to any part of the UK?"

What prompted him to say what he did he'd never know, but Dan said, "Well not exactly, sir. I wouldn't want to be stationed on the Tyne, for instance." A cloud came over the secretary's face.

"Why ever not, it's one of the best parts of England?" The penny dropped: the secretary was a Geordie, a Tynesider! Dan was horrified, he had mistaken his accent for a Scot, and struggled to recover some of the goodwill by saying that he still had some miserable memories of his early apprenticeship days.

The weak excuse was apparently accepted, as Captain Tennant said, "Yes, I can guess what you mean and such things are not easily forgotten. I shall confer with my committee, and advise you of the outcome." Throughout the interview, no mention was made of Dan's visit to Southampton since his given home address was Little Chalfont over sixty miles away.

Dan, on his way home via the underground to Euston Station thence by train, felt so elated he 'shouted' himself a Guinness and a tasty pork pie. After all his earlier disappointments, he felt really happy, on top of the world.

When he got home, the womenfolk could see by his glowing face that he had some encouraging news, and by the end of the week instructions came for him to report for training to Captain Lionnet at Oceanair House. Here was another kindred spirit; Dan and 'France' Lionnet hit it off right from the start. He also met Bill Robinson, already an official with the Association stationed at South Shields, but now on an extended course of training for promotion.

Dan revelled in that month of training, learning how to be an officer's representative under the guidance of Captain Lionnet, a Channel Islander, and former Suez Canal pilot. The three of them spent their time calling on as many officers as they could, on as many ships as they could, from the Pool of London to Tilbury, Thameshaven and beyond to the Isle of Grain where oil tankers abounded. During the week, Bill and Dan lived in a boarding house at Wanstead, all expenses including travel being met by the M.N.O.A., except weekend home visits.

At the end of training, Head Office decided that it would be more economical to appoint Dan to fill the vacancy at Southampton, and retain Bill at South Shields where he was established with the regulars on the Tyne and had his home. It seemed strange that Dan should have raised that objection about Tyneside, when he knew that if he had been offered a post anywhere by, say, the Mission to Deep Sea Fishermen, he would have jumped at it and could have been sent to some far-flung fishing harbour with extremely meagre wages. Whereas here he was appointed as assistant secretary to an organisation dealing with his own profession, in his own familiar and favourite port of the land. It seemed as though it was the fulfilling of that part of the scriptures where it says, "Now unto Him who is able to do exceedingly abundantly more than we ask or think..."

The family travelled down to Southampton in the Morris Traveller and booked into a boarding house. When Dan arrived at the M.N.O.A. office the next morning, he saw the two girls in the outer office and had the greatest pleasure in telling them how he had followed their advice. They all agreed to keep the secret and Dan thanked them with a box of chocolates each.

Later on, Mr Thomas, the new secretary who had taken Captain Jackson's place, introduced him to Jill and Jennie, and everyone smiled and said a polite hello as though they had never seen one another before.

Dan's work involved visiting all British ships in port to call on the officers to see if they were members of the Association and if not, to encourage them to join. To members, he would give a copy of the latest Ship's Telegraph, full of interesting maritime news, and also make available the many services the Association provided. Any pay or service disputes which were beyond his capacity to deal with, Dan would undertake to get a ruling from Head Office. It was a job for which he was ideally suited. He liked talking to the men, listening to their complaints or to their fears for the future of the industry. Yet in all his travelling around the docks, he never met any men he had known in the past.

He met many intriguing characters. One was a Chief Engineer of a large Union Castle liner, a bachelor who, because of his position, was able to take his well-behaved cat on board with him as a permanent traveller. The cat had its own quarters, complete with toilet box, sandpit, scratching post and enclosed promenade deck, and round its neck was a single strip of gold braid with purple edging to distinguish him as engine-room staff rather than just any old moggy. Another Chief Engineer, of a P.O. liner, had no need to go to sea for a living, since his family were the wealthy owners of a leading tea importing company. He made Dan's day on one occasion, by paying his association fees two years in advance.

Dan always got a thrill at being able to board his old ship *Queen Mary* to discuss matters concerning their welfare with the officers. He was surprised to find that some of them, underneath their authoritative exteriors, were as union-minded as miners or dockers. With the expansion of passenger air services across the North Atlantic, it was obvious that liner travel would decline and ships which in the past had been so popular and profitable would be laid-up and their personnel made redundant. The shipping companies were not keen on giving generous endowments to departing servants, no matter what rank they held or how long they had served. One senior Commodore was so disgruntled with the company's retirement plan for him, that he vowed to expose it to the press. He declared he was going to have his photograph taken at the head of the dole queue in Liverpool with a placard inscribed, "Thank you, Cunard."

Dan could empathise with them, looking back over thirty-five years at that point in which he had witnessed the almost complete destruction of the British Merchant Navy as a result of the Depression, then a fairly rapid recovery towards the Second World War. Then decimation as a result of that, followed by another resurgence cresting in the mid-fifties, and now the curve was waning to a point when, in a few years, the Red Ensign would become as rare as once it had been prominent.

Almost two years passed by, during which enthusiasm and acquired Australasian boldness enabled Dan to sign on more new members than had hitherto been the case in Southampton, a fact which brought a letter of commendation and thanks from Captain

Tennant. Dan was immensely pleased with that, it seemed to justify his being given the job, and Jill and Jennie were equally pleased that they had had a hand in bringing it about.

For Dan, everything had gone so well. With the money they had brought from New Zealand, he and Jessie had been able to buy outright a two-storey, three-bedroom brick house in a cul-de-sac off the main Bitterne Road. Then they had been able to startle a salesman in a modest shop in downtown Southampton by selecting a houseful of furniture and furnishings, and paying cash on the spot. That made the salesman's day!

Nevertheless, Dan hadn't lost sight of his original purpose in coming to Britain – full time Christian service – and that objective now resurfaced. He had kept in touch with Mr McLean in Auckland, and when he mentioned to Dan that a new British Sailors' Society Mission was soon to be opened in the South Island, the news played on Dan's conscience. Were all the blessings he was now enjoying to be thrown away? Why had he got the news about the new Mission now, when he was taking root in very pleasant and promising circumstances? Was he being tested by the Lord to see if his earlier commitment to serve Him was to be overwhelmed by the comforts of worldly work? Dan was in a quandary and prayed earnestly for guidance.

A few weeks later, Mr Thomas retired on account of ill-health and his place was taken by a younger man. The harmony of the office was disrupted and Dan decided that if he was offered the South Island post he would accept it and resign from the M.N.O.A. Following the advice of Revd Raymond Phillips in Auckland, he had applied to their Head Office in London for the British Sailors' Society job. With his background, knowledge of New Zealand conditions, and support of the Society's chief representative there, Dan felt he had a good chance, and it came as no real surprise when he was appointed Superintendent of the new Mission.

At the interview at the B.S.S. Head Office in London's East End, Dan wondered whether he was doing the right thing, and for a reason he did not understand at the time, he offered to pay his own and family's passages all the way to Bluff. These fares were considerable, since it is almost impossible to travel farther away from London than Bluff.

To show their appreciation, the General Secretary arranged for Dan to be measured for a good quality brass-button uniform. Later, they advised Dan that he and his family were booked to travel on the *Ruahine* sailing in two months' time, via Curacao, Panama, and Tahiti.

With all this settled amicably, Dan faced the less pleasant task of giving notice to those who had been so kind to him at Oceanair House, two years previously. In the bus he said a silent prayer, but he knew the answer was simply to tell the truth, it all sounded so horribly ungrateful for being taking on in the first place, and he felt absolutely awful.

Douglas Tennant looked intently at Dan for a few moments and then said, "Has Southampton office got anything to do with your decision, Dan? I can easily get you transferred up here to the London docks."

Dan replied, "I'm sorry, sir. Much as I would enjoy working the London docks, the die is cast and I must go." They parted on the best of terms and Dan volunteered to be the Association's unpaid representative in New Zealand.

During his final month with the Association, Dan said goodbye to the men he had met on such fine ships as the *Caronia*, the *Chusan*, the *Windsor Castle* and many others, not knowing that within a few years most of the ships and men would be redundant. Dan felt a particular sympathy for the older officers on ships like the *Carmania* and the *Carinthia* who seemed to be as much a part of a well-established vessel as the well-worn leather upholstery of their wardrooms – well-polished from long service.

Jill and Jennie were sad that Dan was leaving. He had always got on well with them, never adopting the superior attitude so commonplace in some offices in those days. On the other hand, the secretary, while expressing disappointment at Dan's departure, was probably relieved. He proved useful, as it happened, because he bought quite a lot of Dan's and Jessie's furniture.

Connie and Stan couldn't understand why Dan should quit such a good position, adding significantly, "We hope you know what you're doing!" He didn't!

After they sold their house Dan, Jessie and Suzy, and their Sheltie dog, set off for a tour of Scotland. They enjoyed their trip to Edinburgh, Pitlochry and Inverness, returning south via the western

Highlands, sleeping in the little Morris Traveller each night. Dan included in his itinerary a visit to the real Stirling Castle.

While Dan still had mixed feelings on sailing from London, Jessie and Suzy were happy to be returning homewards. They called at Curacao in Dutch Guiana for fuel oil and a chance for the passengers to see the sights. Then it was on to Panama, a new experience for Suzy but not for her parents. The glorious weather continued all the way to Tahiti, where going through the entrance in the reef brought back memories for Dan. Papeete looked just the same, with the traditional Tahitian welcome on the wharf.

It was mid-morning when *Ruahine* made fast to the wharf. Dan had learned that Papa Sharood had long since passed on to his eternal rest and that his daughters had married and had left Tahiti. However, Elise, a close family friend, entertained them during their brief stay. They spent the afternoon at Papenoo beach and the evening at Elise's home near Venus Point. Dan and his family enjoyed true Tahitian hospitality, sitting on raffia pillows at a low table and eating a sumptuous meal by candlelight. The visitors had no idea what was in the dishes, and their hosts didn't know the English words to tell them. The guests wondered if they might have been eating sea snails, or squid, or octopus, but since everything tasted delicious they didn't worry about it too much.

When they returned to *Ruahine*, Elise and her family accompanied them on board for a quick look round, and it was Dan's turn to show his appreciation of their kindness with gifts of chocolates and other sweets.

When the customary call was made for all visitors to go ashore Dan, Jessie and Suzy were bedecked with leis and given baskets full of fruit. The bananas lasted all the way to New Zealand and were enjoyed by all their shipboard friends, particularly a London family who thought it was wonderful to visit the South Sea Islands they had read so much about.

The 'Dream' Evaporates

Apart from the usual shipboard frolics on that voyage of *Ruahine*, an amusing incident remains in the memory of Dan and Jessie. Among their fellow passengers, they had at their table, a young Scottish engineer from Dundee. His accent was such that he was difficult to understand. He made it known that he was emigrating to New Zealand, and was engaged to one of his countrywomen already living in Invercargill.

Another passenger sharing the dining table was a Lancashire lass, a nurse with a brogue as broad as the Pacific ocean, she seemed to understand Scottie better than anyone else, and he likewise had no difficulty conversing with Helen. The shipboard romance developed to such an extent that by the time *Ruahine* reached Wellington, Scottie had proposed to and had been accepted by Helen. Being of Scottish descent, Dan was rather shocked at Scottie's instability, and although he had experienced awkward moments in his lifetime, he was glad that he was not in Scottie's shoes arriving in Wellington with his former fiancée waiting for him on the wharf.

The passage from the Friendly Islands to Wellington gave Dan time to think about the future. Perhaps it was just as well that he was unaware of what lay ahead. His dream of full-time Christian service was about to be fulfilled, but it was also about to be shattered, and all because of misunderstanding on both sides. Dan expected to be the Superintendent of the kind of Mission he had seen in operation all over the world, to be a witness to the Christian faith on which the British Sailor's Society work was based. This, apparently, was not the concept of the local people who had a different view. They had been responsible for the fund-raising and building of the Southland Merchant Navy Centre, which in their eyes, was a club with wholly worldly activities, for visiting seamen, and it was a pity Dan was unaware of this, or he would not have given up his M.N.O.A. job and intruded.

By the time Dan arrived on the scene, a large group of enthusiastic volunteers was already running the club, and they had neither asked for, nor wanted anyone from anywhere, least of all England, to take control. This was perfectly understandable. They were a very clannish group of people determined to support one another in a dispute, though separately contentious, they would not allow any 'outsider' to push them around, and would stick together come what may, so the stage was set for friction right from the start.

The British Sailors' Society was unaware of that attitude and gave the club its blessing, and the prestige of the Society name and flag. Head Office might have thought that appointing a Superintendent from London would make an impression on the good people of Southland and encourage them to give their financial support to the project. The next step came when it was suggested to Dan by one of the many committees, that if he left the running of the club to the volunteers, he could sit back and devote himself to travelling around Southland raising money with talks at the various churches, clubs and other organisations. Dan's eyes were then truly opened to their idea of his role, which was of course in direct contrast to his, and although he tried desperately to adjust, he grew so disillusioned, frustrated, and disappointed, that after six months he resigned.

To his surprise, his resignation caused consternation, and the frantic appeals to stay on puzzled him, until one of his few supporters, a local pastor who also later relinquished his post, told him that his rejection of the job would seriously tarnish their image in certain areas important to them.

Dan stood his ground, which brought Revd Phillips down from Auckland to get him to change his mind, and when he failed, the patron of the Society in New Zealand, a top business tycoon, invited Dan to lunch at his Invercargill hotel. He, too, returned to Auckland without achieving his objective, a failure which Dan felt would be a change for him as he was well known for his aggressive business tactics. Dan certainly wasn't happy at this state of affairs and couldn't understand all the fuss that was being made: it was even mentioned in the local newspaper.

He remembered that it hadn't been plain sailing even at the inaugural meeting when he had unwittingly ruffled feathers. At the function to welcome him to his new post, a local dignitary making a speech was so flowery in his remarks that, to Dan, it wasn't real, he couldn't believe that the stranger was referring to him, so he glanced around wondering who it could be. He then heard the orator stop speaking and, in a very different tone of voice, say, "I am addressing YOU, Captain Robson!"

Now, six months later, he was withdrawing from the scene, having given two weeks' notice. He knew that he had fulfilled his idea of a mission man's role by visiting all ships on arrival in the port, to offer any assistance, and to invite the men to use the facilities of the club. He was happy in his dealings with his own fraternity, and of course met some of the officers he had dealt with when he was their agent in the Merchant Navy Officers' Association.

He left with a clear conscience, although he had been told he lacked sufficient 'grace' for such work, and he was content to leave it at that. It was now that he realised the 'wisdom from above' that had prompted him to pay their fares from London to Bluff: he was free from any obligation to remain, and so ended his dream of 'full-time Christian work'.

What Now?

Dan and Jessie felt suddenly alone, without any clear idea what to do. They felt it best to leave the area and start afresh, so they all piled into the Morris Traveller they had brought out with them, and drove to Christchurch.

Dan was to learn that just because the Master allows what looks like failure to occur in a person's life, it doesn't mean that He no longer cares for them. In Dan's case, with wife and daughter to care for, it was imperative he got some sort of employment right away, and see what developed after that.

Scanning the newspapers on his first morning in the city, Dan saw a job as a clerk in a Credit Office. He was fifty-two and had no office experience, but he decided to apply. His Master Mariner's certificate convinced the boss, a keen yachtsman himself, he could do sums, so he was taken on at £14 per week. Then he and Jessie went house-hunting. They found a suitable cottage in Bryndwyr for £4000, so they negotiated a mortgage, had their possessions sent up from Bluff and settled down again.

With some trepidation, Dan began work at the Credit Office. It was mostly telephone work, contacting the credit managers of the city's leading businesses, and gradually he came to grips with what was required of him. The man who was leaving gave him many tips and warned him about 'Cyclops', the staff's name for the lady office manager, who sat on a swivel chair in a glass enclosure and kept her eye on everyone. Dan discovered it was a mistake to even look idle because 'Cyclops' would emerge with a pile of letters to be addressed, or some other task. No one was allowed to leave the office, even to go to the toilet, without her permission.

Suzy found a job in a picture-framing shop, and helped to provide for her own maintenance, but there was no money for anything other than necessities. Dan therefore, kept his eyes open for something more in line with his own profession, and one day read an advertisement for an Accident Investigator for the Lyttelton waterfront. The successful applicant had to be conversant with ships and cargo-handling procedures and preferably a qualified ex-ship's officer. It was right up Dan's street, so he applied right away, and within a week an interview had been arranged at the Port Line offices in Hereford Street, just around the corner from his office. The appointment time was 11 a.m.

It wouldn't be easy to slip away from the office. Right up until 10.45 that morning Dan had no idea how he would attend that interview at eleven. He was just deciding to ask to go to the toilet, when 'Cyclops' herself called him to do a 'search' at a Government building further up the street. It was 10.55 a.m.! Dan offered a silent prayer of thanks as he sprinted down the street to reach the Port Line offices spot on eleven o'clock.

At the interview, Dan sensed the fraternal atmosphere of fellow seafarers, and felt he made a favourable impression. When he left he was walking on air and bounded along the street to do the errand he was supposed to be on, getting back to the Credit Office with no one any the wiser. Three days later, he received a letter from the Lyttelton Port Employers' Association appointing him to the job and asking him to report to their Norwich Quay office in two weeks' time. Overnight he had become Captain Dan Robson, Accident Investigation Officer, on the Lyttelton waterfront.

'Absolutely fantastic!' thought Dan; he and Jessie were delighted. The bounce from junior clerk to a role more in keeping with his training gave Dan's ego a healthy boost. Also, his wages were doubled, and that made all the difference to their struggle to combat the rising cost of living. Dan, meditating on his good fortune, felt the Lord was compensating him for his great disappointment in seeking full-time Christian work. He was being reinstated into his chosen profession, the maritime world, dealing not so much with ships but with the waterfront work on them.

At the Lyttelton office, he met Captain John Twomey and Captain Robbie Edwards, both master mariners, and melded in with them, and to the work he was given to do as a duck to water. He could not think of anything more suitable for his temperament and abilities than investigating waterfront accidents, and reporting on them with a view to accident prevention. Robbie introduced him to the many officials he would meet in the course of his duties, and gave him plenty of tips for dealing with workers, and their union officials. Dan's own experience with the Harbour Board in Auckland, and his work in Southampton, all helped to equip him for the work, and enabled him to come to grips with it quickly.

As Dan became established in the waterfront scene, he came to know several men who were not afraid to say they were Christians, and with whom he could share matters of vital interest in their spiritual lives. He learnt much from such dedicated men as Captain Bill Drake, Salvationist Bill Ramsay, and waterside workers Jim Stewart, Ray Te Koeti and others, which led him to organise lunchtime meetings of prayer and worship at the Salvation Army Hall every Thursday. This proved to be a time of spiritual nourishment for all concerned. It seemed that Dan had found his niche and was at last settling down to a comfortable, respectable and conventional life.

He had planted fruit trees in his spacious back lawn at Bryndwr, and dreamed of lying in a hammock on warm summer afternoons and being able to reach out to pick a plum, apple or pear from an overhanging tree. What a dream for an ageing seafarer!

At eighteen, Suzy startled Dan and Jessie one day by telling them that she wanted to join the Royal New Zealand Navy as a Wren. The call of the sea was apparently surfacing in their daughter, and though Dan knew it would be unwise and unfair to discourage her, he and Jessie were very reluctant to part with her. He was about to experience a taste of his mother's sadness and grief, when he had left home. Suzy was such a good daughter, and it was hard to see her go. However, Dan was assured she would be looked after throughout her life, just as he had been.

Although Dan and Jessie were happy with the fellowship at their local Anglican Church, Dan never wanted to separate himself from other brothers and sisters in the family of God, so they frequently attended meetings at other places of worship. In that way they had warm fellowship with a wide range of believers, from sober-minded Baptists, Brethren, Methodists and Presbyterians, to Salvationists and Pentecostal groups, and rejoiced in them all. At one post-Lenten exercise, which involved hosting a mixed group of believers at their home every week, Dan and Jessie enjoyed sharing spiritual worship with some Roman Catholic Sisters who, with the permission of their Mother Superior, were allowed to attend and take part. Everyone received a rich blessing as a result, the Sisters were very appreciative.

At Lyttelton one afternoon, Dan was walking towards the wharves, when he suddenly became aware of a sort of spiritual canopy hovering over him. Although he didn't dare to look up, he had the impression it was peachy-pink in colour. The comforting presence of the canopy lasted about ten minutes and then, as suddenly as it had come, it disappeared. He was fascinated by that visitation, something entirely new in his experience, and though he questioned his Christian friends about it, no one could offer a solution. It was not until years later that he heard of people witnessing similar 'theophanies' and was reassured that he hadn't imagined the whole episode.

A few weeks later, the vicar of their parish church invited Dan to give his testimony at a Sunday evening service, and he agreed, as he was always eager to testify to the saving Grace of the Lord. He asked that, when he had completed his testimony, if everyone could sing 'Take my life and let it be consecrated, Lord, to Thee'. The vicar agreed, but when Dan, with a spirit-inspired afterthought, asked if they could sing it on their knees, he thought that was too much to ask of the congregation.

Dan returned to his seat beside Jessie and stood with everyone else while the opening bars were sung. Halfway through the first line he was felled like an ox to his knees. It was so sudden, and he fell so heavily, that it was lucky a hassock was in position to cushion his knees. Tears poured from his eyes on to the hymn-book. He wasn't actually crying, he was exhilarated: to him it was more like a cleansing flow, and he thought of the term 'rivers of living water' which continued until the singing stopped and the others sat down. After the service, it was revealed that two other people in the congregation had had the same experience. The vicar was at a loss to explain what had happened, but the event created animated discussion in the following weeks.

Through his conversations with his dear Christian brother, Captain Bill Drake, who had spent most of his life in the Open Brethren persuasion, Dan understood that though he had a certificate of baptism as a baby, he should undergo Believer's Baptism: total immersion. Dan, always anxious to go the whole way for the Lord, agreed and then did an inexplicable thing. He went to an Assembly of God church, asked the pastor if he could be included in their next baptism ceremony, and was duly baptised by him. He didn't tell Jessie, or even Bill, who had been the one to prompt him in the first place, and needless to say, both were disappointed that he did it without their witnessing the occasion. Later on in his Christian walk Dan realised the joy others have in attending these baptisms, and regretted his thoughtlessness.

About that time, Derek Prince, a noted preacher and evangelist, came to Christchurch and held a series of meetings at the Horticultural Hall. Mr Prince, with his powerful Spirit-directed-intellect, was able to impress people with their dire need of salvation. Dan and Jessie attended a meeting, and found that they were never the same again in that the Lord gave them a fresh impetus, Baptising them in the Holy Spirit, Hallelujah! It was a spiritually thrilling encounter, and for days afterwards Dan felt as though his bones were hollow and filled with the gas that lifts balloons. He was also given a new way of communicating with the Lord, a blessing which generally accompanies Holy Spirit Baptism, and with it, release from the fear of man, and a freedom to witness to anyone who came along.

In that happy and productive way, almost six years were spent in Christchurch and Lyttelton. Dan had mastered his work as Accident Investigation Officer, and, for his Christian activities, was often referred to in a good-natured way as Lyttelton's 'hound of heaven'. As another part of his work, he trained watersiders to qualify as winchmen and hatchmen, he also helped his fellow office workers, and felt settled and secure in the most suitable work he had ever had. He could have comfortably relaxed to retirement, or could he? It was all so peaceful that it reminded him of that part of the scriptures relating to the end of the world; when everyone is talking peace, peace, then the end shall come.

On one of his calls around the various shipping company offices, he saw a poster advertising the sailing of the Italian liner *Angelina Laurro*. There was nothing remarkable about that, but when Dan read her ports of call, his feet started to itch. *Angelina* was to leave Wellington on 30th January, 1969, for Punta Arenas in the Magellan Strait, thence to Buenos Aires, Rio de Janeiro, Tenerife, Lisbon, Vigo and on to Southampton, and just the mention of those places stirred up again Dan's adventure-loving blood. He must tell Jessie, he thought, and was surprised when she showed interest. They agreed that it wasn't worth throwing away everything they had regained after their earlier experiences, to do so would be absolute madness they thought, but despite their protestations they did just that. Dan really suffered in his spirit when he handed in his notice to John Twomey: it was a repeat of the agony of resigning from the M.N.O.A. in London; why must he torture himself in this way, he wondered.

When all their friends found out that Dan had no job to go to, and he didn't know where they would live, they wondered whether he and Jessie had taken leave of their senses. Their only excuse was, perhaps, they had not yet got the longing for their native land out of their systems.

Again there was the awful wrench of selling their little cottage, furniture, car, the giving away of the remainder of their possessions, and the farewells to their many good friends. They visited Suzy, now established in the WRNZS at the Naval Base in Auckland, and then joined *Angelina Laurro* in Wellington. To complete their discomfort, the film shown on the first night out on the Angelina, was a ghastly one about the crime and violence of depressed areas in England.

The ten day passage across the South Pacific Ocean was largely uneventful, other than the usual shipboard frolics to amuse and entertain the full-complement of passengers. Most of these were Australian-domiciled post-war Italian migrants taking advantage of a trip home in one of their own ships, but in fact, *Angelina Laurro* was formerly the Dutch liner *Oranje*. *Oranje* had such a good record for her stability, that during World War Two, she was converted to being a hospital ship and gave invaluable service in that capacity throughout the war.

Dan and Jessie were often fascinated by her graceful movement as she rode the huge swells, steady as a rock, resembling a duck riding the ripples on a pond. As on *Southern Cross* seven years earlier, they made friends with many interesting people, some of them missionaries returning to Chile, Bolivia, Uruguay and Brazil, and that led to meetings for Bible study, prayer and worship. The Italian passengers held regular Masses, conducted by their own Roman Catholic priests.

Wisely, the ship's agents had arranged for the Magellan Straits pilot to join the ship at Wellington to avoid any likely problem in picking him up off the stormy Chilean coast.

There was very little of interest to see at Punta Arenas, the southernmost township in the world. It looked like a frontier town in a cowboy movie with its unsealed streets, plain khaki-coloured buildings and few shops. Here, a young Canadian couple with two toddlers and a baby in a backpack, disembarked with the intention of walking home. It would have been comforting to learn they achieved their objective, but such information never came to hand.

Jessie was impressed with Buenos Aires, its fine wide boulevards and ornate architecture, but Dan was more interested in looking for a café where they could get a decent cup of tea. However, he did notice the bullet-riddled walls of derelict buildings with political slogans daubed on them, signs of the political turmoil of recent years.

At Rio de Janeiro, the Mardi Gras was in full swing, and to avoid the crowds in the sweltering heat, they took a bus to the top of the Sugar Loaf to see the massive statue of Christ. It was an imposing work of art, but lifeless, and meaning very little, it would seem, to the inhabitants of Rio where the Devil's handiwork was evident in the squalor, vice, corruption and poverty on every side.

On to Lisbon, the Bay of Biscay – unusually calm under leaden skies – and then the cold grey waters of the English Channel. Dan's sister Connie and Stan were at Southampton waiting to take them to Aldershot where they now lived, and Dan and Jessie saw they were back in the land of wall-to-wall people, wondering again if they had done the right thing in returning. They planned to stay with Connie for only a couple of days before going on to Southampton, but on the Monday morning Stan took Dan to the busy engineering company in Guildford where he worked, and there Dan was offered a job as clerk at £13 a week. Dan was in no position to bargain, especially as he was now fifty-eight years old, so he accepted.

He found the work hectic and strenuous but he learned that while his colleagues were just as busy, they had a different attitude towards the work. They took it light-heartedly, doing their best, but never letting it get on top of them. At the first sound of the five o'clock hooter they swept their desks clear and went home.

Dan found it difficult to adjust, and when he saw the Project Manager casually scrawl 'three months' in thick blue crayon across a 'Very Urgent Order' he was flabbergasted. The manager explained that there was so much urgent work that there was nothing else he could do, and the client was free to go elsewhere. So it was – no free and easy relaxed Lyttelton style here in this hectic manufacturing world.

After a couple of months Dan's health deteriorated, and Jessie was uncomfortable about imposing on Connie and Stan for so long. They decided to go to Southampton where some good friends would accommodate them until they got a home of their own again. Dan said goodbye to his cheery colleagues, reminding them of their vital need of salvation and that Jesus had said that we must be 'born again', praying that his earlier witness would bear fruit in due course.

Arriving in Southampton, Dan left Jessie with their friends to go down to the docks. As a result of his former association with many officials, and timely help from above, he was offered the post of Mate and Relieving Master with a company operating sand-dredgers. Dan didn't hesitate. He knew it was a gift from above at a critical time. Praise the Lord.

Never Left, Never Forsaken

Even Jessie was amazed, and their friends could hardly believe that someone in his late fifties could arrive in a city with a high percentage of unemployed and land a job within a couple of hours.

That is the normal way to think, but the Master is far above such limitations, and as He has expressed in His Word, 'Open thy mouth wide and I will fill it' to indicate He is ever ready to help His people and nothing is impossible with Him. Dan, though zealous in his Christian walk, often forgot to pray specifically for things, relying on a very brief prayer – 'Lord, Thou knowest' – leaving the outcome to Him. The Master accepted this as evidence of his faith. He has an intimate knowledge of each of His children's foibles, even their innermost thoughts so, in Dan's case, knowing him to be impulsive and inclined to jump at a command, He never kept him waiting for long lest he jump the wrong way.

Dan and Jessie went house-hunting and found a three-bedroom, semi-detached brick house in Bitterne for £4500, and since his pay was likely to be £60 plus per week, they had no difficulty in getting a mortgage.

He soon found that good wages meant long, tiring hours, three weeks on duty, then one week off. For the first two months he relieved other Mates, met different Skippers and discovered the peculiarities of the various ships. It was necessary for him to get acquainted with the art of dredging and the skills required.

Sand Lark, a neat little vessel with comfortable accommodation and well-equipped with navigational aids and radiotelephone, was his first experience in dredging. On this first trip he was Second Mate, the Mate and Skipper being well-experienced in the dredging business. The Old Man was a real character, a Welsh ex-trawler man, an excellent seaman who called a spade a spade. Everyone knew where they stood with him, and Dan developed great respect for him even though he was sometimes made to feel a real novice again. The Mate was different – very competent, but he regarded Dan, a deep sea man, as an interloper, and he didn't bother to hide the fact. He reminded Dan of the North Sea fishermen who wore thick heavy leather sea-boots and had never bothered to learn to swim, their theory being that if they fell overboard that was it, there was no sense in prolonging the agony. The Mate reckoned the difference between deep water seamen and coastal seamen was that the former messed their trousers when they sighted land, and the latter when they lost sight of it; a centuries'-old observation, not necessarily true.

The two main sources of supply of their cargoes were the Pot Bank, off the Needles at the western end of the Isle of Wight, and the Solent Bank, between the Isle and the Hampshire coast. Although the banks had been worked for years by scores of dredgers they were constantly being built up again by the action of the tidal currents bringing together the silt, sand and shingle spewed out by the rivers around the area. For the company it was good business, paying a royalty and harvesting the valuable material for sale at ports all along the south coast.

Sand Lark headed for the Solent Bank to load a full cargo of sand and shingle for Newhaven further along the coast. As they arrived in the vicinity of the bank Dan couldn't help noticing the studied air of indifference adopted by the Old Man to camouflage the precision of his anchoring, and he could see the Mate was pretending not to take any notice either. They were like a pair of anglers jealous of their favourite spots and wanting to keep them a secret to themselves.

When the ship was finally anchored in position, the Skipper in the wing of the bridge lowered the long eighteen inch diameter suction pipe, which worked on the same principle as a vacuum cleaner, hinged at its forward end and raised or lowered by the winch operator. Since it was the most important part of the whole operation, and since the Skipper was responsible for what came into the hold, he was usually the one in control. The winch operator couldn't see the lower, working end so it was largely a hit-or-miss affair until the first gush into the open hold revealed whether the haul was acceptable or not. If it wasn't, the pipe-end was raised to try elsewhere.

Dan was fascinated as he saw the rich golden flow of sand and shingle pour out of the pipe into the hold, bringing a satisfied look to the Old Man's face.

"That's a lovely looking brew," Dan commented, trying to be conversational.

"It 'ud better be" grunted the Skipper.

Three hours later the hold was full, the sea water had been pumped out and they were under way, past Cowes, through Spithead and bound for Newhaven. The Mate and Dan took over the watch-keeping, and maybe to put the wind up Dan the Mate indulged in 'rock-dodging' – keeping as close inshore as possible. Dan pretended not to notice, but it was hair-raising at times with all the shipping, fast cross-Channel ferries and hosts of yachts to contend with.

These busy little dredgers were kept constantly working, provided the weather did not make it impossible to 'work' the Banks, and Dan could see how the company could pay the good wages but, at the same time, extract their pound of flesh.

Their discharging ports ranged from Newhaven in the east to Plymouth in the west, with Shoreham, Portsmouth, Southampton, Poole and Exmouth in between. He found that 'watchbelows' could be anything but peaceful times to sleep. With the engine room bulkhead on one side of his cabin, and on the deck outside the for'ard bulkhead the clattering steam-winch which raised and lowered the loading pipe, his cabin, at times, could be likened to being inside an empty oil-drum with hammers banging the outside walls of it. The time came when Dan was given his first command, the *Sand Snipe*, and sent to the Pot Bank to load for Newhaven. When he got there about dusk there were already four other dredgers working it, and since it wasn't done to operate too close to another ship, he had to anchor about three hundred yards away, lower the pipe and wait to inspect the first suck. When it gushed forth under the glare of a floodlight, instead of being the thick, rich golden colour Dan had so often seen on the *Lark*, it was an ugly black mess of mud and rubble. He spent the next two hours trying to find a better spot, and whenever one of the other ships completed their loading, Dan slipped into its place. He went doggedly on until sunrise when he was virtually shamed into weighing anchor and heading for Newhaven.

He wasn't optimistic about his reception and the depot manager took one look at his cargo, went into his shed, came out again for a closer look, then went back inside. The ship had hardly finished tying up when the manager reappeared to call out to Dan that his cargo wasn't fit for discharge at Newhaven, he was to take it to Southampton for use as fill – in other words it was rubbish! Dan's feelings were somewhat dashed, but the manager told him not to worry too much, it had happened before with beginners and would be forgiven, although repeated failures wouldn't be.

Later Dan heard with relief that even the experts mis-fired on occasions. Nevertheless, he never again collected material that wasn't acceptable. Years later the installation of underwater video cameras at the working end of the pipe took the guesswork out of the operation so there would be no excuse for picking up anything other than what had been ordered.

As Dan got used to the sand dredging business the routine was varied only by the weather or by the occasional comical or dramatic incident. Once when Dan was Skipper of the Sand Grebe they were in Exmouth, his favourite little port tucked away in the corner of Lyme Bay. Two seamen were missing at sailing time, carousing in a dockside pub, and when the Bos'n tried to hurry them back on board they told him to tell the Mate and the Skipper to get lost, and on returning the Bos'n did.

Dan said, "Righto, let go for'ard, let go aft!" and they left port.

While unloading at Portsmouth the next day the missing men turned up, but they got a shock when Dan told them they had been replaced, their gear was ashore in the wharf shed, and they could pick up their wages at Head Office. All this had been arranged by radiotelephone with Southampton en route.

Another time he took *Snipe* to a certain port and berthed as usual. He was leaving the bridge and put on his jacket to go ashore when he heard a hullabaloo on the wharf alongside where he saw the wharf foreman cursing and swearing at the Mate. As Dan approached the two men the yard foreman came up, his face blazing with anger, and told him the ship shouldn't be there and, in the coarsest terms, ordered Dan to move it. When Dan said he took his orders from Head Office and not from yard foremen he almost went berserk, shouting, "You're a lying bastard, Captain!"

What followed happened so fast that most bystanders missed it, but to Dan it seemed like slow motion and completely without his volition.

With icy calm Dan's eyes slowly swept down the contour of the foreman's nose, mouth to his unshaven chin. Then, an inner voice said, "HIT IT!" so vehemently, that Dan immediately obeyed. He landed a terrific right uppercut, better than any he had produced in his boxing days, and the stocky, solidly-built man twenty years younger was literally lifted off his feet to arc backwards and crash heavily to the wharf.

When Dan saw that the man's head and shoulders hung over the edge of the wharf his first impulse was to rush forward to stop him falling into the dock. His second was to think, 'Good heavens, I've started a fight! At my age!' He whipped off his coat expecting rapid retaliation, but instead of scrambling to his feet and attacking Dan, the foreman grovelled away on all fours like a beaten dog, calling over his shoulder, "I'll get my own back, Captain, don't you worry!"

While Dan was collecting his thoughts and feeling rather ashamed at what he thought was his lack of control and a lapse in his Christian witness, he heard the voice of the mobile-crane driver behind him say, "Well done Skipper, that's the best day's work I've seen done for a long time. He sure had it coming to him." Dan thanked him and, picking up his jacket, walked back along the wharf to where the Mate and two seamen were standing. Dan wanted to hear their version of what they had seen, but all three agreed that all they saw was the foreman erect one minute and flat on his back the next; they assured Dan they had seen no blow.

Dan couldn't believe that, and thought they might be adopting that stance in case he was later charged with assault, but they were simply telling the truth. Puzzled, Dan boarded the ship and went to his cabin and, while waiting for breakfast, casually glanced through his Bible. He was comforted to read that the Lord strengthened them that are His, and, 'with arms that can bend a bow of bronze', enemies shall fall at their feet.

From his boxing experience he was sure that to move a man of the foreman's size and weight in the way he did would have damaged his hand, but there wasn't a mark on it. It must have been Someone other than he, the blow had been SO fast, SO accurate, and

SO powerful, it was beyond the capacity of normal fifty-eight year-old Dan.

A week later in Southampton Dan was summoned to Head Office to give an account of the fracas. The Manager listened attentively, and at the end said the company didn't approve of its Captains bashing yard foremen. Then, with a hint of a smile, he went on: "Please don't make a habit of it, Captain Robson!" Two weeks later Dan heard the foreman had been sacked for improperly using the company's facilities.

Another time Dan was on his favourite ship with Captain Evans when they were given an assignment which was certainly not the Skipper's cup of tea, since he was no socialiser. In his younger days the Skipper had been a heavy drinker. A deep sea trawlerman's life was tough enough to drive a man to strong liquor, but a serious liver complaint and his wife's Chapel friends combined to encourage the Skipper to see the Light, and sign the pledge. But he had never been seriously tested.

Sand Lark had been chosen to host a group of South Coast businessmen for a party at Shoreham. The ship was specially cleaned up, she was dressed with flags to hide the blemishes, and the company had organised the catering. To impress their guests, the Skipper was asked to wear a uniform, but he said he had never worn one in his life and he wasn't going to start now. Finally, Dai Evans reluctantly agreed to wear a uniform cap, but as he didn't have one, the office borrowed one that looked like a relic from some maritime museum – the peak covered with dull gold laurel leaves and the whole cap looked frayed and tatty. It was also a size too big, and on the Skipper's balding head, the cap swivelled and wobbled whenever he moved his head. This didn't add to the dignity of the occasion, but gave the proceedings a rather comic opera touch. With so much free liquor on hand, the Skipper's resolve to remain a teetotaller was swept temporarily aside, and only a substantial lunch at one o'clock slowed him down a little.

He soon abandoned what diplomacy he had, and at one point, a guest sidled up to him, and said loudly, "I say, old man, you passed quite close to my yacht off Worthing the other day, didn't you see me?"

Turning to glare at him the Skipper said, "If you're one of those bloody idiots who clutter up our shipping lanes, it's just as well I didn't see you, or I would have bloody well run you down!" Everyone round about laughed, except the recipient of the blast, who backed away muttering, "I say, I say..."

During the afternoon, a trio of women came on board to prepare and serve afternoon tea, and this arrangement upset the ship's cook. Bizarre though it may seem, the cook had a 'crush' on the Captain, and seeing those women attending to duties he felt were his alone, he was smitten with jealousy and tried to drown his damaged emotions. Emboldened by the Johnny Walker whisky, he staggered up to the bridge, pushing through the crowd, to declare himself. The Skipper glared at him through his own boozy haze and then, in the crudest terms, ordered him off the bridge and out of his sight. But that was not going to be the end of the matter.

With the food and drink disposed of the festivities started to wind down and when the last of the die-hards finally went ashore, the Skipper was decidedly the worse for wear but anxious to get away from it all, and back to normal work. By 6 p.m. the ship was ready to depart. Dai Evans took his place on the bridge, and with a flourish ordered, "Let go for'ard, let go aft!" and slammed the engine-room telegraph down to 'full ahead'. Then, with his feet planted firmly pointing forward, he swung his upper torso round to order the helmsman, "Hard a'starboard!" and promptly collapsed, a senseless heap on the wheelhouse floor.

Dan, having alerted the engineer, expecting something like this to happen, swiftly brought the telegraph back to 'slow ahead' and took over the piloting out of port, while the Bos'n and two seamen carried the Old Man down to his bunk. Once outside the breakwater, Dan looked at the helmsman and said, "Well, thank goodness that's all over and done with!" meaning the party with people coming and going. The words were scarcely out of his mouth before they heard shrieks from down below. The Bos'n rushed up to report that the Cook had slashed his wrists, so after a hasty glance round for other ships, Dan told the helmsman to hold his course while he went down below to investigate. The Cook was writhing around on the tiled galley floor with blood all over it, a bloody mess indeed, so Dan grabbed a couple of tea-towels and with the Bos'n's help, applied a tourniquet to each wrist. Then, dashing back to the bridge, he called the shore station on the radio-telephone to say he was on his way back with an injured man.

The port doctor came out to meet the ship in the pilot launch, and after sedating, bandaging and treating the Cook, he supervised the transfer of the patient into the launch and off to hospital.

With the Captain happily oblivious to all that was going on, and the Cook on his way to hospital, *Sand Lark* again set course for the Owers lightship off Selsey Bill. Their orders were to proceed to the Solent Bank to load for Poole, and after navigating through the busy shipping of Spithead and the Solent, they arrived in the early hours of the following morning. By that time Dan was dog-tired. He had been on duty since dawn the previous morning, and while he would have liked to let Captain Evans sleep on, he knew that the Skipper preferred to choose his own loading spot. Dan woke him up and organised a mug of strong tea for him, and his respect for the old sea-dog grew as he watched him recover from the effects of falling off the wagon the day before. As soon as the Skipper set foot on the bridge, he was in command again and able to locate one of his favourite spots in which to anchor. Later in the day they heard that the Cook was recovering and hoped to return to *Sand Lark*, to which Captain Evans replied, having been told the events of the previous evening, "Only over my dead body!"

One day in late October, when Dan was on leave, Jessie told him she wasn't looking forward to being at home alone in the long, dark, winter months. The following Sunday afternoon when Dan and Jessie were out for their usual walk, they came upon a large complex of buildings with a six-storey office block in front. They had not been up that way before, so it was new to them.

The thought occurred to them both that it might be a good place at which to try for a job. They went home and Dan wrote a brief letter to the personnel manager saying that he, Dan, would call on him the following morning at ten o'clock to ask about the prospects of getting work.

They retraced their steps to the office block and tried to slip the letter under the door, when a voice behind them said, "'Ullo, 'ullo, what's goin' on 'ere, then?" It was the security man, and when they explained that they were trying to find the letter box to post their letter, he told them that letter boxes "were out" on account of letter box bombers. However, he offered to take their letter and see that it reached the personnel manager. He reached into the depths of his old overcoat to fish out his wallet and placed Dan's letter in the centre of it.

As they walked away, they thought, "Well, that's probably the end of that," sure the man would forget all about it, but the following morning Dan decided to go to the office anyway. At the reception desk he was told that his letter had been received, and the personnel manager suggested he should go and see Mr Brooke, the warehouse manager. Dan, having asked the Lord to go before him, felt relaxed, although he knew only too well he had very little to offer.

Mr Brooke looked up from the mass of papers on his table to ask: "Yes, what can I do for you?"

Dan answered, "I've come to see if there are any vacancies on your staff, sir."

"What experience have you had in warehouse work?" asked the manager.

Dan, deciding that come what may he would be strictly truthful, said, "None, sir."

"Well, what line of work have you been used to?" was the next question.

"I've spent most of my life in the shipping world, both at sea and ashore, sir."

That dear man wore very thick-lensed glasses and Dan couldn't be sure whether he was looking at him, at his papers or at the ceiling. After a long pause he said, "So you don't know anything about the builders' merchants' business?"

Fearing the interview was coming to an end, Dan muttered "I'm afraid not, sir, but I'm fairly versatile and feel I could adapt myself to what was required of me."

In answer to further questioning Dan explained that he wanted to work ashore, because he was fifty eight years old and wanted to spend more time at home with his wife. As the interview progressed, Dan had the sinking feeling that he was not going to be acceptable to Mr Brooke, and yet he hadn't been dismissed and the man seemed deep in thought. Dan waited for the verdict, then to his surprise he heard: "The hours are 8 a.m. to 5 p.m., five days a week, the starting wage is £14 per week, with some overtime available."

Dan wasn't sure whether that was a statement or an offer of employment, but then Mr Brooke continued, "If that is acceptable to you, when can you start, Mr Robson?"

'That's fantastic,' thought Dan, then realised his answer would most likely spoil everything. He explained that he had to give a month's notice to the shipping company he was employed with. It was Mr Brooke's turn to be surprised, but then he looked at the wall calendar and said, "Oh all right, we'll make it Monday, 30th November. Report to me then, okay?"

Dan couldn't get back home quickly enough to tell Jessie, who was delighted. They worried a little about the drop in their income, but decided that being at home together would be well worth it. As long as they could make their mortgage payments on time there was no need to frighten the building society.

For Dan's last spell with the dredgers, he was plagued with all sorts of problems: bad weather, fog, machinery breakdowns, sick engineers. One night he would never forget he was on watch on the bridge with only the man at the wheel, crossing that normally very busy area between Owers lightship, off Selsey Bill, and St Catherine's Point, the southernmost extremity of the Isle of Wight. The fog was so dense he couldn't see the fore part of the ship, so he buried his head in the radar set which stayed unusually blank, to seaward. He just could not believe there was no other shipping, and imagined a fault in the radar, and running full-tilt into the side of a supertanker or huge container ship. With the helmsman gazing stolidly into the compass and Dan into the radar, both were straining their ears for the fog signals of other ships. All they could hear was the swish of their own progress through the water. At least in the radar panel Dan could see the coast clearly outlined on the starboard bow, the Isle of Wight etched from Sandown Bay to St Catherine's Point, and that was comforting.

As they neared St Catherine's Point, he spotted a small echo on the radar screen approaching from the direction of the Pot Bank. He put out a call on the radio-telephone and was relieved to hear the familiar Welsh accents of Captain Evans, and after exchanging news and views regarding the fog, they continued their courses, passing each other unseen, apart from the radar screen.

Snipe loaded a cargo at Pot Bank for Portsmouth, and after discharge, Dan was anxious to get out again to catch the tide. He saw ahead of him a German cargo ship leave a wharf and move towards the fairway. Dan knew that he should allow the German ship, with a pilot on board, to go ahead of him, but he could see by its slow progress that he could just slip past quite nicely. He rang for full speed on the engine-room telegraph, and they just got ahead of the other ship when the engineers phoned Dan to say that they must stop the engines immediately because there was mud in the intake valve of the cooling system. What a time for that to happen.

They just had to drift, hoping *Snipe* would keep heading down the fairway as it was strictly forbidden to anchor in that area. They were right opposite the top-brass establishments of the Royal Navy and feeling that Admirals galore were glaring down at them through their telescopes, aware that the pilot and officers of the German ship had their binoculars trained on *Snipe*'s bridge, Dan restrained himself from giving a friendly wave, and chose instead to peer anxiously astern as though someone had fallen overboard. Fortunately, *Snipe* maintained her heading and in due course the engineers reported the intake problem had been solved and the ship could proceed.

At Poole, Dan said goodbye to *Snipe* and joined *Sand Grebe* for his last trip with the dredgers. She had her problems too. His orders were to load a full cargo of sand only, at Pot Bank for Plymouth, that meant the shingle had to be screened off and returned to the sea, prolonging the loading operation. Breakdowns and a low swell held up the work even further, but at last the pipe was brought aboard, the anchor weighed and a course set for Prawle Point.

It was Sunday morning, with church bells ringing, as Dan piloted *Sand Grebe* past the Hoe, where Sir Francis Drake played bowls within sight of the Spanish fleet, and berthed for unloading in the inner harbour. There were delays and frustrations all day, the generator intakes got fouled with mud, two men went adrift before sailing, a gale was forecast, and neither the compass, nor the radar were working properly. The concentrated electrical power of the nearby R.N. ships might have been the cause. They lost two hours waiting for the two men who eventually turned up somewhat the worse for wear, and by the time the ship emerged from the relative calm of the harbour into the channel, the gale was doing its worst.

One of the groggy truants was at the wheel and when *Grebe* started to buck into a short, steep sea, it wasn't long before he asked to be relieved. His watch-mate wasn't fit enough to take over the steering, so Dan told them both to go below and sober up. He took over the wheel, keeping the Eddystone Light on the starboard bow until he could change course for Prawle Point. With the compass being so erratic, visual aids proved invaluable, so with Prawle Point Lighthouse opening up on his port bow, and the westerly gale building up, the Grebe wallowed and yawed her way up Channel.

At two in the morning, Dan was relieved by the Mate and on going down below he found the two truants sound asleep on the warm floor of the galley. Dan decided to leave them there; it would definitely be their last trip too. At eight in the morning, when Dan returned to the bridge, the Isle of Wight was plainly visible, *Grebe* was bowling along with a fair wind and sea. It was a fitting climax to Dan's nautical career. With the exhilaration of the gale, Dan told the Bos'n to give his two watchmen work to do on deck while he himself would savour the thrill of being at the wheel to take *Grebe* south about the island through busy Spithead and Solent to the Solent Bank. They had received orders to load there for Southampton.

There would be a few more hassles to contend with yet, and Dan's last day of an eventful last spell of duty convinced him that it was time to give it up with no regrets. Arriving at the Bank at sundown, he found other ships already there, so he had to wait for a suitable anchorage. The whole pump-up was fraught with problems. An unwanted swell rolling in from the westward made pumping difficult and the suction pipe was damaged. To make matters worse, the pumping machinery broke down three times and the winch wire once. Dan began to wonder if they would ever load enough aggregate to fill the hold and let them proceed to Southampton, but of course they eventually did. At seven they berthed alongside their depot in the River Itchen. It had been the longest pump-up ever, a thoroughly miserable night, and Dan was thankful it was all over.

After handing over *Sand Grebe* to her new master and paying off the two delinquent seamen, Dan went to the company's office to terminate his contract officially and to say goodbye.

That Distant Horizon Draws Nigh

Dan presented himself at the warehouse on the Monday morning and was introduced to Steve Cupper, Mr Brooke's second in command, and to Lou Strong, foreman of the heavy goods section. Lou tried to explain the intricacies of the catalogue system which were double-dutch to Dan at first, but he was teamed with a young man named Tony who knew the system and initiated Dan into its mysteries. It wasn't as easy as Dan imagined and without Tony's know-how he would have been at a loss; a catalogue number XP368-940 was not that but, 548-200, and so on. He was also unused to lifting heavy weights, so by five o'clock, he was mentally and physically worn out. But as he walked home he was delighted to think he was back home with his dear Jessie, to have the evening meal together, and relax in front of the fire.

Dan persevered with the manhandling of heavy boxes of nails, bales of fencing wire and other weighty goods, but after six months he wondered if he could keep it up, and looked enviously at husky young men in departments dealing with lighter items like wallpaper and electric-light fittings. He didn't want to mention a transfer for fear of losing what he had, but he did make it a matter for prayer, with his favourite short one, 'Lord, Thou knowest'.

One morning during tea-break, the new personnel officer came into the warehouse section where Dan worked and asked Lou Strong if he could have a few words with Dan, privately. His first words were, "I understand you hold a Master's foreign-going certificate, Mr Robson?"

"Yes sir, that's correct."

"Well, why are you working in the warehouse?"

"I wanted to come ashore, sir, so I took any job I could at the time," Dan said.

When the next question was, "Do you think you could handle office work?" he said,

"Yes, sir, I have had some office experience."

"Well, I'll see what I can do for you," replied the young man, and then in a friendly manner he confided that he was an ex-Royal Navy officer, and had been looking through the personal records of the firm's employees. Dan felt that this was an answer to his prayers, the young man's appointment and the prompting of him to take this step. Who better than a Naval Officer would appreciate the value of a Master Mariner's Foreign-Going certificate?

Jessie, being the thrifty and excellent housekeeper she was, found that she had been able to manage on five pounds a week for living expenses, enabling Dan to bank the remaining eight pounds ten shillings for the mortgage, rates, gas and electricity. So it was a bonus when Dan was transferred to the Customer Services department on the third floor with an increase in salary of two pounds per week. What's more, he no longer had to clock on and off. It was also pleasant to work with a mixed group of women as well as men again, a situation that added a little zest to the working day. The Creator initiated the feminine capacity to fascinate males ever since Eve beguiled Adam into sharing her act of disobedience in the Garden of Eden, and they have been using the gift ever since. He knows, since He gave it to them, that this feminine trait is the spice that whets the male appetite, so that there's no reluctance on their part to ensure the continued propagation of the race.

Dan settled down to the work on the third floor and learned how to handle the problems that arose in the course of a day's business. When he compared this new life with the humdrum existence on the dredgers, he really praised the Lord for His provision, although in financial terms, he was forty-five pounds a week the poorer.

As in Guildford, Dan was amazed at the light-hearted approach his young workmates had to their work, and the young man whose place he was taking, horrified him by saying, "Get on your bike, mate," to end conversations with people he was there to serve. When Dan took over he tried to restore courtesy and respect when dealing with the firm's customers, especially as he was a new chum. They seemed happy to make allowances, as long as they had someone polite to discuss matters with. So in an unusual way, Dan's introduction to his new role was actually helped by his predecessor's rudeness.

Of course, there were minor pitfalls, such as the time Dan took an order for a long list of builders' requirements including, "one teeny weeny waste disposal unit."

Dan, thinking that the man had been reading too many children's stories, confirmed the order as, "one very small waste disposal unit."

There was a pause, and then came a schoolmaster's tone: "Would you mind repeating what you've just said?" Dan did so.

"That's not what I said, is it?"

"No, sir."

"Well, what did I say then?"

"If I remember correctly, you said, 'one teeny weeny waste disposal unit'."

The voice now rang out like a sergeant major's: "And that is what I want, got it?"

Meekly Dan answered, "Yes sir, sorry about that!" He found out that 'Teeny Weeny' was a trademark, not a description.

Living a normal life ashore enabled Dan and Jessie to visit many different churches to have fellowship with their spiritual brothers and sisters in their various settings. This wasn't as easy as it sounded. Some were too conformed, others too relaxed, some cold and unfriendly, some seemed to devote too much time appealing for funds, not for missionary enterprises, but for extensions and improvements to church or manse. So while Dan and Jessie indulged in church window-shopping, they broadened their minds and concept of true Christianity. They attended some churches more often than others, perhaps because of excellent teaching, or the sincerity of the praise and worship, which reflected the fervency of that particular fellowship. A positive advantage of this visiting was the breaking down, in their own minds, of the denominational walls that separate believers from one another into their own little pens.

About this time, Dan and Jessie received a cheery letter from Suzanne to say she was due out of the Wrens and was planning to join them in England, and would it be all right if she brought three friends to stay for a while? Of course, it would be lovely to be together again, they replied warmly. Then they thought about feeding four extra mouths, young ones at that.

They had not forgotten their section at Taipa, so now, needing some extra cash, they instructed an old solicitor friend of theirs in

Auckland, to sell it. Property values, especially choice sites such as theirs, had soared, so they more than doubled their money, and when these extra funds were made available, Dan and Jessie were able to buy more furniture, bedding and other essentials. They also managed to buy a Bedford minibus, and with this they met Suzy and the girls off the Northern Star to take them home, what a joy that was to see their dear daughter again.

It was like a tonic to Dan and Jessie having these cheery companions in the house, but anxious to fend for themselves, the girls soon got temporary jobs to break themselves into English working conditions, they took on anything available. Their presence made a big difference to the quiet life of the elderly couple, but Dan and Jessie got used to the added noise, later nights, and youthful exuberance, and so missed the girls a lot when they eventually left to go their separate ways.

The minibus proved a Godsend on many occasions, not only for sightseeing with the girls and other overseas visitors, but for conveying Girls' Brigade groups to camps and also to the Royal Albert Hall for really big occasions. In all this, Dan was mindful that the Lord was his provider and sustainer, so always gave thanks to Him.

The Bedford also served as a small meeting place for a lunchtime group of fellow Christians Dan had been able to locate, hiding their lights under filing cabinets. Much blessing was obtained, digested and passed on at those small fellowships of prayer and Bible discussion that produced at least one addition to the Father's family in the course of its existence.

One Sunday morning when Dan and Jessie were visiting Suzy in Bristol, they walked into town and came upon a church with a noticeboard outside which said, "In a city of ancient churches, this is the second oldest, but we are also the youngest because we have been 'born-again'. We offer you a warm welcome. Join us."

Who could pass by untouched by such a message? They needed no second bidding to enter and savour the inviting fellowship of this old yet new church.

As soon as they passed through the outer porch into the body of the building they sensed an atmosphere of warmth, love and happiness to an extent they had never encountered before in any denominational hall, chapel or church. Although early for the service, they were greeted cordially, handed the usual paperwork, and ushered to a pew three rows from the front. The usher told them that the policy was to fill the church from the front, and if people preferred the rear they should time their arrival accordingly, but they might miss out altogether. This was later proved correct when latecomers were seated on plain chairs in the aisles.

Having attended many different Anglican churches, they were conversant with the usual pattern, but here there was obviously a departure from the norm. There were redemption hymnals in the racks behind the pews, and as Dan's trio moved into place, the people already assembled began to sing, 'Let the Fire fall, Hallelujah, let the Fire fall', with their arms extended to the heavens and expectantly joyful, eager faces. Dan and his family were thrilled they had ventured in.

The singing continued until the vicar gave the signal for the normal service to proceed, but as soon as it was over and some of the regular parishioners withdrew, the vicar removed his outer vestments and laid them over the pulpit rail as though to say, "and now let's get down to business!" There followed one of the most open, uninhibited sessions of worship and praise Dan's family had ever witnessed, and needless to say they enjoyed it to the full. In fact, so much so, that they returned for the evening service and another full house, it was a privilege to be there.

Dan couldn't help comparing the liberated style of worship in this Bristol church, known by its young ones as the "Pip 'n' Jay," (their version of St Phillip and St James) with some other churches he had attended.

One in particular came to mind. Seeing a notice board in front proclaiming, "Moody and Sankey hymn night tonight. All welcome," he and Jessie as lover's of good Christian music decided to join in the festival of praise.

The chapel was long and narrow, and when their eyes became adjusted to the feeble illumination they were surprised to see only about half a dozen people sitting at the front, then rows of empty pews until the last two right at the back, which appeared to be full with twenty or so people. While Dan and Jessie waited expectantly for some evidence of a choir or bright singing to burst forth from somewhere, a formal type of service droned on.

When it finally ended Dan asked the man who had taken up the collection, "What's happened to the Moody and Sankey hymn night?"

"Oh, I think that was last week, they've forgotten to take the notice down," he said.

'Yes,' thought Dan, 'That matches the whole scene,' and when shaking hands with the minister at the door, who looked relieved it was all over, he asked, "Isn't it a strain to have to talk across all those empty rows to reach the folk at the back? Couldn't you ask them to move nearer the front?"

"Oh no," he shuddered at the thought, "I couldn't do that, they would be awfully offended."

"Well, why not shift your lectern down the aisle and get closer to them?"

The poor man actually laughed and said, "If did that they would all leave the church and never come back." It seemed he too, had a cross to bear.

Dan had often realised he had much to learn in his Christian walk and was yet to find out the learning process never ceases as long as more enlightenment is sought, and one's spirit and mind are prayerfully open to receive.

The Bedford taught him a lesson one summer's day. He had parked it after only a short run, and noticed that it was moaning and groaning, so Dan opened the bonnet, to investigate and find that the radiator was red hot. The car had proved a faithful servant; instead of letting down its neglectful owner, it had brought him safely home before expiring through lack of water. The previous car Dan had owned was always demanding attention: oil, water, batteries, tyres, the lot, so he had to pay attention to it and try to anticipate its needs. With the Bedford, he had been casual, taking advantage of its undemanding ways. It was revealed to Dan that this could apply to everyday life; one person could take another's kindness, patience, and gentleness for granted, and show no appreciation, while giving constant attention to a troublesome, touchy, self-centred and ungrateful, person.

Before buying the minibus, Dan had owned a smaller car and when he sold it he had tried to recover the unexpired portion of the insurance premium he had paid. Despite many letters, the answer was always the same - no, no, NO. On the company's letterhead the list of directors was headed by a Viscount, and it was only through being in the Customer Service Department, that Dan discovered he was a customer, and he was able to write to his private address, a stately mansion deep in the Sussex countryside. He described his attempts to get a refund, adding that years ago the unfortunate poor of this country were transported for life to Australia for stealing much less than his insurance company was now doing with impunity.

After posting the letter Dan didn't really expect a reply, but about three months later a scrawled letter arrived from the Viscount.

"Dear Mr Robson," it said. "I received your letter yesterday on my return from an overseas trip which included Australia. I am very happy to inform you that those 'poor people' we sent out there so long ago are now doing very well indeed. I trust you will be relieved to hear that. Regards..." Dan appreciated the Viscount's sense of humour but he appreciated even more the enclosed postal order for twelve shillings and sixpence, the sum he had been battling for. He acknowledged receipt of the money with thanks, and went on to say that by virtue of long residence 'Down Under,' he could claim to be an Australasian and hoped one day to rejoin those valiant folk.

Dan had met an Australian working in the warehouse and they became great mates. Harold was from Victoria, he and his English wife Ida had settled in Southampton where, with Jessie, the four of them had become close friends. Dan just had to mention the gospel good news of salvation, and though Harold was blunt and seemingly unconvinced for a long time, he eventually succumbed to the convicting power of the Holy Spirit. From then on, he and Ida joined Jessie and Dan at all the seminars and Bible conferences that came within 'cooee' of Southampton or London, visiting such places as Sunbury Court, once the headquarters of William Booth of the Salvation Army, Treacle Towers, the superbly situated stately home of one of the sugar barons of the previous century, and now used as a conference centre.

So the years rolled pleasantly by. The minibus was used to take visitors on scenic trips to Winchester and Salisbury and for trips around the beautiful Hampshire countryside. Dan had converted the Bedford into a mini-caravan with a portable stove and sleeping quarters for two, so they could join the campers at the conventions they attended.

One day, during a holiday in the West Country, Dan took Jessie to the lovely seaside town of Exmouth, his favourite port of call while on the sand dredgers. From there they visited Sidmouth, and the donkey sanctuary just out of town where a soft-hearted benefactor had provided a haven of rest for ageing donkeys to die in. The visit made Dan wonder about his own approaching retirement in a few months time; what would he and Jessie do, and where? That would be an adventure yet to unfold.

Dan had a pleasant surprise one afternoon when he was told someone was asking for him down in the showrooms. On going down, who could it be, he pondered, then he saw his old friend Captain Evans, with wife and married daughter. He was now retired, being well over the retirement age, and his wife wanted to buy a new bathroom suite, could Dan advise them? Among other problems Dan had had to deal with, many had been in connection with bathroom suites, but it was not his job to sell them, so after putting Mrs Evans and daughter in touch with the salesman of that section, he and his old shipmate enjoyed a few minutes catching up on one another's news. For Dan it was like a breath of sea air, the affinity that binds seafarers together, but, sadly, that was their last meeting, at least, in this life. Dai Evans was truly an unpolished 'diamond' Dan respected.

When Dan's retirement day came, it was with a mixture of relief at completing the course, and sadness at leaving such a friendly group of workmates who had made his last working years pass so happily. He spent his last afternoon going around saying goodbye to all the people he had come to know, then at three o'clock there was a presentation by the manager. With all the cards, kisses and tears, it was an emotional experience for him. However, as though to say 'enough of that' a small incident occurred that caused laughter all round. Dan's swivel chair crumpled up under him as though it, too, had had enough and was retiring with him, he was later told, it was a 'write-off' beyond repair!

Dear faithful Jessie welcomed him home with his retirement gift and farewell cards. His long working life was finally over, and now it was time for a quiet celebration of their own. Hallelujah!

Neither of them had any idea, at the time, that the following twenty years would be just as active and eventful as their pre-retirement ones. The rocking chair stage was not yet in sight.

And So ends the worst
Seafaring memoir I've
ever come across.
No wonder the author
remains anonymous!

Epilogue

Dan, on his voyage through life, had encountered ships from the largest to the smallest and those in between. He had served on many of them as already reported, had met hundreds as shipmates, some, really good first-class men, others not so. The same yardstick could be applied to his workmates in the various capacities ashore, male and female, where at first, he had felt like a fish out of water and was surprised at his own naïveté. Although shipmates and shoremates were much the same in many respects, they were individually, as different as their fingerprints, and that is as it should be since all are part of God's wonderful creation. As for the 'distant horizons', yes they had been very much in evidence on ocean voyages, but in the Spiritual sense they are just as real. The assurance of knowing that without any merit of his own, but relying wholly on the promises of God in His Word, the Bible, he could and would share, with countless millions of others, the vista of Eternity with the Creator of ALL GOOD THINGS. What a prospect... what an horizon!! HALLELUJAH! AMEN.

A suitable epitaph for Dan would be,

I've anchored my soul in the haven of rest,
I'll sail the wide seas no more,
The tempest may sweep o'er the wild stormy deep,
In Jesus I'm safe evermore.